The Good Health Guide

The Good Health Guide

The Open University in association with the Health Education Council
and the Scottish Health Education Unit

HARPER & ROW, PUBLISHERS

LONDON

Cambridge
Hagerstown
Philadelphia
New York

San Francisco
Mexico City
Sao Paolo
Sydney

Copyright © 1980 The Open University

All rights reserved
First published 1980
Harper & Row Ltd
28 Tavistock Street
London WC2E 7PN

Publisher: Michael Forster
Production Editor: Martin Creese
Design/Art direction: Richard Dewing & Nigel Soper
Millions Design
Editor: Denise Winn

Open University Core Course team: Lorna Bailey,
Carol Haslam, Sue Ingold, Rosemary Randall,
Brian Sayer and Christine Schofield

Consultants: Paul Brown, Monica Darlington,
Katherine Dunn, Peter Fentem, Rod Griffiths, John Logan,
Jane Madders, Lisa Miller, Elizabeth Morse, Jenny Popey,
Robert Priest, John Rowan, Jane Scullion and David Tuckett

External assessor: Alan Beattie

Secretarial support: Margaret Bruce, Corinne Dowle,
Sybil Meacham

Librarian: Joyce Barlow

Academic co-ordinator for Community Education: Nick Farnes

British Library Cataloguing in Publication Data
Open University. *Health Choices Course Team*
    The good health guide.
    1. Health
    613   RA776

    ISBN 0–06–318150–9
    ISBN 0–06–318173–8 Pbk

Phototypeset by Oliver Burridge & Co Ltd, Crawley
Printed and bound by New Interlitho Ltd, Milan

Contents

A community education course from the Open University

We are sure that you will find this book interesting and enjoyable to read on its own. However, this book has been written as part of an Open University course called *Health choices.*

Health choices is one of the Open University's new-style community education courses which deal with the practical concerns of everyday life. It has been produced by the Open University in association with the Health Education Council and with the Scottish Health Education Unit. It is not part of the Open University's undergraduate programme so you won't end up with letters after your name. But you can, if you wish, obtain a Letter of Course Completion from the Open University by completing successfully four questionnaire-style assignments which you can send to the Open University for marking.

If you have already signed on for this course you will have received this book direct from the Open University as part of the course materials. If so, you will not need to read the rest of this section as you already know what is in the course.

However, if you bought this book from a bookshop you may wish to register as a student on the 'Health choices' course.

Health choices is a learn-at-home course. There are no classes, no teachers and no set hours. You can study where and when you like and you work through the materials in whatever order you choose. To give you a rough idea of how much work is involved we estimate that if you were to study the course during the eight week period of the linked TV and radio programmes you would need to spend about five to six hours a week on it. However, you *can* spread the work out over a longer period because there is plenty of time allowed to finish the assignments.

What's in the course?

A **This book** – The Good Health Guide – is the course book and forms the core of the course.

B **Four television and four radio programmes** – which have been specially made for this course. These eight pro-grammes will be broadcast in Autumn 1980 and again in early 1981. The programmes follow the theme of personal relationships. To find out when these programmes are broadcast, look in the *Radio Times* from October to December, and again in January to March each year. Registered students are sent a Broadcast Calendar and detailed Broadcast Notes about the programmes.

C **A resource pack** – which you will receive when you sign on for the course. This resource pack contains the following things.

Broadcast notes – which suggest what you should do as preparation for each programme. They also contain activities which help relate the issues raised in the programmes to your own life.

A cassette tape and notes – which teach you relaxation (side one) and how to wake yourself up and keep fit with a simple programme of exercises ('Moving to music', side two).

A study guide – which explains how all the parts of the course are related. It suggests various ways to follow the course and helps you choose the study plan which best suits you. The table overleaf shows an outline of how the course could be studied during the eight week broadcast period.

A self help study group booklet – this booklet explains a scheme we have organised to help students contact each other and form a group. Of course, you might like to form your own group by persuading some of your friends to join at the same time as you. The course is specially designed to help you learn on your own. You take what you want from it – you do not need to be 'taught' it by anyone. But you may find it helpful to share your learning, your experiences and problems with other students.

Assignment booklet – this contains four quiz-style assignments to help you check your understanding of the course. If you wish, you can send them to the Open University where they will be computer-marked, and if you complete them satisfactorily you will be sent a Letter of Course Completion.

The resource pack also contains a selection of health related booklets and leaflets from the Health Education Council and the Scottish Health Education Unit.

Want to sign on?

If you already own a copy of this book write to:
ASCO
The Open University,
PO Box 76
Milton Keynes, MK7 6AN
and ask for form HR1 which will tell you the fee and contains an application form.

If you are reading a copy which belongs to someone else, you can either buy a copy from a bookseller or register directly with the Open University as a student, in which case you will receive a copy of this book by mail with the other course materials. (Write for an ordinary application form to the above address.)

Other community education courses

The community education courses from the Open University deal with the practical concerns of everyday life. They're written for anyone who wants to make his or her life better. All of the courses are presented in a lively, easy-to-read style which helps you get to the root of matters that concern you. They help you decide where you need to make changes in your life and to weigh up what's best for you.

There are three courses for parents, *The first years of life, The pre-school child* and *Childhood 5–10*, which deal with the problems, worries and joys of bringing up children. There are two courses for consumers, *Consumer decisions*, which help you decide the best ways of managing and spending your money, and *Energy in the home*, to help you save on your fuel bills. And there's a course to help school governors called *Governing schools*. Future courses will consider adolescence, food, and planning retirement.

The course fee in January 1981 is £14. If you want more details of any of these courses or wish to sign on directly for *Health choices*, write to the address given in 'Want to sign on?'

An eight week study period

Some people like to follow the course over the eight week period of the broadcasts, starting either in October or January. If this appeals to you we suggest you follow this plan which involves five to six hours of study a week.

	The book	Broadcasts	Cassette*	Assignments*
Week 1	Read and do the activities in Chapter 1 'A new look at your old life'	Read the relevant broadcast notes.* Watch television programme 1 'Stormy weather'		Complete questions 1–10 of the first assignment
Week 2	Read and do the activities in Chapter 2 'Person to person'	Read the relevant broadcast notes. Listen to radio programme 1		Complete questions 11–20 of the first assignment
Week 3	Read and do the activities in Chapter 3 'Looking after yourself'	Read the relevant broadcast notes and watch television programme 2 'Home Cookin'	Listen to and practise the activities on side 2 'Moving to music'	Complete questions 1–10 of the second assignment
Week 4	Read and do the activities in Chapter 4 'Breaking old patterns'	Read the relevant broadcast notes and listen to radio programme 2		Complete questions 11–20 of the second assignment
Week 5	Read and do the activities in Chapter 5 'Work and health'	Read the relevant broadcast notes and watch television programme 3 'See-saw'		Complete questions 1–10 of the third assignment
Week 6	Read and do the activities in Chapter 6 'Stress and emotions'	Read the relevant broadcast notes and listen to radio programme 3	Listen to and practise the activities on side 1 'Relaxation'	Complete questions 11–20 of the third assignment
Week 7	Read and do the activities in Chapter 7 'Your sex life'	Read the relevant broadcast notes and watch television programme 4 'Tell me when it hurts'		Complete questions 1–10 of the fourth assignment
Week 8	Read and do the activities In chapter 8 'A healthy community'	Read the relevant broadcast notes and listen to radio programme 4		Complete questions 11–20 of the fourth assignment. Post off all the assignments to the Open University

These are sent to registered students with their course package.

The Good Health Guide

This book is about health – your own health and how much control you have over it. It's about choices you can make.

What's it all about?

You will find that certain themes run through the book. We, as authors, approach health from a particular point of view.

○ We are interested in *health* not illness. This means that we don't talk much about illness. We're not concerned with the sort of diagnosis that a doctor offers or with telling you what's wrong with you.

○ We think health has as much to do with minds as with bodies. Your feelings, your relationships and how you get on with others are just as important as your physical well-being.

○ We think health is concerned with lifestyle. It's about the choices you make in your life about how you want to live. Just as importantly, it's about the obstacles that may stop you living as you wish.

What can you do?

There are constant reminders today that the modern way of life is by no means a healthy one. TV, radio, newspapers and magazines paint a gloomy picture. We're told we eat, smoke and drink unwisely. We take too little exercise. We work in stressful conditions. Our environment is polluted and dangerous. Many people have feelings of anxiety and depression.

And of course you are offered many solutions. Conflicting advice springs from the pages of the press. Try this new diet. Or that new exercise programme. Take up this. Give up that.

So what *can* you do?. And how do you decide what to do? This book is designed to help you make your own choices.

In it we concentrate on what you as an *individual* can do to affect your health. Throughout you will find activities, quizzes and suggestions for things to do.

These will help you:

○ **look** at the way you live now.

○ **decide** whether there are things you'd like to change.

○ **find out** the things you need to know in order to make changes.

○ **act** on your decisions.

No man is an island

Of course health isn't just an individual matter. There are all sorts of things you can't do much about on your own.

○ Solving some health issues needs collective action. You have to join together with others to get things changed. Enforcing safety regulations at work would be one example.

○ Solving some health issues needs political action. For example if you want to improve the health services that are provided for you you would first need to explore the way those services are organised. You would need to find out how the money is shared out, and who makes these decisions. You would have to discover how to work with others to put pressure on central government departments or on local health authorities.

○ Solving some health issues needs a change in society. In some cases the way society is organised is at the root of health problems. Environmental pollution, such as heavy smoke from factories, is one example of this.

These are all important areas of concern in health. At the end of this book, in a section called *What next?*, you will find a list of other books and organisations that will help you follow up these kinds of issues.

In this book we concentrate mainly on what you can do personally to change the way you live. We hope it will help you become clear about what you can do as an individual, that it will open up possibilities of personal change and that it will help you to become aware of the limitations of personal action. And – most importantly – that it will help you to start on the process of change itself.

Good luck!

A new look at your old life

When did you last sit down and look at where your life is going?

It's not something that most people do very often. But, if you are going to change anything about your health, it's the first step. You've got to sit down and take stock.

In this chapter...

The topics in this chapter are designed to help you do this. We begin by asking you to think about *What is health?* Health means different things to different people and it can be important to know what you are aiming at when you decide to change. We take a look at some of those different views and ask you to work out your own ideas. But ideas without information are not much use.

The second topic, *Your body*, quizzes you on what you already know about health. When did you learn what? Who told you such and such was true? If you want to change your approach to health you've got to be sure you've got the facts right. We point you to some reliable sources.

The next two topics are more personal. *Body and mind* helps you explore the way you think about your health. How does the way you see yourself affect what you do? If you see your body as a machine, for example, how are you likely to treat yourself? How do you think your emotions affect your physical health? How does your physical health affect the way you feel?

Good times, bad times tries to pull all this together by focusing on the kind of things that have made you feel really healthy or unhealthy recently. What's going on in your life at the moment that's making you feel the way you do?

Finally, in *Making changes*, we come down to the nitty-gritty of what you are going to do about all this. How do you decide on which things you'd like to change? How do you go about it?

Only you can choose
If you want to make changes in your life, you can start by doing these things.

Review the way you live now.
Decide what you would like to change.
Find out if you need to know more about how your body and mind works to do this.
List all the changes you would like to make.
Choose which change you want to tackle first.
Work out ways to bring about this change.
Consider possible snags. What might make it difficult for you to put your plan into action?
Arrange ways of getting extra support to help you change.
Put your chosen plan into action.

What is health?

We all talk about health, but what do we really mean?

Talking about health

It's much easier to talk about illness and being ill than it is to talk about health and being healthy. Most of us can say what it means to be ill, but can we say what it really means to be healthy?

When we talk about our health we are usually talking about something that is wrong with us. Try the following activity and see if you agree with us.

'How are you today?'

In the next few days, try and notice the answers you get to the following questions. They are common questions which we all ask our friends and relatives every day of the week.

'How are you today?'
'How are you feeling today?'
'Are you better now?'
'What is your health like these days?'

Almost certainly you will find that the answers you get are all about illness and feeling unwell. Most people will mention their aches and pains and operations. Hardly anyone will tell you how well they feel or how good life is. They won't tell you about the things they do that make them feel good. This isn't really because people are gloomy. It's just very hard to talk about good health and much easier to talk about bad health. We don't have many words for good health in our language.

Next time you're in a queue or on a bus or train listen in to the conversations around you. It's quite likely they will be about health. But people will be talking about what's wrong with them, not what's right with them. Ill health seems to be more interesting to talk about than good health. No one gives you much attention or sympathy if you are blooming with health!

What does being healthy mean to you?
Being healthy means different things to different people. What do *you* mean by health and being healthy? The following quiz will help you find out.

There are three columns in the quiz. The first is for you to fill in. Tick all the statements you agree with. The other columns are for your partner or friend to fill in. Ask them to tick the statements they agree with. Then compare what you've all said. There will probably be large differences.

For me, being healthy is:	You	Partner	Friend
1 enjoying being with my family and friends			
2 living to be very old			
3 being able to run for a bus without getting out of breath			
4 hardly ever taking any pills or medicines			
5 being the ideal weight for my height			
6 taking part in lots of games or sports			
7 having a clear skin, bright eyes and shiny hair			
8 never suffering from any thing more than a mild cold or tummy upset			
9 being able to adapt easily to changes in life, eg, getting married, becoming a parent, changing jobs			
10 feeling glad to be alive when I wake up in the morning			
11 being able to touch my toes or run a mile in 10 minutes			
12 enjoying my job and being able to do it without too much stress and strain			
13 having all the bits of my body in perfect working condition			
14 eating the 'right' foods			
15 enjoying some form of relaxation or recreation			
16 never smoking			
17 hardly ever going to the doctor			
18 drinking only moderate amounts of alcohol			

Now look across to the next page. Under each heading on pages 17 and 18 ring the numbers which you ticked.

Health is ... not being ill

If you ticked 4, 8, 13 or 17 you probably think of health as something to do with medicine. Perhaps you think that you can only be healthy with the help of doctors and the National Health Service. Unfortunately doctors and the health service can do little to help us to be healthy. They usually only help when we are ill. When scientists try to measure how healthy we are as a nation they look at the amount of disease and death that occurs. 'Health' itself is not measured.

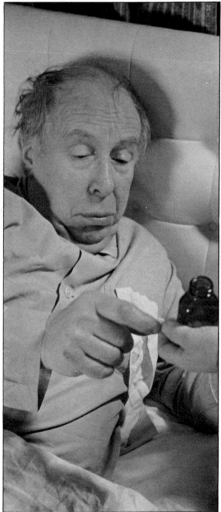

Health is ... being fit

Statements 3, 6, 11 or 15 suggest that, for you, health is something to do with being physically fit. But can you be fit and still be unhealthy? Or unfit and still be healthy?

Norman Croucher lost both his legs below the knees before he was 20. Despite this disability he continued his rock-climbing career and has climbed several hard routes in the Alps and Andes. Losing your legs doesn't sound very healthy but we'd probably all agree that he must be fit. When you are fit your muscles are so well trained that they can do more work without putting extra strain on your heart. This is why athletes have a lower heart rate (pulse) than ordinary people. Another benefit of fitness is that blood pressure is lower. This means it is easier for the heart to pump the blood around the body. Being fit is part of being healthy.

Health is ... living to an old age

If you ticked statements 2, 5, 14, 16 or 18 you probably think being healthy means reducing your chances of dying young. Insurance companies want to know how long someone is likely to live. They work this out by asking about past illnesses in the family such as:

How long did your parents live?
What illnesses did they suffer from?
How heavy are you for your height?
Do you smoke or drink?
What sport and recreation do you do?
What work do you do?
Where do you live?

They know that a person's chance of a long life depends on all these things.

But is living to 100 really a good measure of health for *you*? Some people live to be very old but don't enjoy their life very much. Living to a ripe old age is only one aspect of health.

Health is ... adapting

Ticking 9 and 12 suggests that you think of health as the ability to adapt so that you are always on top, whatever your surroundings. This is certainly a very useful ability. But adapting has its costs. Sometimes people are pushed into ways of adapting that produce other strains on them.

What about the young mother on her own who takes anti-depressant pills so that she can cope with looking after her baby?

Or the man who has to have five pints in the pub before he can go home to his family?

Or the factory worker who is frequently off work with back trouble because he is bored with his job?

These people have all found ways of adapting so that they can cope with their lives. Are these adaptations healthy or unhealthy? If their surroundings were changed instead, perhaps they could cope without cost to their health. Many of us are only as healthy as the society we live in allows. To cope in society we have to adapt at a cost to ourselves, perhaps by taking pills, being off work, talking to a psychiatrist. In an ideal society no-one would need to 'adapt' in these ways.

Health is ... positive health

Statements 1, 7, 10 and 15 see health as something quite different from illness and medicine. Positive health starts where not being ill stops. Although this is quite an ancient idea, we have only recently begun to take it seriously. We cannot measure wellness as easily as we can measure illness. Some people do not believe it exists and say there is no such thing as positive health, only absence of illness. Positive health covers all the things we can do so that we don't become ill (prevention) plus all the things we can do to become even more well (promotion). It means being happy, communicating well, eating well, taking exercise, coping with stress and achieving our full potential.

What are your ideas?

Did you tick statements from different groups?
Did you tick different statements from those your partner and/or friends ticked?
Have any of you changed your ideas as a result of doing this activity or through discussing it with each other?

 In fact, health is a mix of all the things we've mentioned. The aim of this book is to help you find the right mix for yourself.

Who's healthy?

The following case studies are about people with different lifestyles and at different stages of life. Write your own 'story' on a separate sheet of paper.

Anne is a young married mother of 22. She has three children under five and feels this is why she never got her figure back. Her husband does shiftwork. All the responsibility for the children falls on her and she's always tired when her husband comes in. She rarely gets out of the house except for shopping trips and doesn't see her friends much now. She feels rather low and depressed. Recently she has began to smoke more and to snap at the children. She also gets bad headaches.

Robert is 40. Seven years ago he broke his back in an accident and has been in a wheelchair ever since. His wife, 10-year-old son and many friends help him to lead a full life and are quite used to his disability. Each day he drives himself to where he works as a bookie's clerk and goes to the races whenever he can. In his free time he plays wheelchair basketball and archery, at which he is becoming very skilled. Robert's biggest grouse is that he can't get into his local library or cinema.

Edith is 45 and going through the change of life. She and her husband Jack are overweight. They smoke a lot and always have a drink at lunch and dinner. This worries Edith because last month a good friend of Jack's age died of a heart attack. Everyone has been saying it's because he was so unhealthy, but he wasn't as fat as Jack, and Edith has high blood pressure. Their children have grown up, married and live far away. She feels she has little to do now, and can't wait for when the grandchildren arrive.

In the table below we have made some judgements about these people's health and suggest changes they might decide on to become healthier. There are often many choices that could be made and we have suggested just a few. Now try to fill in the table for yourself. This will give you a guide to what health is for you and so help you to use this book.

Are they healthy?				Why might they want to be healthier?	What could they do?	Which chapters in this book are important?
ANNE	Ill	Not ill Not healthy ✓	Healthy	To enjoy life more For the children To keep her husband	Send older children to playgroup Talk to husband Get help from mother Go to doctor	See Chapter 2 *Person to person* Chapter 4 *Breaking old patterns* Chapter 6 *Stress and emotions*
ROBERT	Ill	Not ill Not healthy	Healthy ✓	To get in the team for the Paraplegic Olympics Just to show others what can be done despite his handicap To make his son proud of his father	Robert's doing pretty well but how about pressing his local community health council or social services department to make local facilities better for the disabled?	See Chapter 8 *A healthy community*
EDITH	Ill	Not ill Not healthy ✓	Healthy	To live longer So that she can be a glamorous grandmother To look after Jack	Go on a diet Buy a dog and take it for walks Get a job Stop drinking and smoking Take up yoga	See Chapter 3 *Looking after yourself* Chapter 4 *Breaking old patterns*
YOU	Ill	Not ill Not healthy	Healthy			Look at the list of chapters at the beginning of the book

Your body

How you feel about your body may depend on what you know about how it works and where everything is.

It is possible to be quite healthy without knowing anything about how your body works. But if you know little or your information is wrong, you may worry needlessly about your health. We think that understanding your body helps you to take better care of yourself.

What do you think?

The following activity will help you check some of the 'facts' you know about the human body. Maybe you need to ask yourself if you have always believed certain things just because you first heard them when you were very young. Where exactly did you get your information from?

   Go through the questions circling just one of the answers as the right one. Then read the comments at the end to find out where to go from here.

1 *High fibre foods such as wholewheat bread are said to be good for us because:*
A the fibre contains vitamins and minerals
B other animals eat fibrous foods
C the extra bulk helps the body to pass out waste matter more easily

2 *Alcohol has a very fast effect on the body because:*
A it is absorbed quickly by the gut
B the smell goes straight to the brain
C it poisons the liver and kidneys

3 *When we talk about someone having clogged arteries we mean:*
A that particles in the blood are sticking together
B fat-like substances are lining and narrowing the tubes through which the blood passes
C that part of the heart is damaged

4 *Bath salts in a bath relieve aches by:*
A encouraging you to relax and release tense muscles
B making the water softer
C soaking into your muscles and bones

5 *Indigestion tablets work by:*
A bringing up wind
B balancing the acid in the stomach

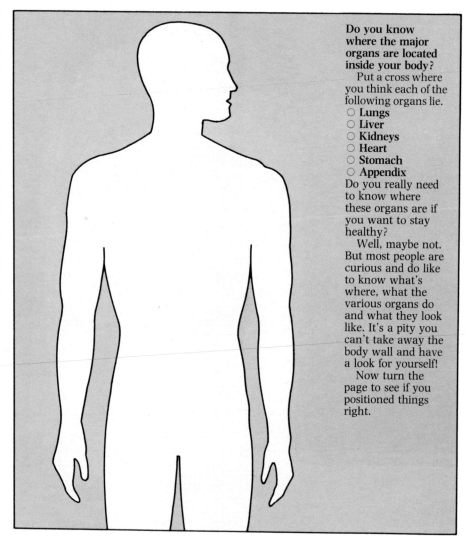

Do you know where the major organs are located inside your body?
   Put a cross where you think each of the following organs lie.
○ **Lungs**
○ **Liver**
○ **Kidneys**
○ **Heart**
○ **Stomach**
○ **Appendix**
Do you really need to know where these organs are if you want to stay healthy?
   Well, maybe not. But most people are curious and do like to know what's where, what the various organs do and what they look like. It's a pity you can't take away the body wall and have a look for yourself!
   Now turn the page to see if you positioned things right.

C speeding up the digestion

6 *Menthol vapour rub, massaged into your chest when you have a cold, brings relief by:*
A being inhaled and making the air passages feel clearer
B making your chest feel warmer
C passing through your chest wall into your lungs

7 *Cigarette smoke damages the lungs because:*
A the hot smoke burns the tubes to the lungs

B some of the ash collects in the lungs
C the smoke contains tar and other harmful substances

8 *You catch a cold because:*
A Your body's low on Vitamin C
B you got wet through in the rain
C you caught the germ from someone else with a cold

9 *Vigorous exercise is good for you because:*
A it prevents heart attacks
B it makes you feel fitter and healthier
C it will make you a better lover

So what did you know?

Now check the answer you chose (A, B or C) against the answers below.

1 High fibre foods

C Fibre has almost no food value for humans because our guts cannot break down the fibre cell walls. But some foods which have a lot of fibre also contain useful vitamins and minerals (eg, fruit and vegetables). Fibre passes through the human gut almost untouched. But because it is bulky and absorbs water it makes waste matter pass out of the bowels easily and regularly. If you would like to know more about the importance of fibre and how to include more of it in your diet, Chapter 3, *Looking after yourself*, will help you.

2 Alcohol

A Alcohol gets into the blood faster than anything else we eat or drink. The blood carries it to the liver where some of it is broken down. If there is too much for the liver to cope with at once it stays in the blood. When the blood reaches the brain the alcohol very easily passes into the brain cells. This causes the typical mood changes that occur after drinking alcohol. But smelling alcohol will not affect you. Too much alcohol over too long a time can damage your liver. But this is not the only harm it can cause. To find out more about the dangers – and benefits – of alcohol, see Chapter 4, *Breaking old patterns*.

3 Clogged arteries

B Arteries carry the blood away from the heart and out to all parts of the body. It is returned to the heart along the veins. Sometimes – for reasons that are not yet fully understood – fat-like particles carried in the blood are deposited on the inside of an artery wall and make the passage narrower. Eventually it may become so narrow that blood cannot pass through. The part of the body supplied by that artery is then starved of vital oxygen carried by the blood. If this happens in the coronary arteries (the heart's own blood supply) part of the heart muscle dies. For further information, including how to avoid this happening, see Chapter 3, *Looking after yourself*.

4 Bath salts

A Many aches and pains are caused by nervous tension. Relaxing the tense muscles helps relieve the aches and pains. The salts themselves can't affect your nerves, bones or muscles. They just make the water feel and smell inviting. There is more on how to relax and reduce stress in Chapter 6, *Stress and emotions*.

5 Indigestion tablets

B The stomach produces a weak acid to help the digestive juices break down (digest) the food. Normally a thick coating of slimey mucus protects the stomach wall from these digestive juices. If, for some reason, this protective lining fails, then the digestive juices start to attack the stomach wall and an ulcer can develop.

6 Vapour rubs

A The natural warmth of the chest makes the menthol vapours pass into the air which is then inhaled. The menthol vapours help clear blocked noses and make breathing easier. But there is still no cure for the common cold. The menthol vapours cannot pass through the skin and go straight to the lungs. The warm feeling they give is comforting but won't help cure your cold.

7 Smoking

C The air passages leading to the lungs are lined with little hairs which sweep out unwanted particles and sticky mucus. The irritating smoke stops these hairs moving and so tar – from the smoke – and mucus collect in the lungs. This may lead to chronic bronchitis or lung cancer.

Ash does not get into the lungs. The temperature of cigarette smoke does not damage the lungs, so smoking cool menthol cigarettes will not protect your lungs from harm.

The smoke contains a poisonous gas – carbon monoxide – which goes into the blood stream instead of the oxygen which the body needs to live. (A pregnant woman who smokes reduces the amount of oxygen that gets to her baby.) Another poison in the smoke – nicotine – also enters the blood. The heart may eventually be damaged.

Most people nowadays know about the dangers of smoking, what they don't know is how to give up. This is where we will try to help you. If you are interested, see Chapter 4. *Breaking old patterns*.

8 Colds

C Colds are caused by germs – usually viruses but sometimes bacteria. They are passed from person to person. You can't get a cold by getting wet. But being soaked through may weaken your defences and make a cold worse when you might easily have fought it off otherwise.

There is no firm evidence yet that taking lots of vitamin C either prevents or cures colds. Your body can't store this vitamin, so buying and taking lots of it is probably money down the drain.

9 Exercise

B Despite what the adverts say, exercise and being fit won't make you a better lover. (But reading Chapter 7, *Your sex life*, might help.) However, because being fit makes you feel better, you may feel more attractive to the opposite sex. Exercise makes you fitter and healthier because it tones up your muscles and improves your blood circulation. We still can't say for sure that exercise, in itself, prevents heart attacks but it may help to do so.

Finding out more

Now that you have done this quiz, do you wish you knew more about your body and how it works? You should be able to get reliable information from: ○ your family doctor ○ health visitor ○ midwife ○ district nurse ○ the Health Education Council or Scottish Health Education Unit (their addresses are in *What next?*) ○ the books listed in *What next?* (See end of this book.)

What's where?

Did you do the test on page 20 and try to pinpoint where our organs fit in our bodies?

Well, these diagrams show what you would see if you could take away the body wall. On the left is a diagram of what you would see from the front; on the right, the view from behind.

The trouble with marking a few crosses on an outline figure, as you did, is that you can't take into account just how many organs there are altogether, what size they are and how tightly they are packed into our bodies. It certainly is a neat packaging job but difficult to understand at first glance.

To see properly how the organs are connected to each other you would need to take them out of the body and spread them out. But then you would lose the picture of whereabouts in the body they lie.

We have described for you how some of the major organs are connected together. The numbers in the text match the labels on the diagrams. There is much more to the body than we have shown here, of course. You would need a separate diagram to see clearly, and understand, the bone structure, the blood system, the nervous system and the male and female reproductive systems, for example.

If you would like to look at such diagrams, the books suggested in *What next?* will be useful for you.

How things connect

These diagrams show only a few of the major organs in the body.

When we breathe in, air passes down the windpipe (*trachea*) **1** to the main breathing tubes (*bronchi*) **2** and into the *lungs* **3**.

The tubes end in tiny grape-like sacs (*alveoli*) **4** in the lungs. Here some of the oxygen from the air which is needed by the body is passed into the blood stream. A waste product, carbon dioxide, passes from the blood into the air in the lungs and is then breathed out.

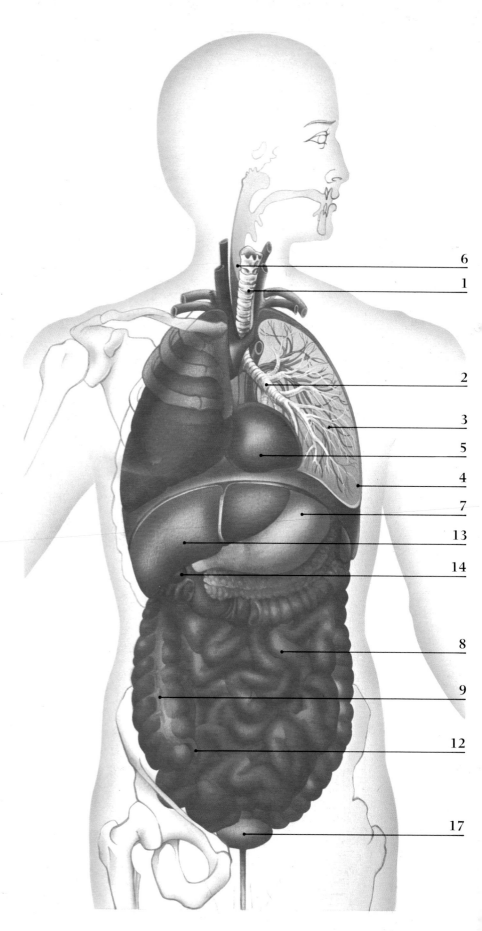

6

1

2

3

5

4

7

13

14

8

9

12

17

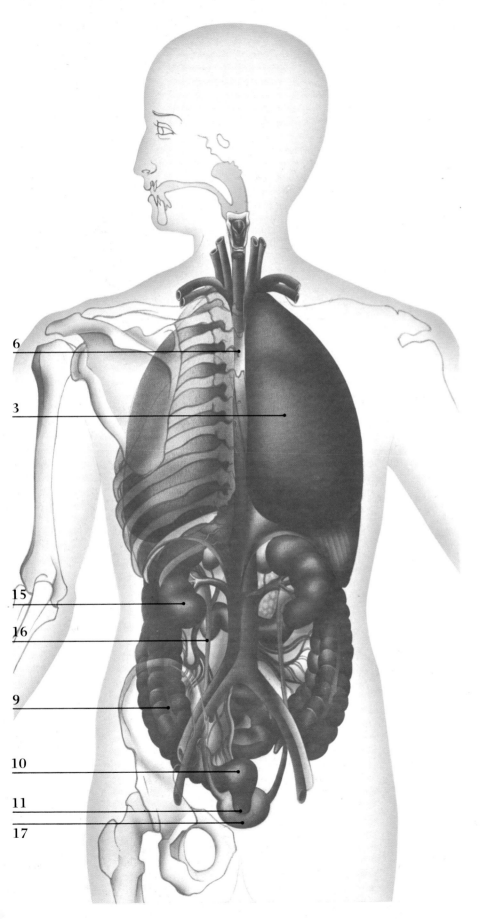

6

3

15

16

9

10

11

17

The *heart* **5** has thick muscular walls and four chambers. It pumps blood out through the *arteries* all round the body. Blood, from which the body has removed the oxygen it needs, comes back along the *veins* to the top right-hand chamber. It passes down to the bottom right-hand chamber and is pumped out to the lungs where it picks up a fresh supply of oxygen. It then comes back to the top left-hand chamber, passes down to the bottom left-hand chamber – and then sets off round the body again carrying its new supply of oxygen.

Chewed food goes down the foodpipe (*oesophagus*) **6** to the *stomach* **7**.

The stomach mixes the food with digestive juices and churns it up – then squeezes it out into the *small intestine* **8**.

The small intestine completes the digestion of the food which, once it is broken down into fats and proteins, can then pass through the wall of the intestine into the blood stream, via which it is carried off round the body.

The small intestine leads to the *large intestine* **9** which separates out most of the water that's left in the remains of the food and passes it into the blood. What is left – the faeces or stools – goes on to the *rectum* **10**.

The rectum stores the stools – which are eventually passed out through the *anus* **11**.

The *appendix* **12** is a short finger-like tube which is no longer of any known use to us – and easily gets blocked and inflamed in the young or the old.

The *liver* **13** is involved in many of the body's processes. It purifies the blood by breaking down and removing poisonous waste products and also any alcohol or drugs we take. It controls the amount of sugar that goes round in the blood. It also makes a special fluid called *bile*.

The *gall-bladder* **14** stores the bile – and squirts it into the small intestine, when needed, to help break down fatty foods.

As blood goes through the *kidneys* **15**, waste products, salts and water are filtered out as urine.

The urine passes down the tubes (*ureters*) **16** into the *bladder* **17** from where it is passed out of the body.

Body and mind

How you see yourself may affect how you feel.

How do you see yourself?

How do you think of your body? Is it a machine that works well enough but could get rusty if it's not kept serviced? Is it some kind of monster that may get out of hand if it isn't watched? Do you think you are a superman and that nothing could ever go wrong with your body really? Is it a source of endless pleasure? Is it a 'good runner', always in good condition? Or do you try to forget it? Consider that everything below your head is a nuisance? Is it a mystery to you, always doing unexpected things?

Perhaps one of these descriptions rings a bell for you. Or perhaps you feel good about your body on 'good' days and differently on 'bad' days. However, there are good and bad sides to all these body images. See right for our ideas.

Responding to body signals

How people feel about their bodies may determine what they do when they become aware of anything being wrong. For example people's responses to a simple headache range from imagining their death from a brain tumour to working even harder so that they can ignore the pain. Where would you put yourself on this scale? The responses on page 25 are graded from 10 down to 1. Put a circle round the number of the response that sounds most like you.

Mind and body

Some of the ways you see your body probably make it seem that your body and your mind are separate parts of you. Some people do think of them as quite separate. They may take care to stay physically healthy – but give little thought to their mental health. Or neglect their bodies – but be concerned with their emotional life. But in fact they are closely linked together. What happens to your body can affect your emotional health and your emotions can also affect your physical health.

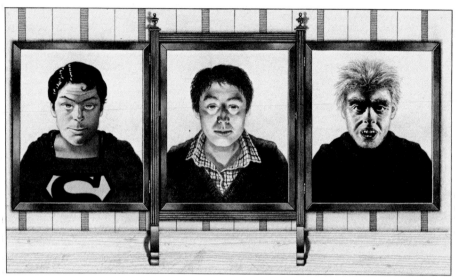

On good days, do you think of your body as:

A machine?
You expect your body to work well without any attention from you

A monster that could get out of hand?
Once you give in to your body you might as well go on a binge and enjoy it

Like superman?
It never crosses your mind that you might get ill

A source of pleasure?
You find there are many super things your body can do

Like an olympic athlete?
You feel proud of your body and take good care of it

Of no importance?
You never notice your body it doesn't 'get in the way'

A container for your mind?
You are too concerned with other things to be worried by minor aches and pains

A great mystery?
You treat your body carefully – even pamper it

On bad days, do you think of your body as:

A machine?
You think you should hand your body over to experts who will repair it if anything goes wrong

A monster that could get out of hand?
You want to punish your body if it gets out of hand

Like superman?
You tend to take silly risks and may feel your body has let you down if you get ill

A source of pleasure?
You may push your body too far in having fun

Like an olympic athlete?
You can get too concerned about keeping your body running well

Of no importance?
You may not pay attention to important symptoms and delay seeing your doctor

A container for your mind?
You don't value your body enough and may not take good care of it

A great mystery?
You may worry when there is no need because you don't understand your own body

Bodies react to feelings

When something upsets you – or excites you – it often produces a physical reaction. Some signs may be obvious.
○ You flush with anger or embarrassment or excitement.
○ You tremble or feel sick with fear.
○ You get a headache through worry.
○ You get tense or shout with anger.

Feelings can produce 'illness' symptoms too. Some common symptoms that arise as a result of emotional upsets or problems are headaches, skin rashes, vomiting, diarrhoea, toothache, constipation, fainting, paralysed limbs, a dry cough or a runny nose.

Of course these can all have physical causes too. Sometimes the cause will be purely physical. Sometimes a physical problem will be made worse by emotional upsets. Sometimes the physical symptoms arise solely as a response to emotional difficulties.

Emotional health

No-one likes to feel ill. No-one likes to feel unhappy. So what can you do about the emotional side of health? Emotional health can be affected by:
○ how you were brought up.
○ what happened to you as a child.
○ where you live.
○ the work you do.
○ money – even having too much.
○ how you get on with people.
○ sexual relationships.
○ what you do with your feelings.
We think that emotional – or mental – health is so important that many of the chapters in this book deal with it.

Most people know when they are physically ill. It's easy to recall a time when you felt ill. But what happens when you try to remember when you felt really healthy? Some people's first thoughts about health may well be about physical fitness. But, thinking a bit more deeply about it, the 'good times' we remember are often those when we have felt particularly healthy emotionally. The next topic will help you think about your own good times and bad times.

Response to body signals

10 You worry yourself silly over the slightest symptoms

9 You know so much about how your body works and what could go wrong with it that you put the worst interpretation on any symptom

8 You know you are a 'hypochrondriac' and tend to explain away as imaginary what might be an important symptom

7 You occasionally worry about a symptom but seek your doctor's advice and explain your worry as well as the symptom to him

6 You know the basics of how your body works and what symptoms you should consult a doctor over

5 You not only know how your body works but how to keep it working. You plan for positive health

4 You feel your body is very complicated and needs regular servicing from an expert – so you go for regular check ups

3 You think if you push your body just a little bit harder the tiredness, backaches and headaches will go away. So you ignore early warning signals that you are overdoing it

2 You believe that symptoms are all in the mind and that there is never anything wrong with your body. You are surprised and feel betrayed by your body if you do get ill

1 You ignore major red light signals and only see a doctor when you finally collapse

Want to change?

10 Admitting you do get worried opens the way for you to ask for help for your worries rather than your symptoms. Worrying in itself can make you feel ill – so ask for help

9 Maybe you need to learn more about statistics so that you can appreciate the things you worry about are exceedingly unlikely? Taking an interest in positive health will help you switch from being 'illness' to 'health' orientated

8 Your worries have been switched away from physical symptoms and on to mental ones. So you still have the problem of worrying too much about yourself. See *What next?* for a book on the symptoms for which you should visit your doctor

7 This is a good way of coping with your worry and should reduce the number of times you worry unnecessarily

6 Good! Now how about keeping fit so that you have even fewer symptoms to take to your doctor?

5 This course is a good positive approach to health. But remember it's not just your body you need to keep fit: how's your mental health?

4 Experts disagree about the importance of regular check-ups. You can reduce the chance of such check-ups revealing worrying problems by learning more about how to stay healthy

3 Why do you push yourself so hard? You need to look at the stress in your life; see Chapter 6 on *Stress and emotions*

2 Knowing more about how your body works and how to keep it running well will help you to value it more. Everyone gets ill occasionally – treating yourself or getting help quickly is the best course of action

1 Some people need a major shock to make them think about their health. It's not the best way to approach it. The rest of this book should help you find some alternatives

Good times, bad times

What really affects your health? Is it other people? Your work? The place you live? Your habits? Things you do?

It's clear that health is more than just whether your body works well. It has an emotional side too as we showed in the last topic. But there's more to it still. Your individual health is affected by the people around you, the things you do, the things that happen to you, the places where you live and work and so on. In fact a great deal of everyday life could be said to affect your health one way or another. So how do you decide what's really important?

If you look at the times when you've felt really good or really bad, you may get a clearer picture of how different things affect you. This is what we want you to do in this topic.

Look at your life

We want you to recall events from the past year that stand out in your mind. Events that have happened to you personally. Events that have made you feel particularly good or particularly bad.

Perhaps you think it strange that we are saying that feeling good is the same as being healthy and that feeling bad is the same as being unhealthy. It is true that they're not *always* the same thing. But quite often they are. When you're feeling good about yourself and about life in general you are often in good condition physically. You are not under stress. Relationships are going well. When you feel you're having a bad time, you're quite probably under stress. Physically you may be a bit below par. Relationships may not be going well.

You can decide for yourself about this by doing the activity which follows. It will take you about 20 minutes. Choose a time when you can be quiet and on your own. Let your mind wander back over the things that have happened to you in the last year or so. Remember some of the things you have done. Think about the people you have known. Remind yourself of places you have been to. When you are ready, fill in the space on the two charts on page 27 and 28. On each one there are examples from two people, Jackie and Graham, who tried this activity. These are to give you an idea of the kinds of events we are asking you to recall. Remember – your events will not be the same as theirs. They are just given as an example to help set you thinking.

Remember ...

In the charts on pages 27 and 28 we want you to write down six things that happened to you in the last year or so.

Good times

The first three are 'good times' – times when you have felt really good in yourself. You may remember at some time feeling really healthy. Or of being really pleased and satisfied. But it will have made you feel good *in yourself*.

Bad times

The second three are 'bad times' – times when you have felt really bad in yourself. Maybe you remember feeling sick or ill. Or being drained of energy and worn down. Maybe you remember feeling anxious, confused or worried. But it will have made you feel bad *in yourself*.

○ Write one event in each of the spaces on the charts.

○ If you do not want to mark the book you can write your events in a notebook or on a sheet of paper instead.

○ For each event try to describe:
where you were.
what you were doing.
what other people were doing.
how long the feeling lasted.
what made it begin and end.
whether the event changed anything in your life.

Good times

An example from Jackie

At home alone with John for the weekend. Kids had gone to mum's. We decorated the front room. I felt very energetic. Got lots of exercise. Felt good to be doing something with John. Good feeling lasted till I went to work on Monday. This was the first time we'd had a weekend alone together for at least two years. Feel determined to do it again.

Good times

An example from Graham

I decided to leave my job. The good feeling started when I knew I'd really made up my mind and went to see my supervisor. I had a terrific feeling of freedom and energy. The world opening up. Other people were much more positive about my decision than I'd expected. The real 'high' feeling ended quite quickly but I've gone on feeling good.

Good times
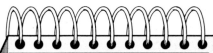

An example from Jackie

I took the kids to the seaside at half-term. We went swimming. The feeling began with breathing in the fresh air and then getting excited. Forgot about work. Ended when one of them was sick on the coach coming home.

Bad times

An example from Jackie

Tuesday. Alone. Ate a whole packet of biscuits and felt sick. Hated myself. Started after queueing all day in the housing office. Stopped when the children came home from school and I had to think about them.

Bad times

An example from Graham

My father died last summer. I don't know what I felt except it was bad. Didn't want to talk to anyone about it. No-one I could talk to. The really bad feeling lasted a few days. You get back to normal but things aren't really the same.

Bad times

An example from Jackie

John away for two days. No adult to talk to. I felt very lonely and sorry for myself. Children around but I didn't want to talk to them. Feeling ended when John came home. Made me realise how dependent I am on him.

How does remembering make you feel?

Recalling good times and bad times can arouse strong feelings. Remembering bad times can bring back feelings of sorrow, loss or anger that you may have forgotten about. Remembering good times can bring feelings of regret that the good times are in the past, particularly if your life isn't so happy now.

But there's a positive side too. Remembering good times can help you realise exactly what it is you like about your life. It can help you plan to make sure 'good times' happen more often. Remembering bad times can help you pinpoint the things that cause them. Jackie, in our example, could see that her bad times were connected with the fact that she tended to be on her own with the children too much. Understanding this started her thinking of ways to change things. Remembering bad times can also help you to work through the painful feelings linked with them. There are some bad times where the most important thing is to come to terms with what has happened. Graham, for instance, could do nothing about the fact that his father had died. But it would probably help him to tell someone his feelings about his father's death.

Who can you talk to?

Doing this activity may have aroused strong feelings in you. If it has, do try to find someone you can talk to. A chat with a friend or a member of your family may help. If there is no one in your immediate circle whom you can discuss things with, this may be a problem in itself. Two of the chapters in this book, *Person to person* and *Stress and emotions*, look at different aspects of emotional health and may help you here. The *What next?* sections at the end of the book list a number of organisations that offer counselling services. You might find that talking through 'bad times' with some professional help is just what you need.

What else can you do?

If you want to plan for more 'good times' what should you look for in the events you wrote down in this activity? Can you see some common threads running through them? For a lot of people who do this activity the common threads seem to be these.

The good healthy times are connected with –
○ relationships with people you love.
○ being in the country or on holiday.
○ being free from some of the usual constraints of everyday life.
○ feeling full of energy.

The bad unhealthy times are connected with –
○ being parted from people you love.
○ feeling helpless or alone.
○ feeling constrained or tied down.
Which are most important to you?

Choices and Obstacles

For many people the 'good times' are closely connected with their relationships with others. It can be important to look at any obstacles that get in the way.

People often think that the only way to improve their health is to do something about exercise and diet. You have probably gathered by now that we don't entirely share this view. You may be beginning to think, like us, that health is about every aspect of your life. It's about the things you want for yourself and those close to you. It's about the things that may prevent you getting what you want or make it a difficult struggle. For example, your working life may mean that you cannot come and go as you please. Living in a city may make it difficult to take exercise, breathe fresh air or go into the countryside. Relationships with family and friends can be stressful as well as joyful.

Changes

So if you want to make changes in your life, where do you start? It can be confusing. It can be hard to know which parts of your life you *can* change. It can be hard to imagine what will happen if you try to change.

It may be that looking at your diet or realising what you need actually is the best place for you to begin. It may be a change you can manage easily. It may be a change that will lead to other changes. Making new relationships, for instance. Or feeling more confident about taking a new job.

But it may be that you want to start somewhere else. Looking directly at your relationships and emotional life, for example. Or seeing what can be done about your work situation. In the next topic we look at what is involved in making changes.

Making changes

What happens when you decide you want to change some aspect of your health? How can you keep up any changes?

Any change, whether large or small, goes through several steps. When you have made changes in the past you may not have been aware of this process. We want to spell it out because we think it is helpful to be aware of it. Then you can know how to put it into practice consciously. You can know how it can go wrong. And know how to put it right.

What happens?

In its simplest and ideal form the process looks like this.

1 You have a goal, you are excited by the prospect of producing something or achieving something. This is what gives you motivation and energy. Your goal might be: ○ getting thin ○ finding a sexual partner ○ improving your work conditions.
2 You decide on an activity you will enjoy that will help you achieve your goal. Like: ○ joining a slimming club ○ chatting someone up ○ enforcing health regulations at work.
3 You carry it out. You achieve your goal.
4 You relax and reflect on what you've done.

Of course most changes are more difficult to make than this. Simply knowing what your goal is doesn't tell you how to achieve it. All sorts of things can get in the way. Look at the following possibilities.

You don't enjoy what you're doing
You may really desire to get thin but choose a rigid diet that makes you miserable. If you don't enjoy what you're doing you're unlikely to keep it up.

You're not tackling it the right way
The activity you've chosen won't achieve your goal. For example, you desire to be thin. But all you do to try to lose weight is take up jogging.

You don't know enough
You desire to be thin. But you don't know that beer is very fattening and you carry on drinking six pints a night.

Something is stopping you
Maybe you want to take up cycling. But you can't afford a bike. Or you desire a more fulfilling job. But there's high unemployment in your area.

Someone is stopping you
What someone else wants gets in the way. You may be a man whose goal is to lose some weight. But one of your wife's pleasures is producing marvellous meals. Her enjoyment is spoilt if you don't eat them.

There's a conflict inside you
For example, you may want to get into the football team. This will involve you in giving up drinking in order to become fit enough. This conflicts with another desire of yours which is having a booze-up on Saturday nights.

Part of you feels afraid
You may have the goal of losing weight so that you look more attractive to the opposite sex. But you're afraid of making relationships. So, every time the pounds begin to drop off, you get scared and rush out on another binge.

If you don't face the fact that something is stopping you achieving your goal, you may end up doing one of these things.

You lie to yourself
You want to diet but you just can't resist food. So you give up trying and tell yourself that you don't really care if you're fat or have a heart attack. But you're still unhappy.

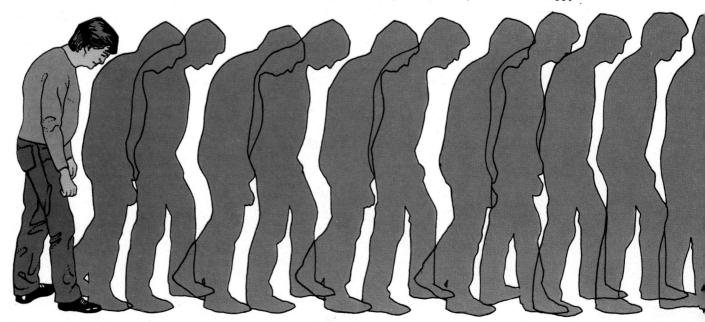

You delude yourself
You put your faith in magical solutions that involve you in no real effort to stop eating. You think that five minutes' exercise a day or a session on a slimming machine will get rid of the inches whilst you still consume cream cakes. Then, on the scales, you feel shocked and hurt that all your 'efforts' have failed.

You torture yourself
You eat only greens and fruit and cottage cheese. You spend your whole day thinking about the food you'd like to eat if you could. You punish yourself so much that the craving for bread or chocolate overwhelms you. You have one bite and then, overcome by guilt, you say, 'what the hell' and eat three loaves and six Mars bars.

In each of these solutions you ignore the fact that something has gone wrong. You stick rigidly to your decision even if everyone else can see that it is pointless.

Don't get caught out this way. Instead of battling blindly on, take a fresh look at your problem and try a more realistic approach to its solution. You may have been thinking of yourself as 'a slimmer' but you haven't done anything to make you lose weight.

Coming unstuck

What can you do when you get stuck? The first step is to become aware that there is a

PROBLEM

You need to become aware of the things that are stopping you from reaching your goal. You will then be in a better position to decide on a course of action that will help you achieve it. Try working it out in the way we suggest overleaf.

Your changes

What changes are you thinking of making?
○ Write out on a piece of paper six things about your life and health that you would like to change.
○ How many of these are goals you *really* want to achieve?
○ Put a star by the ones that make you feel really enthusiastic.
○ Now choose the two that you would most like to achieve. Make sure you choose things you *really* desire, not

things you just think you ought to do or other people think you ought to do.
○ Enter them in the first two blank columns of the chart overleaf.
○ Then work through the activity to look at the problems and obstacles that might arise for you.

In the right-hand columns there are examples from Kevin and Edna. Kevin is 26. He lives on his own. He works a night shift in the bakery and has few friends. He spends most weekends visiting his mother. Edna is 45, she has been married for 20 years. She doesn't work. Her family are growing up and are almost ready to leave home.

What to do

When you have read Edna and Kevin's chart and filled in your own, perhaps you will see things differently. You will see that Edna's problem has one main aspect. She doesn't really know enough about what other people feel and want. Until she finds out she won't be able to start on a sensible course of action. She needs to talk to her husband and children to find out what they really want. At this stage the next chapter, *Person to person*, would be most likely to help her.

Kevin's problem is harder. You can see that for him getting a girlfriend is no easy matter. He might decide to tackle the problem from a number of different angles. He could decide to see a specialist about his stammer. He could put some effort into finding places to meet girls. He could find out the kinds of things girls are interested in talking about. He could try joining that social club.

Several of the other chapters in this book might help him. Chapter 7, *Your sex life*, would tell him about sexual relationships. Chapter 2, *Person to person*, might help him reconsider what harm his job is doing to his social life. The final chapter, *A healthy community*, might point him towards resources in the community that could help.

To decide which of the course books would be most helpful to you, look back at the analysis of your problem. Then, on page 33 (top), tick the factors that are involved. You will see that each of them leads out into different chapters.

If at first . . .

Like the people in the examples, you probably have ticks against more than one chapter. Any problem has many aspects: decide where *you* want to start. But remember that you may need to look at other chapters too.

Making changes can be difficult. You may find that you're on the wrong track. You may find it discouraging if you don't succeed at first. Don't punish yourself for failure. You'll only make yourself feel worse. Go back to your problems. Try to decide what's stopping you. Try to decide what's frustrating you. Is there something you've missed out? What else could you do that would help?

Think about:

○ joining together with others for mutual support.

○ taking small steps which will move you gradually towards your goal.

○ making sure there is something enjoyable about what you are doing.

○ looking at the other topics in this course, as you read on, which talk about how to make changes.

	Your Answer 1
1 What is your goal?	
2 What other goals do you have that might conflict with this?	
3 What fears are you aware of that might conflict with this?	
4 What might prevent you from achieving your goal?	
5 What might help you to achieve your goal?	
6 What knowledge do you need to achieve your goal?	
7 What resources do you need?	
8 Do other people in your life have goals that might conflict with yours?	
9 Do other people in your life have goals that coincide with yours or might help you achieve yours?	

When you've finished the topic think about what you'd like to read next ...

Themes	You	Kevin	Edna	Read this chapter
Nutrition				3
Diet				3
Losing weight				4
Alcohol				4
Smoking				4
Drugs				4
Sexual problems				7
Sexual relationships		✓	✓	2, 7
Talking to people		✓	✓	2
Social life		✓		2
Friendships		✓		2
Loneliness		✓		2, 6
Family relationships		✓		2, 6
Frightening feelings				6
Depression				6
Madness				6
Stress				6
Relaxation			✓	3
Leisure				3
Taking up exercise				3
Work				5
Enjoying work				5
Health at work		✓		5
Doctors				8
The health service		✓		8
Voluntary organisations		✓		8

Your Answer 2	Kevin	Edna
	Having a girlfried	Having a more exciting relationship with my husband Derek
	Liking to be on my own	None I can think of
	I'm afraid I'll stammer when I talk to girls	Life's comfy. I'm afraid of upsetting the apple-cart
	There doesn't seem to be anywhere to go to meet girls. They all seem to be married. I work nights	I have to look after the children and spend a lot of time on housework and cooking. I get very tense if the house isn't just right
	There's a social club at work but I'm too nervous to go along	The children are actually growing up now and could do more for themselves
	How to talk to girls	I wish to know what my husband feels and what kind of relationship he wants
	Confidence	Courage to bring the subject up!
	My mum. She thinks girlfriends are a waste of time	Jack seems happy with things the way they are
	I don't know many other people	Some of my friends say similar things about their husbands. Perhaps the children would like to be more independent

Person to person

Personal relationships are one of the great pleasures of life.

There's a lot of joy to be had in doing things together. It's good to feel understood and cared about. It's good to understand others and care about them.

But personal relationships are also one of the great problem areas in life. Nothing makes you so miserable as those times when they're not going right.

This chapter looks at ways of communicating well and improving your personal relationships. In it we ask you to pay attention to things you probably don't usually notice.

Who am I? asks you to look at the sort of person you are and the way you feel about yourself. Confidence and your opinion of yourself are very important in how you get on with others. This topic explains what confidence and self-esteem depend on and suggests ways you can improve your own.

Personal space and *Isolation and loneliness* take up the issue of whom in your life you relate to. *Personal space* explores the need for a good balance between the time you spend with others and the time you have to yourself. *Isolation and loneliness* looks at a problem that many people face – simply not having enough people around.

The next four topics are all about the basics of how you communicate. *Expressing your feelings* and *Thoughts and feelings* look at the part played by emotions. Are you able to tell others what you feel? What's the best way to do it? *Feedback* and *Asserting yourself* look at different ways of saying clearly what you want from others. Good communication is a skill you can learn. The more you practise the skills we outline in these topics the better your relationships should become.

Finally we come to a question that's often in people's minds when they think about improving their relationships with others. Is change possible? We think it is and we hope you will too. It can also be difficult. *Changing*, the final topic, helps you understand why it may be hard and suggests effective ways of starting to make changes.

Who am I?

This is not a question people often ask themselves.

We assume we just know.

Outside appearances

When you start asking who you are you think first of the things that are obvious to all the people who know you. You might start by thinking about the roles you have and the things you do. This is a list a person called Sandra wrote.

Who I am

I'm Kevin and Sally's mother
I'm Tracy's granny
I'm Bob's wife
I'm a machinist
I'm a member of the tenant's association committee
I'm a keen gardener
I'm a dog-lover

Take a pencil and paper and write a similar list about yourself.

Next you might think of things that make you the *kind* of person you are. Try imagining what someone else would say about you if they were describing you to someone who'd never met you. This is the list Sandra wrote.

She's short and a little bit dumpy
Her hair's beginning to grey
She's pretty even tempered
She's a good friend if you're in trouble
She fusses a bit too much
She likes a joke
She gets depressed sometimes
She's got green fingers

Now write a similar list about yourself.

These kinds of statements don't really tell you very much however: they tell you about how you seem on the outside. They're things other people might notice about you. They're things anyone might know. But how does it feel on the *inside* being you. How do you feel about yourself?

Inside feelings

We'd like you to use the next activity to take a look at the way you feel about yourself. What do you like about yourself? What do you dislike about yourself?

Most people find it easier to describe the things they dislike about themselves.

Saying what you like about yourself can be embarrassing. You may feel afraid other people will think you big-headed. You may fear that they'll disagree with you. When you describe the things you dislike there isn't any danger. Other people disagreeing in this situation can seem an advantage. You appear modest by pointing up your faults, while they disagree and tell you that, really, you're great!

In the activity we want you to list things that you like and dislike about yourself. You'll see that there are two columns, one for your likes and one for your dislikes. *Make sure that every time you enter something in the 'dislike' column you also enter something in the 'like' column. If you can't think of any-* thing to put in the 'like' column leave this activity until another day when you can. Don't let yourself get away with putting yourself down. At the top of each column you'll find an example from Sandra. These are to give you an idea of the kinds of things we mean.

You'll find it easier to do this activity if you think specifically about a particular time. Think back over the past week. What have you done? Who have you seen? Who have you spoken to? How have you felt?

If you prefer, you could do this activity with a friend. In this case you don't need to write anything down unless you want to. Instead, take it in turns to tell each other the things you like and dislike about yourselves.

1 Your appearance How do you feel about the way you look? Start by entering at least three things you like about your appearance in the left-hand column. If there are things you dislike, enter them in the right-hand column.

	LIKES	DISLIKES
SANDRA	My blue eyes and clear skin	I'm a little bit overweight
YOU		

2 Things you do What have you done this week that's made you like yourself or feel pleased with yourself? Maybe you did something that was an achievement for you? Maybe you did something that helped someone else? Start by entering at least three things in the 'Things I like' column. Then if there are things you've done that make you dislike yourself enter them in the 'Things I dislike' column.

	LIKES	DISLIKES
SANDRA	Helping a neighbour	Shouting at Bob
YOU		

3 Things you say What have you said this week to someone else that's made you like yourself? Maybe you said something to someone else that was difficult for you to say? Something you'd wanted to say for a long time? Enter at least three things in the 'Things I like' column. Then if there are things you've said that make you dislike yourself, enter them in the 'Things I dislike' column.

	LIKES	DISLIKES
SANDRA	Told Bob I wanted him to spend more time at home in the evenings	Snapped at a neighbour's child for no reason
YOU		

4 Things you feel Which of the following feelings and attitudes have you had towards others this week? Tick the ones you can recall experiencing.

	SANDRA	YOU
LOVE	✓	
HATE		
LIKE		
DISLIKE	✓	
INTEREST	✓	
ANGER	✓	
APPROVAL		
CONDEMNATION		
AGGRESSION		
WARMTH	✓	
TOUGHNESS	✓	
TENDERNESS		
PITY		
CONTEMPT		
PLEASURE		
ANGUISH		
FRUSTRATION		
FULFILMENT		
JOY		
SADNESS		

Now decide whether you like or approve of the fact that you felt these things or had these attitudes. If you approve of them, write them in the 'Things I like' column below.

	LIKES		DISLIKES
SANDRA	Love	Anger	Dislike
	Interest		Toughness
	Warmth		
YOU			

You should now have some idea of the kinds of things in yourself that you like and dislike. Different people like different aspects of their personalities. One person may like the fact that he is aggressive. Someone else may dislike this same quality. You must now decide whether any particular qualities that you have worry you. This is closely tied up with your sense of self-esteem.

Self-esteem

Self-esteem is how you value yourself.

When you've got self-esteem you value yourself. You feel confident. You trust your judgement. You know what you're capable of. You respect yourself for what you do and who you are.

When you lack self-esteem you feel weak and helpless. You are uncertain of the value of anything you do. You don't trust yourself and you don't trust other people's reassurances. You're unsure of who you are. You may find it hard to make satisfying friendships. Life gets on top of you very easily.

If you have grown up feeling loved and secure you are more likely to have a high sense of self-esteem. You will have grown up with a true sense of who you are. You will have learnt how to trust the reactions you get from the outside world. Your picture of yourself will be accurate. You will feel secure.

Many people, however, grow up without a secure sense of who they are. As children they may have struggled to be what someone else wanted. They may have been given confusing messages about what they should and shouldn't do. They may never have been praised for the things they achieved. They may never have been given helpful criticism. Love may always have been conditional on doing what someone else wanted them to do.

Test your own esteem

Place a tick against any of the following points that apply to you.

When you were a child did people often:
☐ admire you for things you hadn't done?
☐ praise you for qualities they saw in you but you didn't feel you possessed?
☐ sometimes praise you and sometimes blame you for doing the same thing?
☐ laugh at things you'd made or done?
☐ compare you unfavourably with brothers, sisters, or other children?
☐ nag at you to do better?
☐ say they were disappointed in you?
☐ show little interest in what you did?
☐ interfere in everything you did?
☐ worry unnecessarily about you?

If you answered yes to most of these questions it is likely that you grew up with just such a feeling of insecurity. You may have a low sense of your own worth. You may find it hard to believe other people's opinions of your value.

Self-esteem comes from outside

Self-esteem is developed through childhood experience but it is only maintained through your day-to-day contact with other people. You continue to need them to value who you are and what you do.

You still need people to say things like 'I like what you're doing', 'I value what you're doing', 'I believe in you'.

Building up self-esteem

If you lacked self-esteem as a child, what can be done about it in adult life? It doesn't work to seek continual reassurance from other people. Momentarily you feel better, but within a short time you are again full of self-doubts. 'Did you really mean that?' 'Perhaps she only said that to make me feel better', 'It's only because she's blind to my weaknesses. She can't see the real me. She can't see how horrible I really am'.

Perhaps the fact that someone admires some quality of yours or something you've done just feels like a terrible weighty expectation you have to live up to. If you're not always smart/clever/witty or whatever, he or she won't love you. You start to hate yourself for not living up to what you think is expected. Your self-esteem gets shot to pieces once more.

If you are trying to build up your own self-esteem, what can you do?

Concentrate on things you do that you like. Rather than thinking of the things you *are* (or think you are) remind yourself in detail of some of the things you do. So, for example, instead of telling yourself that you're friendly and likeable, try remembering some incidents when you showed these qualities. Who were you with? What was it you said or did that made you come across in this way? What else can you do that will help you feel good about yourself?

Similarly when you ask others for their opinions of you, ask them what they think of what you did. If you just say, 'Was it all right?' or 'I'm afraid I didn't do very well' people tend to reply, 'Oh, you're fine, don't worry'. You may be left with the nagging doubt that

perhaps it *wasn't* all right after all. If you say things like, 'Tell me what you liked about such and such' or 'Tell me how I came across to you', you are more likely to get helpful replies.

Again, watch how you compare yourself with others. If you compare what you think you are with what you think they are, you'll probably find you lower your sense of self-esteem. Other people seem marvellous. You feel you can't live up to their standards. So, if you must compare yourself with others, again concentrate on what you and other people *do*. Saying, 'Oh, she's a much better cook than I am' probably leaves you feeling miserable. Saying, 'She makes better fruit cake than I do' could lead you to find out how she does it and learn how to do it. You'll even improve your sense of worth a little bit by showing that you too can do some of the things you admire in others.

You may now be getting a clearer picture of who you are. The rest of the topics in this chapter look at other aspects of people's personalities and the ways they relate to each other. They should help to fill out the picture you have of yourself and answer any questions you've been left with.

Personal space

We all need personal space. But what exactly is it?

And how do you know if you've got enough?

Do you have enough?

Everyone needs space and time to themselves. What they do with this space and time varies. The amount different people need also varies. When you don't have enough, however, you usually know by the symptoms.

Perhaps you feel overwhelmed, or irritated when other people are around.

Perhaps you feel overwhelmed by the demands people make, or by the demands you fear they *might* make.

Perhaps you feel hemmed in. You feel you have little choice over what you do.

Personal space is often marked by a place that is particularly yours. Your *own* room, littered with *your* things, as *you* want them. It's a place where you can be utterly yourself. You're free to do what you like – write poetry, talk to yourself or pick your nose without fear of interruption.

Most people live their lives in close proximity to others, however. Bedrooms are shared with flat-mates or spouses. Houses are shared with family or friends. Most work-places by definition involve the presence of others. The demands of work itself often prevent privacy. On our travels to and from work we stand jammed against the rest of humanity on trains, in buses and in traffic jams. Actual physical space that is truly your own can be hard to come by. For many people the nearest they get to it is the lavatory or a precious half hour in the bath.

Yet a bit of privacy where you can give all your attention to yourself is essential for emotional health. It's a time when you think about the day's events, fantasise, day-dream, let your thoughts wander where they will, solve problems in your imagination.

How much do you really need?

Before you think about how much of this kind of personal space you need it can be useful to look at how much you have at the moment. A rule-of-thumb guide is to look at how much time you spend on your own *doing something for yourself.*

You can check this out by keeping a diary like the one opposite. Try to fill it in at the end of each day.

In the column headed 'What I did' write the things you were doing, which you considered to be totally for yourself.

In the column headed 'How long?' write down how much time you spent doing each of the activities.

Only fill in the times when you were really doing something for *you*, when your desires and interests and your attention were on yourself. To help you, here are two examples. Jim spent half an hour digging the garden because his wife had been going on at him about it. Although he was on his own his mind was on getting the job done as fast as possible. He felt resentful at his wife for encroaching on him with her demands. Not an example of genuine personal space. Bob, on the other hand, spent 20 minutes in a crowded pub. He spoke to no-one but day-dreamed about his holidays, blissfully unaware of the noisy arguments going on around him. Paradoxically, an example of taking personal space.

Peter's Diary

MONDAY

What I did	How long?
Had a bath	30 mins
Sat and stared at the wall	15 mins
Thought about our holiday going home on the bus	20 mins
Total	1 hour 5 mins

TUESDAY

What I did	How long?
Did yoga at home NB. Rest of the day I was rushed off my feet	30 mins
Total	30 mins.

WEDNESDAY

What I did	How long?
Sat on the loo at work	20 mins
Pretended to read the paper so I didn't have to join in the talk at dinner time	15 mins
Yoga class in the evening	40 mins
Total	1 hour 15 mins

THURSDAY

What I did	How long?
Thought about last Saturday's football match during a boring meeting at work	15 mins
Pretended to be asleep when the others were watching TV and thought about next Saturday's football match!	20 mins
Had a bath	30 mins
Total	1 hour 5 mins

Not enough personal space?

You probably don't have enough opportunity for personal space, if:
○ you are never alone.
○ you often feel bothered by thoughts of things you must do.
○ you often feel bothered by the demands people make on you.
○ you find it hard to enjoy the company of others in case they make demands on you.

Too much?

You probably have too much opportunity for personal space, if:
○ you spend a lot of time alone.
○ you don't enjoy your solitude.
○ when you're on your own you have feelings of isolation and deadness.

The quiz below may help you decide whether you have too much or too little opportunity for personal space.

Place a tick against each statement in *one* of the columns. For example if you often feel too fatigued to make much effort place a tick in the 'often' column next to this statement.

On questions 1–6 score:
0 each time you ticked often
1 each time you ticked sometimes
2 each time you ticked rarely
3 each time you ticked never

On questions 7–12 score:
3 each time you ticked often
2 each time you ticked sometimes
1 each time you ticked rarely
0 each time you ticked never

If you scored *high* on questions 1–6 (12–18 points) and *high* as well on questions 7–12 (12–18 points) it is likely that you don't really have enough personal space.

A *low* score on questions 1–6 (0–6 points) and a *low* score as well on questions 7–12 (0–6 points) indicates that you probably have more personal space than you find comfortable.

Mid-way scores (6–12 points) on both sections suggest that you have the balance about right.

Deciding to change

If you want more personal space you may find it useful to check your answers to the following questions:
1 When are you going to make the time?
2 Do you need to give up some other activity?
3 Who (if anybody) do you need to talk to about it?
4 What are you going to say to him/her?

The topic *Asserting yourself* later on in this chapter will help you here.

Some people find it easy to be with themselves and give themselves attention. For others it is difficult because they feel guilty about time spent on themselves.

Active personal space

There's another aspect to personal space too. It's the areas of your life that *you* control and manage. These may be quite small things like, for example, the garden is your territory and you won't put up with anyone else trying to organise it. Or they may be large things like, for example, the upbringing of the children is your territory and you feel angry if other people try to interfere.
○ How far do *you* dictate the terms of your relationships?
○ How far are you subject to the wishes of others?
○ How many activities, tasks or fields of knowledge do you feel are your prerogative?
○ Where do you bow to others?

	Often	Sometimes	Rarely	Never
1 I feel too fatigued to make much effort				
2 The weekend is just an empty stretch of time				
3 I feel I am an uninteresting person				
4 Small tasks multiply and fill my day				
5 I respond automatically to my children				
6 I feel cut off from others				
7 My whole day is planned in advance				
8 I visit friends because I feel I ought to rather than for pleasure				
9 I resent my children's requests for attention				
10 I feel irritable when other people ask me to do things				
11 I have difficulty in saying no to others' requests				
12 I keep going long after I'm exhausted				

Isolation and loneliness

Being alone can be pleasurable – but only if you want to be alone. If you don't, it can be miserable.

You're sitting on your own. You're pleased to be by yourself. You're enjoying your own company. You're alone.

You're sitting on your own. You wish someone else was around. You feel cut off from human contact. You're lonely. You're isolated.

Why does it happen?

It's one thing to enjoy being alone, it's another to feel lonely. When you are lonely, you can't enjoy being alone. Loneliness and isolation aren't really individual problems. They're *experienced* by individuals sure enough. Thousands of separate people sitting in their separate rooms alone. Each feeling lonely, miserable and inadequate. Each wondering, 'What's wrong with me that I don't seem to have friends, companions, lovers?'

In reality, loneliness and isolation are social problems. Their origins lie in the kind of society we live in.

People have to be socially mobile because of their work. If you have to move in order to find work you lose contact with old networks of family and friends. This is particularly true for young people coming from areas of high unemployment into other towns to look for work.

Housing tends to be designed for families, small units just big enough for parents and children. There's usually no room to take in another relative or a lodger. Single people often find themselves living alone through no choice of their own.

The basic social unit is the family. And families are becoming smaller and more private. Thirty years ago 'family' might include aunts, uncles, cousins, grandparents all living in nearby streets. Today, family usually just means parents and children. New housing developments have meant that old patterns of living have been broken up. Each individual family tends to be isolated from the next. People who used to be included in family or neighbourly circles are now excluded and on their own. This is particularly true for old people and for people who have never married.

Television reinforces the idea that there is something wrong with you if you're not surrounded by family and friends. Many advertisements show smiling happy families or groups of energetic young people all having a whale of a time. In fact, a lot of people *don't* live in families. Twenty-one per cent of the population actually live alone.

All this is probably cold comfort if you are lonely and isolated. But it may help a bit to know that some of the causes are social. It may help a bit to know that it doesn't mean you're crazy. It may help a bit to know that there are a lot of other people in the country in a similar position.

But what can you, as an individual, do about it if you're lonely? The activities and suggestions in the rest of this topic aren't going to change the society you live in. But they *are* steps you can take as an individual. They may help you to make things a bit more pleasant for yourself. Read through the whole of the topic before you start on the activities.

Finding other people

One of the hard truths about dealing with loneliness is that it's you who has to make the efforts. You're probably going to have to decide on something you like doing and use it as a means to meet people you have something in common with.

These are some of the usual possibilities.

A sports club Most large towns have sports complexes where you can join in a variety of activities – swimming, jogging, yoga, squash, etc. Often there are clubs attached to them. Smaller towns usually have a number of clubs for sports activities – tennis clubs, darts teams, swimming clubs.

An evening class These are run in a wide variety of subjects. They're usually quite cheap to join. Local libraries can tell you what's available.

A voluntary organisation Something to consider if you like the idea of helping others. Most organisations are always looking out for volunteers. Many towns have a council of social service which coordinates local volunteers. Again your local library should be able to help with names and addresses.

A political group The major political parties all have branches in most areas. Membership is usually open to anyone who agrees with their policies. Many towns also have branches of smaller pressure groups, such as the ecology group, Friends of the Earth. Again your local library should be able to provide information.

A club or special interest group There are all sorts of organisations for all sorts of interests. A mother and toddler group, the Women's Institute, gardening clubs are a few examples.

A match-making organisation These usually advertise in the local and national press. Some are more reputable than others. Be careful that you're not throwing your money away if you join one of these.

Building up your confidence

If you are feeling lonely the list on page 42 probably doesn't make you feel much better. You may have told yourself hundreds of times that you ought to get out, join something, meet people. In order to do this, you need to build up your confidence first. You need to remind yourself that you are an interesting person, that you are able to make friendships, that other people might like to know you. Try the following activities. They're designed to help you build up your confidence about yourself. They're aimed at helping you take advantage of everyday situations where you can make contact with people.

What's good about you?

In the first space below or on a separate sheet write down five things you like about yourself. Things you feel good about. 'I'm proud of the way I do my job', 'I like my independence' would be examples.

Things that are good about me

1 _____
2 _____
3 _____
4 _____
5 _____

What's interesting about you?

In the next space write down five things that other people might find interesting about you. 'I come from Liverpool', 'I know how to play chess', 'I give good racing tips' would be examples.

Things that are interesting about me

1 _____
2 _____
3 _____
4 _____
5 _____

What are you interested in?

In the third space below write down five things that you like to talk about. Politics, your family, horse-racing, anything you like that interests you.

Things that interest me

1 _____
2 _____
3 _____
4 _____
5 _____

You now have 15 statements about things that are good and interesting about you. Remind yourself of them throughout the day. If you like you can write them out on bits of paper and pin them up where you can see them. Put one on the bathroom mirror for example. Another in your wallet or handbag. Another by the cooker. Another by the phone.

When you do the next activity keep all these things in your mind. Remember:
○ there *are* good things about you.
○ there *are* interesting things about you.
○ there *are* things you're interested in.

Making social contacts

Next is an activity to help you get used to making contact with people. It's a list of tasks for you to do. Plan to do them over a period of several weeks. You might like to keep a diary of how you get on. Write down how each task went, how you felt about it, what the other person said or did.

Before you begin, a word of warning. This activity will be most useful to people whose loneliness and isolation is recent: if you've just moved or just given up work, for example, and have got out of the habit of making conversations easily with others.

If, on the other hand, you are someone who has never been able to make friends and has always led an isolated life, this activity may not be very useful. If you have always found yourself isolated it is likely that you lack the social skills that make conversation and friendship easy. You may have difficulty in picking up the signals other people give which indicate they want to continue or end a conversation or are interested or bored by what you say and do and so on.

These skills can be learnt but are best learnt with the professional help of a counsellor who can talk through the problems with you. If you think this might apply to you don't do the activity as you may just be setting yourself up for more disappointments. In *What next?* you will find addresses of counselling organisations that could help you acquire the skills you lack.

Read the list of tasks opposite. Cross off any that you can't do because of your particular circumstances. (For instance, you're not likely to talk to a petrol pump attendant if you don't have a car.) Now write the figure 1 beside the task that you think looks easiest for you. Write 2 beside the next easiest one. Carry on till you have put all the tasks into an order of difficulty for yourself.

Your Number 1 is the task you are going to try first. Decide when you are going to do it. Carry it out. Write it up in your diary. Give yourself a reward for doing it. (This could be anything – watching your favourite TV programme; buying your favourite food; having a lie in.)

Work through the tasks gradually. Take your time. Each one you complete successfully will help build your confidence and get you more used to meeting and talking with people.

Meeting the people you want to know

Of course these tasks aren't going to make you permanent friends. Most of them will just help you discover that it's not so hard to strike up conversation with a stranger. This is important if you've got out of the habit of being with people. But if you want to find more lasting friends you're going to have to do more. Look back at our list of possible places to meet people. Where are *you* going to begin?

The tasks

Introduce yourself to a new person in the place where you work or study or at your local shops. Show interest if they reciprocate

Ask a neighbour or someone at work if you can borrow something from them. Make arrangements to return whatever it was, and return it on time

When you are standing in the queue at a bus-stop, cinema, bank or supermarket, strike up a conversation with the person standing next to you

Chat to the petrol pump attendant as he's filling your car. Talk about the weather or your car or the news

Look out for someone who needs help of some kind – could be on the street, at the shops, at work. Offer to help

Organise and hold a small party for three to five people. Invite at least one person you don't know well or ask a friend to invite someone

Make enquiries about an organisation or club you think you would like to join. Have a chat with someone who runs it

Approach someone at work whom you don't know well and ask if they will come to lunch with you, to get acquainted

Say hello to three people today who you wouldn't usually greet. Try to get a smile and a return hello from them

Expressing your feelings

Which of your feelings do you let other people know about? Which do you keep to yourself?

Sometimes it's a good thing to say what you feel. At other times it's better to keep quiet about your feelings. Sometimes it's hard to know exactly what it is you do feel. At other times feelings are so strong they seem to overwhelm you. How often do you express what you feel?

Controlling feelings or letting them out

The stereotype of the English is that they are cold, reserved and unemotional. Compared with the extravagant French or the explosive Italians the English are an uptight lot. If they do feel anything they're not likely to let you know. It's a caricature but it has some truth in it.

We grow up in a culture which tells us that it's good to control our feelings. We learn that it's best to restrain our warmth, our tears, our anger. We learn that it's better to be rational. But is it? What happens to feelings you don't express? Many people argue that they don't just disappear. They continue to exist under the surface and affect the way you feel and behave.

Anger that you don't express to others can become anger that you turn against yourself. Fears that you don't talk about may make you timid in all things. You may put on a brave front but inside you're fearful and anxious. Hurts and disappointments that you've never cried over may make you protect yourself hard against any possible new hurt and become over-cautious about getting close to others.

How do you show your feelings?

The following quiz looks at some feelings that are common to us all and some of the different ways that people react to them.

Reactions can range from expressing the feeling spontaneously and directly to finding some way of denying that it exists at all.

For each section circle the answer that is most often typical of you.

1 Anger
When you feel angry, which of the following reactions would be most typical of you?
a Raising your voice or shouting at the person you're angry with
b Explaining quietly why you're angry
c Trying not to be angry (perhaps because you think it's wrong or unfair)
d Saying or feeling that your anger isn't important
e Telling yourself you're not really angry or that you've not really got anything to be angry about

2 Feeling sad or upset
When you feel sad or upset, which of the following reactions would be most typical of you?
a Crying about it to someone else
b Talking to a friend about what's upset you
c Going away and crying on your own
d Telling yourself it's silly/childish/self-indulgent to get upset
e Telling yourself you don't really feel upset or sad or that you don't really have anything to feel upset or sad about

3 Feeling frightened or worried
When you feel frightened or worried, which of the following reactions would be most typical of you?
a Trembling, shaking or crying as you tell someone how you feel
b Talking to a friend about the things that are frightening or worrying you
c Going away on your own and crying about it or feeling bad
d Telling yourself it's silly or irrational to feel frightened or worried and pushing the feeling away
e Telling yourself you don't really feel frightened or worried or that you don't really have anything to feel frightened or worried about

4 Feeling embarrassed or ashamed
When you feel embarrassed or ashamed, which of the following reactions would be most typical of you?
a Laughing in embarrassment as you try to explain to someone why you feel embarrassed or ashamed
b Telling a friend later about how you felt embarrassed or why you felt so ashamed

c Swallowing hard and wishing the floor would open so that you could disappear from sight
d Telling yourself the feelings aren't important
e Pretending you're not in the least embarrassed or ashamed and putting an arrogant or cocky face on it

5 Feeling happy
When you are feeling happy, which of the following reactions would be most typical of you?
a Laughing and smiling, telling someone how you feel
b Analysing to yourself or others the reasons why you're happy
c Going around with an inner glow
d Telling yourself the feelings aren't important
e Telling yourself this can't last, it's not really true or it's not right to be happy when others aren't

6 Feeling disgust or dislike
When you feel disgust or dislike, which of the following reactions would be most typical of you?

a Screwing up your face, grimacing as you say what you feel
b Telling a friend how much you dislike or feel disgust about something or someone
c Controlling your disgust or dislike
d Telling yourself the feelings aren't important
e Pretending that nothing's happened. Ignoring the things or people that make you feel this way

7 Feeling warmth or affection for others
When you feel warmth or affection for others, which of the following reactions would be most typical of you?
a Touching, holding, embracing, kissing other people
b Talking to a friend about the way you feel
c Deciding not to express how you feel, perhaps because you're afraid you might get hurt
d Telling yourself the feelings aren't important
e Telling yourself it's sloppy and sentimental to feel like this about people and pushing the feelings away

Do you…

Express feelings directly?
The (a) statements show ways in which feelings can be expressed directly. You feel something and you show it. This is usually a good thing to do, but can you think of occasions when it wouldn't be?

Talk about them?
The (b) statements show ways in which feelings can be partially expressed by talking about them. Talking about your feelings can help you get clear about what you feel. You can get support. You may start to build up the confidence to express feelings more directly.

Keep them to yourself?
The (c) statements are about trying to control your feelings. Sometimes you may feel it's best to keep quiet about what you feel. You may not want to make yourself vulnerable before others. Or you may decide that expressing your feelings would be destructive to someone else. If you *always* keep your feelings to yourself, however, you may find that they start to come out in other ways. Anger that's not expressed, for instance, can come out in feelings of self-hate or emerge as a headache. Fears that you never talk about can make you behave more timidly than you need to.

Explain them?
The (d) statements are about ways of dealing with your feelings by making them seem unimportant. You think you shouldn't feel the way you do. This isn't really a good idea. When you push your feelings away you get out of touch with what you want from others. Your relationships may suffer.

Deny them?
The (e) statements are about ways of denying your feelings altogether. For some reason you think your feelings are quite unacceptable. You may think they're not nice. Or you may be frightened of their strength: you push them away by pretending they don't exist. Again, these denied feelings may emerge in other ways.

When should you express your feelings?

Our quiz may make it look as if the best thing to do is always to express a feeling. This isn't entirely true. Different people feel happy with different degrees of expressiveness and what is right for one person is wrong for another.

It is also true that there are good times and bad times to express how you feel. What do you think of the following two examples?

Mary is very angry with her husband Tom. She feels he ignores her when they go out with friends. She feels he puts her down if she tries to give her views. Things come to a head one night in the pub where she feels quite shut out of the conversation. She walks home feeling really steamed up and ready for a row. She decides not to say what she feels, however, because Tom is going for a job the next day. She knows that rows and arguments always upset him far more

than they upset her. She gets rid of some of her aggression by energetically cleaning the bath and doing the ironing. Then she tells him the following day how annoyed she was. What would you have done if you were Mary?

Joanne is upset with her boyfriend Dick because he is always breaking arrangements at the last minute. She feels hurt and angry but doesn't say anything to him directly. In her family, rows always led to physical violence and she is afraid of what might happen if she brings the subject up with Dick. She tells herself that it's not really that important as she knows Dick cares a lot about her. What would you do if you were Joanne?

Mary makes a decision based on the present
She decides not to tell Tom about her anger because she knows him well. She knows what effect her anger will have on him and decides it's not a good idea to tell him *at the moment*. She resolves to talk to him the next day instead.

Joanne makes a decision based on the past
She decides not to tell Dick that she is upset because of the effect that saying such things had in her family. Her decision doesn't really have much to do with the present situation. It doesn't have much to do with Dick. He may not react like her family did at all.

Mary's decision is a good one. She decides to express her feelings but to wait for a better opportunity. Joanne's decision isn't so good. She pushes her feelings away because she's afraid of what might happen. If she never talks to Dick about how his behaviour upsets her she may start to resent him or to get back at him in niggling ways. If she never tells him what's wrong he's unlikely to change.

Becoming more expressive
The next three topics look at different aspects of expressing what you feel to others. If you'd like to become more expressive you may find some of them useful to you.

These pictures show six different emotional expressions. The seventh shows a neutral face for comparison. Researchers have found that the six expressions are basic emotional expressions in most cultures. They show happiness, sadness, anger, fear, surprise and disgust. Can you see which picture is expressing which?

Now check your answers:
In picture 1 the woman shows surprise. In picture 2 her expression is anger. In picture 3 she is showing disgust. In picture 4 the expression on her face is fear. In picture 5 she is showing happiness. And in picture 6 her expression is sadness.

Thoughts and feelings

What is a feeling? How is it different from a thought or an idea?

Sorting out the feelings

Thoughts and feelings are often confused. This is because people simply don't know *how* to express feelings. Brought up to believe that feelings are sissy, sloppy, a sign of weakness or self-indulgence, many people lack the words for what they feel. Sometimes this is simply because they've never learnt how to talk about their feelings. Sometimes the muddle and confusion is a form of defence. People have all kinds of fears about expressing their feelings. They may fear exposing themselves to ridicule. They may fear making them-selves vulnerable. They may fear losing control. Confused communication can help you keep your distance from your feelings. But it also makes for difficult relationships in the long run.

Read through the following statements
1 I feel you don't care about me.
2 I feel you just push me around.
3 You're so arrogant.
4 You're such fun to be with.
5 I feel attacked.
6 I feel you admire and idealise me.
7 I feel we ought to make a decision.

Most of them look as if they're expressing feelings, don't they? If you look more closely at them, however, you may see that they don't. None of these statements really expresses a feeling. In some, feelings are disguised. In others, feeling-type words are used to hide a thought.

1 I feel you don't care about me This statement expresses what I *think* the other person is doing to me. My *feelings* in this situation might be: 'I'm hurt', 'I'm sad', 'I'm angry'. A clearer and more expressive way of putting it would be to say: 'I feel hurt and angry because I think you don't care about me'. With the thought and feeling separated, it is easier for the other person to respond to both. He might reply 'You're partly right. I don't feel the same as I did six months ago. But I didn't mean to hurt you'.

2 I feel you just push me around
This statement says what I think my situation is. *The thought* might be better expressed as (for example), 'I think you people took advantage of me when you left without doing the washing up last night'. The *feelings* might be better expressed as, 'I felt annoyed and let-down'.

3 You're so arrogant This one says what I think about you. It's a judgement. The feelings I have could be quite different. For example: 'I feel jealous', 'I feel resentful', 'I feel critical'. Making a judgement can be a way of avoiding saying what you feel. It can also be a way of hiding your feelings.

4 You're such fun to be with This one also says what I think about you but this time it's a compliment. Again, this kind of statement may be a way of hiding your feelings from the other person. There's nothing wrong with paying people compliments but the feeling would be better expressed as, 'When I'm with you I feel so invigorated/happy/joyful/loving/satisfied/stimulated', etc.

5 I feel attacked This is a sneaky one. It certainly looks like a feeling but what it does is blame the other person. It's really just 'You're attacking me' turned the other way around. It would be better to say, perhaps, 'I feel upset and defensive because I think you're attacking me'.

6 I feel you admire and idealise me This is like our first statement though it's more positive. The feelings behind this thought are not at all clear though. They could be, 'I'm worried'. Or they might be, 'I'm pleased'. If you really want to get a clear response you need to make a clear statement.

7 I feel we should make a decision This needs to be expressed as a thought. 'I *think* we ought to take a decision'. Women are particularly likely to fall into this trap if they assume they have no right to their opinions, ideas, values and judgements. They dress them up as feelings that fit the stereotype of women as intuitive and emotional.

Getting it clear

Listed right are eight more statements where thoughts and feelings are confused. In the space opposite each one write in your 'translation' of the statement so that the feelings are expressed as feelings. The first two have been completed as examples. Use the list of 'feeling words' on page 53 to help you complete the remaining six.

At the end of this topic you will find our suggested translations for these statements. There aren't any right answers. Each statement could be translated in a number of ways. Try getting a friend to do the activity as well and compare your answers.

Of course it's one thing to be able to do this on paper. Putting it into practice in the heat of the moment can be more difficult. You shouldn't expect to be able to do it overnight. Start with small steps. If you are interested, try the following activity.

Saying what you feel

Think of someone in your life to whom you'd like to be able to express your feelings more clearly. Your boss or your husband, perhaps. Now make a list of the kinds of things that pass for feelings, which you usually say to that person. Try to include both positive and negative things.

When you have made your list, place a tick against any statements that are real expressions of feelings. Then write a 'translation', using the list of feeling words to help you, of all the ones that are really thoughts.

(On page 53 there are a few items from someone's list about her husband.)

As you translate your statements you may find you are introducing some new words into your vocabulary. They may seem unfamiliar. It may seem as if they don't really belong to you. You may feel embarrassed to say them. Some time when you are on your own, have a practice. Stand in front of the mirror and try them out. Imagine you are with the person concerned and say your sentence. Experiment with different tones of

1 I feel you're so aloof	*I feel miserable because you don't talk to me*
2 I feel we could have some good times together	*I feel excited when I'm with you; I'd enjoy seeing you again*
3 You're so confident	
4 I feel like you never really listen to what I say	
5 I feel you're the most marvellous person in the world	
6 I feel messed around	
7 I feel you're putting me down	
8 You're driving me crazy	

When people have to resort to deceit, there must be something fundamentally wrong with their relationship. Hiding resentments or disappointments can often be the root of the trouble.

voice and different gestures until you feel happy with them.

You will of course have to wait for the right opportunity to try your expressions out in practice. Life may not offer you the perfect moments. So instead you could actually explain to the other person what you are trying to do. You could try getting them to consider their feelings towards you in a similar way. You might try working through this topic together.

This may not be possible however. Remember that getting good communication is a two-way process. As you get better at saying clearly what you think and feel, other people are more likely to respond in a similar manner. You can't guarantee this, however, so don't be disappointed if you sometimes fail.

Suggested translations for statements 3–8 on page 52

3 I'm happy to be with you. I feel secure in your company, *or*

I feel jealous because you have abilities I lack. (Note how confusing a simple statement like 'you're so confident' can be!)
4 I feel depressed and irritated. I think you shut off when I talk to you.
5 I feel exhilarated and spell-bound when I'm with you. I think you're great!
6 I feel puzzled and unhappy. I don't know what to think about the way you behave towards me.
7 I'm angry with you because I think you criticise me unnecessarily.
8 I feel crazy. I think it's got something to do with you being around.

Compliments

Statements		Translations
You're pretty smart		*I feel proud of you*
I love you	✓	
I think we make a good pair		*I'm really glad I'm married to you*

Criticisms

You ignore me		*I'm angry with you*
I'm irritated with you	✓	
I'm fed up and annoyed	✓	

Feeling words

Many people are so un-used to expressing their feelings that they are hard-put to find words to describe them. Look through the following list of feeling words and count how many you regularly use.

Pleasant	Unpleasant
absorbed	afraid
affection	angry
alert	anxious
amazed	bad
amused	bitter
appreciation	blue
astonished	bored
breathless	brokenhearted
calm	confused
carefree	cross
comfortable	depressed
confident	disappointed
contented	discouraged
cool	disgusted
curious	dislike
delighted	dismay
eager	distressed
elated	disturbed
encouraged	exhausted
enjoyment	fearful
enthusiastic	frightened
excited	frustrated
exuberant	furious
fascinated	gloomy
free	grief
friendly	grumpy
grateful	guilty
happy	hate
helpful	helpless
hopeful	horrified
inquisitive	hostile
interested	hurt
involved	impatient
joyful	insecure
keyed-up	irritated
loving	jealous
moved	lazy
optimism	let-down
overwhelmed	lonely
overjoyed	mean
peaceful	miserable
pleasant	puzzled
proud	resentful
quiet	sad
relieved	sorry
satisfied	surprised
secure	terrified
sensitive	tired
splendid	troubled
stimulated	uncomfortable
surprised	uneasy
tender	unhappy
thankful	upset
touched	weary
trust	worried
warm	wretched

Feedback

Feedback is information you give other people about how you feel towards them and what you want from them.

Why do you need it?

Imagine that you've been cast away on a desert island. You live completely alone. You have enough to eat and drink. You have shelter. It may even be quite pleasant. But there's no-one else around. After a while you start to feel that some of the things you're doing may be rather strange.

One of the things you're lacking is *feedback*. No-one is giving you any information about how you're getting on. No-one is responding to what you do. Without feedback it is difficult to regulate what you do.

Did you say too much or too little? Is your work good or bad? Was she pleased to see you or not? If you don't receive feedback that helps you make sense of what you are doing you can be left feeling uncertain of the effect you have on other people. It can sometimes make you feel quite insecure.

Many simple kinds of statements are feedback. You don't have to deliver a complicated opinion for it to count. The following are examples:
○ Please don't do that
○ Thank-you
○ It's OK
○ Take your hands off me
○ You'll manage better if you hold the screw-driver in your other hand
○ That was a really nice meal
○ I think you're driving too fast
○ I don't think that was a very kind thing to do

What do you get?

Think back over what you've done to-day. Write down five feedback statements that you have said to someone else. Then write down five feedback statements that other people have said to you.

Some of the statements will be *negative*. They'll be criticisms, gripes, moans, complaints. They may have been said with irritation, anger, resignation or embarrassment. Others will be *positive*. They'll be praises, congratulations, compliments. They may have been said with pleasure, joy, matter-of-factly or again with embarrassment.

Some feedback, whether negative or positive, is *helpful*. It gives you a clearer picture of how other people see your actions. It helps you understand what effects you have on other people. It helps you change things if you want to.

Other feedback, some of it negative, some of it positive, feels *unhelpful*. It confuses you. You feel muddled about the picture other people have of you. You don't know what to do as a result of what people say to you.

Helpful feedback

So what makes for helpful feedback?

It's concrete. It's specific It says exactly what the other person is doing.

For example: 'You're holding the screw driver at the wrong angle' rather than 'That's not right' or 'You're holding it badly'.

'You're treading on my toes' rather than 'Get off' or 'Mind what you're doing!'

It talks about actions It says what people are *doing* rather than what they *are*. It doesn't label people. For example: 'You'll spill the coffee if you hold it like that', rather than 'You clumsy pig!' 'You dance beautifully' rather than 'You're fantastic!'

The speaker owns his feelings or thoughts and separates them from the actions of the other person. He makes 'I' statements, instead of doling out blame or praise.

For example: 'I felt really angry when you arrived late for work this morning' rather than 'You make me so angry the way you turn up late for work'.

'I'm enchanted when you look at me with that smile', rather than 'You're enchanting'.

It's immediate It's said at the time, not hours, days or weeks later when neither of you can really remember what happened.

Unhelpful feedback

Unhelpful feedback is the opposite.

It's vague or abstract 'Your manner offends me', 'I like your style'.

It labels people 'You're stupid/pretty/ amazing/incompetent'.

It simply blames or praises the other person 'You wipe me out', 'You turn me on'.

It's delayed 'Yesterday', 'last week', 'some time recently', 'the other day'.

Helpful negative feedback allows the other person to alter their actions if they wish. Helpful positive feedback encourages the other person to continue the things that are giving pleasure. Unhelpful negative feedback makes the other person feel angry, confused or upset. He doesn't know how to change things. It's like being told everything's your fault without being told what you've done. Unhelpful positive feedback is likely to make the other person feel pleased, flattered – and confused. There's no guaranteeing they'll continue to do the things you like so much if you don't tell them exactly what they are.

Deciding which is which

Look through the list of statements below and place a tick against the ones you think would be helpful feedback and a cross against the ones you think would be unhelpful feedback to the person in the situation described.

Clare has just started work as a filing clerk in the sales department of a large factory. She tends to chat and gossip a lot. She often arrives back late from lunch. A set of completed invoices has gone missing. Her supervisor suspects it's due to Clare's carelessness. She decides she must talk to Clare.

Which of these statements do you think would be helpful and which ones unhelpful feedback for Clare?

1 You're putting your job in danger by coming back late from lunch
2 You'd better buck your ideas up if you want to stay here
3 I'm fed up with your laziness
4 You do nothing but cause trouble
5 Some invoices went missing today. I think you were handling them. Do you know what's happened to them?

6 I've been wanting to talk to you for several weeks

Some answers

1 is an example of helpful feedback. It's concrete, tells Clare what she has been doing and what the consequences may be.

2 is vague. Which ideas?

3 blames. The supervisor feels fed up all right. But is it true that Clare has caused this? And is it true that Clare is lazy? It's a difficult statement for Clare to reply to.

4 is an example of labelling. Clare is pigeon-holed as someone who causes trouble. How can she get out of that one?

Often when you label people you find that they start to live up to their label. If Clare doesn't get any better information about what she's doing wrong she won't change her behaviour. People will continue to see her as a trouble-maker. Eventually she may start to accept the role and a vicious circle has been created.

5 is an example of good feedback. It's concrete. It describes actions. It's immediate.

6 is an example of delay. If you've been wanting to talk that badly you should have got on with it!

Asserting yourself

Relationships are a matter of give and take. You tell people what you want. You try to understand what they want.

How can you do it without falling into the traps we talk about in the earlier topics? Look at the cartoons on these two pages and decide which is most typical of you when you try to stick up for yourself.

Passive, hostile or assertive?

The first cartoon shows a passive exchange. Mabel approaches Bill timidly. She is apologetic. She is vague about what she wants. Bill hardly bothers to listen. He doesn't even register that there is a problem.

The second cartoon shows a hostile exchange. Mabel is really steamed up. She attacks Bill but she doesn't really say what she wants him to do. The conversation escalates. They exchange insults. Bill slams out of the house.

In the third cartoon strip, Mabel gets what she wants. Bill agrees to 'talk about the problem'. Why? What has happened that is different? Mabel has asserted herself. She has worked out beforehand what she wants to say. She is concrete about exactly what she wants Bill to do. She persists. She is not put off.

Asserting yourself or asserting your rights is part of good, clear communication. People sometimes think that being assertive means being pushy, selfish or manipulative. It doesn't.

You are more likely to be manipulative if you adopt a passive role like Mabel in the first cartoon. This Mabel will probably get back at Bill by sulking, crying or secret acts of revenge. She might 'forget' to wash his socks.

You are more likely to be selfish and pushy if you adopt the hostile approach. The hostile approach assumes that no compromise is possible. The only gains will be those won by force. Blaming, anger and making others feel guilty are the weapons in both cases.

Asserting yourself means first working out what you want, then saying it clearly and negotiating with others. If you are assertive, you retain your dignity and leave others the chance to retain theirs.

What do you do?

Most people have times when they find it difficult to assert themselves. Someone puts you down. Someone takes advantage of you. You get bad service in a shop. You can't stand up to someone in authority. You feel timid, anxious, or shy. You find a 'good reason' for not making a fuss. And you don't get what you want.

Think of some occasions where this sort of thing has happened to you recently. Write them down, on a separate piece of paper, like the example from Mabel below. For each one make sure you write down what happened, who you were with, where you were, when it happened, how often this has happened before.

Think of at least four events of your own to write down.

What happened?	Who with?	Where?	When?	How often has this happened before?
When I made a comment about politics to Jane, Bill said 'Oh Mabel, you don't know what you're talking about'	Bill	At a party	Last week	Every time we meet his friends

For the four events you have written down, tick any of the following feelings you experienced at the time:

	1	2	3	4
sad				
hostile				
bewildered				
frightened				
shy				
resigned				
inadequate				
self-conscious				
stupid				
inferior				

Tick any of the following bodily reactions you felt:

	1	2	3	4
'butterflies in the stomach'				
blushing				
going weak at the knees				
dry mouth				
increased pulse				
heart thumping				
shallow breathing				
hot flushes				
sweating				

And any of the following rationalisations you made to yourself:

	1	2	3	4
it's not worth making a fuss about				
perhaps I'm being selfish				
it's only once				
no-one else is complaining				
it won't make any difference				
I don't want to make a scene				

You now have the information you need to start changing your behaviour to become more assertive. Look through your list of situations. Decide which was the most threatening to you.

Decide which was the least threatening. And which came in between. The more ticks you made on the three checklists above the more threatening or upsetting the situation probably was. Use this as a rough guide to help you judge.

Now pick one of your medium-threat situations. This is the situation you are going to work on for the rest of this topic. If you choose a very threatening situation to work on it is likely to be too upsetting for you to do much about at first. If you pick one with very little threat it will be such a pushover that you won't learn anything.

Becoming more assertive

What can you do to be more assertive in this situation? How can you get more of what you want?

Don't be vague

The first thing is to describe concretely the situation where you need to assert yourself. *Who* is involved? *What* do they do? *When* do they do it and how often? Describe *what* happens rather than what you think the reasons for the other person's actions are. Below are some examples of vague descriptions with concrete translations of them opposite.

Vague	Concrete
1 You're always trying to take advantage of me	Last week, when I babysat for you, you came back two hours late
2 You never listen to me	Last night in the pub you ignored my remarks about car maintenance
3 You keep wittering on about the same old boring things	Every time we've met this week you've talked about football

Now 'translate' the following three vague statements. Use your imagination.

You're forever nagging
You're always so aggressive
You make me feel fed up

Look back at your situation that you've decided to work on. Describe it concretely to yourself. Write out your description on a piece of paper.

Say what you feel

The next thing is to be clear how you feel about the situation. Express your feelings calmly and accurately, instead of being hostile. Look at our examples to see what we mean. If you want more information about this look back to the *Thoughts and feelings* topic earlier in this chapter. This should help you become clearer about what you want to say.

Hostile ways	Assertive ways
1 I'm really fed up	I'm angry because I had other things I wanted to do that night when you came back late
2 Do you always have to dominate every discussion?	I enjoy having a good discussion as well
3 You're so tedious	I feel bored listening to the same conversation over and again

And some statements for you to translate:

Stop going on at me!
You scare me
You're such a let-down

Now look back at your situation that you've decided to work on. What would be an effective way of expressing your feelings to the people concerned?

Say what you want

It's easier for the other person to change his attitude or behaviour if you say exactly what you want him to do. Give him some feedback. Ask for a small change. Ask for changes one at a time. Think about whether it's possible for him to meet your demand.

Again, here are some examples of good and bad ways of doing this.

Hostile ways	Assertive ways
1 Don't think you can count on me as your stooge anymore	Please don't ask me to babysit for you again
2 You'd better start paying attention to me	I know a lot about car maintenance. Next time I'd like you to listen to what I have to say
3 Stop trying to chat me up	Could we talk about something else over lunch?

And some statements for you to translate:

Get out of here!
Take your smart ideas elsewhere
You need to practise the art of conversation!

Now look back at your chosen situation. What exactly do you want? Write down what you think on your piece of paper.

The consequences

Finally you need to say what will happen if the other person agrees with your suggestion (a reward) and what will happen if he doesn't (a penalty). This is where you are negotiating. You are offering something pleasant for the change in behaviour you desire. You are promising something unpleasant if the situation continues as it is. Rewards and penalties must be realistic. You must be prepared to carry them out. You must be able to carry them out.

Here are some examples of good and bad versions of rewards and penalties.

Hostile	Assertive
1 I'll get you thrown out of the babysitting circle if you keep staying out over time	**Reward** If I know you'll be back on time, I'll be happy to babysit any time **Penalty** If you do ask me to babysit I shall say no
2 If you don't pay more attention to me I shall leave you	**Reward** I'll be better company if you pay me some attention sometimes **Penalty** I shall stop coming out with you if you keep ignoring me
3 I'll get my brother and his mates to sort you out if you don't stop chatting me up	**Reward** I respect you for respecting my wishes **Penalty** I won't come to lunch with you anymore

Now look back at your situation. What rewards and penalties are you offering? Be realistic. Choose something you will carry out. Don't make exaggerated threats.

Carrying it out

So now you are ready to act. You know what made you uncomfortable. You know what you feel. You know what you want. When are you going to make your case for getting it?

Do choose a time when you're feeling fairly relaxed, calm and confident. *Do* choose a time when the other person is feeling relaxed as well. If you get someone in a corner when they're feeling tired or irritated they're likely to react badly. Stick to what you want. Don't get deflected.

Looking assertive

Finally, it is no good trying to be assertive if your body belies you.

Do	Don't
Look at the other person as you speak Relax your facial muscles	Blink, stare, shift your head around Tense your forehead, purse your lips, cover your mouth, keep swallowing or clearing your throat
Sit or stand in a comfortable position	Shift from foot to foot, fiddle with your clothes, wander up and down
Speak clearly, taking deep breaths	Mutter, swallow your words, whisper

If you like you can practise in front of a mirror. Imagine you are speaking to the person concerned and watch what your body is doing. Practise until you look and sound assertive.

Changing

We've suggested all kinds of things you can do to improve your relationships. But how far is change really possible?

Difficult subjects

'I was born this way.' 'You can't teach an old dog new tricks.' 'There's too much water gone under the bridge.' 'Why bother? We muddle along OK?' These are common statements. People often feel that changing an aspect of their emotional life is impossible or else it is not worth the bother. Why should this be?

Perhaps the changes that you want to make centre around something that is difficult for you to talk about. Strong feelings that you're not sure how to voice may be aroused. Let's take a look at how this happened in one family.

Jane and her daughters

One thing Janet had always held against her mother was that she would never talk about anything to do with sex. She felt particularly strongly that it was all wrong for her mother to have been so agonisingly embarrassed when she had had to explain to Janet about menstruation. Janet was sure that she had suffered needlessly from not being able to confide her worries about menstruation to her mother.

Janet decided to bring up her own daughters differently. She regarded her mother's hesitations as nothing but stupid. With her daughters Janet spoke freely about menstruation from the time they were small. She always stressed that it was perfectly ordinary, nothing to bother about. When the elder daughter, Debbie, started her periods, Janet told the younger one, Sarah, all about it in front of Debbie, ending up saying, 'Hooray! That's two of us – you next, Sarah!'

However, both her daughters developed difficulties over their periods. Debbie missed a lot of them. Sarah complained of feeling ill and wanted to stay in bed. Obviously somewhere they had worries. What had gone wrong?

Feelings and facts

It looks as though both Janet and her mother had in a funny way been hampered by the same thing. The thing that

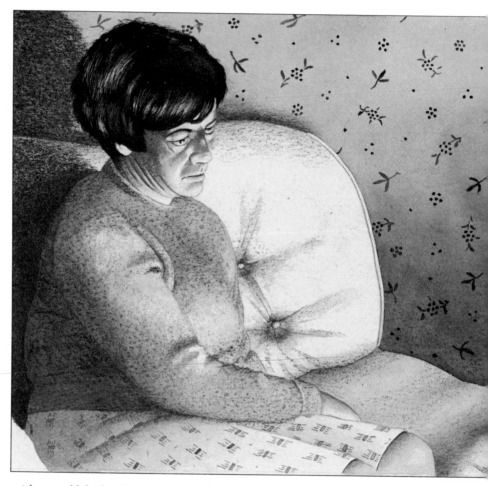

neither could deal with was the fact that a subject like menstruation (and indeed sex, pregnancy, birth) arouses a great deal of feeling, especially when discussed between mother and daughter. There really is no absolutely trouble-free way of talking about these things, though of course some people manage much better than others do.

Mothers are bound to have strong feelings about their daughters growing up to be women. The beginning of child-bearing age in the daughter often coincides more or less with the end of child-bearing age in the mother. The mother wouldn't be human if she didn't feel some pangs somewhere at the sight of her daughter blossoming just when she is starting to fade.

And the daughter must contend with feeling pretty nervous about now being on a level with her mother, two grown-up women together, capable of sexual rivalries just as much as friendship.

Janet's mother tried to squash the feelings that the topic aroused in her by just avoiding the topic. Despite her good intentions Janet made the same mistake. She was determined to talk about the *facts* – but she didn't realise that there were feelings that needed to be talked about as well. She treated the coming of womanhood as if nobody had any feelings or worries about such a 'natural' thing and conveyed to her daughters the notion that it's stupid and wrong to worry. So instead of acknowledging their worries and being able to share them, the

they were as he was that they should change. Although finding better ways of talking about their problems helped Dick and Ellen, they also had to face the fact that in some ways they wanted different things. And that may be an irreconcilable problem.

Is the problem really in your relationships?

Often, difficulties in personal relationships can be caused by other things or at any rate be made worse by them. Physical illness, bad housing, isolation, an unsatisfactory job are all examples of things that can rebound on your close relationships. Anything that puts you under stress tends to make you place greater demands on those close to you. Although many difficult situations can be easier if you're able to have good, clear communication with those around you, good communication in itself can't solve all problems.

So when you're trying to make changes in your relationships you need to think not just about the changes you'd like to make but also about the things that may make change hard for you.

In this chapter we have suggested a lot of practical things you can do. We've suggested some ways of looking at what happens when you communicate with the people around you. We've suggested ways of making that communication clearer. But it's not always easy to change. If the activities in this chapter *have* been difficult for you you may want to look deeper into what is causing you problems.

If you feel that the problems are mainly personal to you, the best chapter for you to read next is *Stress and emotions*. Here we look in more detail at the individual aspects of emotional life.

If, on the other hand, you feel that there are external aspects of your life that put your personal relationships under strain you may want to look in more detail at these. Look back to the answers you gave to the quiz at the end of Chapter 1 on page 33. Which subjects did you tick as being of interest to you? Turn now to those chapters.

girls both became physically upset.

So it can be that the subject matter itself is so emotionally loaded that difficulties arise if you try to ignore these. But of course there is usually a conflict inside you. Your fears are as strong as your desire to do things differently.

Conflicts with others

Changing personal relationships always involves other people. If others don't share your desires for change you may find that your efforts are thwarted. Let's look at an example of how this happened for one couple.

Dick felt very trapped in his marriage to Ellen. Her life centred around looking after him and their two children. She had few interests of her own and was content to spend most of her time making their home a comfortable place to live. She liked him to be around in the evenings, just watching TV or chatting about the day's events. She found it hard to understand that he often found their life together boring and lacking in stimulation.

When he suggested that they went out or invited friends round she felt he was saying there was something inadequate about her or the way she ran the home. She would quickly become upset and tearful and accuse him of not caring for her.

Basically she was happy with things the way they were. She was as determined that things should remain as

Looking after yourself

Many people wish to adopt a lifestyle that is likely to improve their health.

Many people hope to live in a manner which will not harm their health and so they take care over exercise and diet.

Experiments to investigate whether these factors can directly influence our health are difficult to set up and have to run for many years before their results are meaningful. So at present there is little firm evidence about the effects of diet and exercise. But by taking a look first at the kind of food people eat and how much exercise they take and then at the illnesses they get and how long they live, a relationship between lifestyle and illness becomes clear.

There is certainly plenty of evidence that becoming more active and maintaining a better diet creates a sense of well-being. People who have made these changes claim that their attitude to life also changes. They feel happier, brighter and more positive. Because of this they communicate better with others, find it easier to do their jobs and feel better able to cope with the stresses and strains of everyday life. Some even say that more exercise and better eating habits helped them cut down their intake of tobacco and alcohol.

In this chapter we look at what is involved in becoming more active and eating well and how it gives you a feeling of well-being. In the next chapter we look at other changes you could make to avoid harming your health. But these changes are more difficult, as they involve giving up activities which are often enjoyable, such as smoking.

The first part of this chapter, helps you to keep active. *You are more active than you think!* gets you to look at how active you are already and suggests some simple ways by which you can become more active if you wish. The second topic, *What's in it for you?*, shows you what you can expect to get out of being more active. The fact and fiction of what exercise can do for you is discussed. The third topic, *Getting and keeping fit*, is a guide for those who want to start a regular exercise programme as a way of getting fit. The fourth topic, *In the swing*, helps you decide what sort of sport or exercise you might like to take up. The idea is to pick something which helps you to relax and enjoy yourself whilst keeping you fit. Taking up, doing, and reviewing your chosen activity are all discussed.

The second half of the chapter is about the food you eat. *Eating well* takes a look at modern diets and how they have changed in the last half century. How you feel about your food and why you choose what you eat are very important factors when it comes to changing your diet. The next topic, *How do we choose what we eat?*, explores all the factors which affect this choice and looks at what foods the body really needs. In the final topic, *Striking a balance*, you see how to get the right balance in your diet. Easy ways of making changes are suggested.

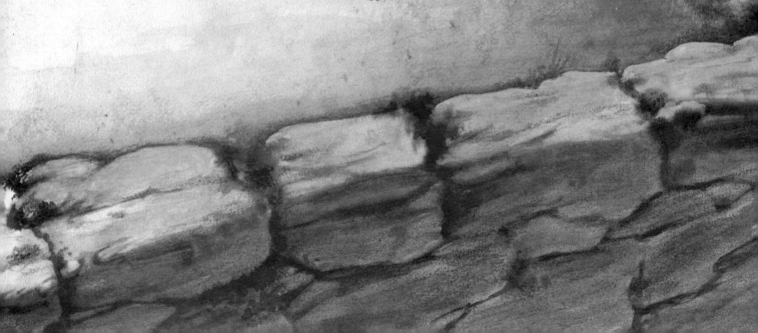

You're more active than you think!

Some health campaigns imply 'If only you were more active your problems would vanish.' But can exercise cure all your ills?

How active are you?

You still have many opportunities to be active in your everyday life even though there are many labour-saving machines at work and in the home and most travelling is done by car, bus or train. By looking at how you spend your time you can find out just how active you really are.

Vigorous activity

Our everyday activities can be divided into four grades according to how vigorous they are.

Grade	Examples	Your activities
A No conscious activity	Sleeping, lying down	
B Minimal activity	Sitting down, motorway driving	
C Light activity	Standing while doing something, eg, shaving, washing-up. Moving around a bit, eg, sweeping the floor, washing the car	
D Vigorous activity	Brisk walking, gardening, scrubbing floors, polishing furniture, washing clothes by hand, light manual work, active love making, climbing stairs, running, cycling, most sports, heavy manual labouring	

Think through your day and grade your activities in this way, then fill in the boxes in the chart. You will need to have another look at your grade C activities later on in this topic.

But now you should concentrate on your grade D activities because **if you do a total – not necessarily all at once – of 30 or more minutes each day of grade D activity then you probably have all the exercise you need to keep physically fit.**

It's only grade D activities that count. Doing more of a less vigorous activity doesn't have the same effect on the body. Vigorous activity gets your heart pumping fast and hard which it needs to do each day.

Try to keep a diary for four days. Two week-days and a weekend will give you the most useful information. If you've got a good memory you can note down at the end of each day all the Grade D activities you did and how long you spent on them, or you may find it easier to keep an accurate record if you make a note each time you do a grade D activity. Here is Jane's diary:

Jane's Diary

Activity	How long?
Date Fri 13th	
Walked – fairly fast – to the station to go to work	*20 mins*
Walked round shops at lunch time	*15 mins*
Walked home from the station – carrying the shopping	*25 mins*
Cleaned up the house like mad for the weekend	*40 mins*
Total	*1 hour 40 mins*
Date Sat 14th	
Gardening – did the lawn with a hand mower	*20 mins*
Emptied out the kitchen cupboards, scrubbed them out, put all the things back. A lot of bending and stretching!	*55 mins*
Total	*1 hour 15 mins*
Date Sun 15th	
Walked round the park after lunch. Just about brisk enough for Grade D	*40 mins*
Total	*40 mins*
Date Mon 16th	
Walked to the station. (Didn't walk home at night, got a lift home from the station – it was pouring with rain.) Didn't do any housework in evening, watched TV	*20 mins*
Total	*20 mins*

On most days Jane gets 30 or more minutes of vigorous activity. She is busy and active often just walking to and from work or doing the housework. However, getting a lift to and from the station each day would cut out most of her vigorous activity!

In your diary your days' scores will give you an idea of how your weekday activities compare with your weekends. You can also see, for instance, how much that game of football on Tuesday, or walking to work when the car was laid up, increased your score. Remember, to keep fit you should be doing 30 minutes (or more) of a grade D activity every day. About one hour on three to four days a week would probably be just as good.

Jane, for example, reckoned she could offset her Monday score against her vigorous Friday. You need to keep the score balanced within the week. One week's holiday – say, pony-trekking – won't offset three months of sitting down at a desk all day and in front of the television at night!

Do you need to do more?

Did you find that you don't usually do enough vigorous activity? To do enough isn't nearly as bad as it sounds. You don't have to take up a special exercise or sport. You can become more active through quite small changes in your life. The following list shows the energy saving way and the more active way of doing some common activities. Place a tick against the 'active ways' you already do and an asterisk (*) against those you *could* do.

You may have a good reason for not being able to do some of these activities in a more active way. Think of some of your other activities that you *could* put more energy into doing.

Easy way	More active way
Take the lift or escalator	Use the stairs
Take the bus or train	Cycle or walk all or part of the way
Shopping trolley on wheels	Hand held shopping bags
Spray polish the furniture and floors	Hand wax polish the furniture and floors
Wash clothes in washing machine	Wash clothes by hand
Tumble dry washing	Hang washing on line and iron it
Use an electric drill or saw	Use a hand drill or saw
Buy and cook convenience foods	Buy, prepare and cook fresh food
Amuse children by turning on TV	Amuse children by playing with them, taking them for walks
Ask your workmates/secretary/ partner to fetch and carry for you	Get up and do it yourself!
Power mow the lawn	Hand mow the lawn
Your examples	
a	a
b	b
c	c

You probably realise that most of the things we suggest mean going back to an old way of doing things. You may think this a waste of time and would rather have time free for more exciting things than chores. Fine. But if you do want to be more active then you will have to use some of your spare time on exercise or sport.

Being fit

A leading fitness expert has suggested that in addition to this vigorous activity the average person needs to:
○ **twist and turn** the major joints through a full range of movement each day to keep the body supple. (Most grade D activities would do this.)
○ **stand** for a total of two hours a day, not necessarily at one time, to help the circulation of the blood and put stress on the bones to maintain their structure.

To check if you are standing for a total of two hours a day you may need to go back to the chart of the four grades of activity. All grade C activities are done standing up. So are most of grade D activities (except vigorous activities like cycling and rowing).

It should be quite easy for you to do more grade C activities if you need to increase the time you spend on your feet.
○ **each day lift** a heavy load for at least five seconds to maintain muscular strength. (Be sure to lift carefully and bend your knees rather than your back when you lift.) Just lift ordinary objects such as a full shopping bag, a typewriter, a basket load of wet washing, an average suitcase or a small child.

To sum up ...

It is not hard to get fit and stay fit. It really doesn't have to be a difficult and unpleasant process. This topic has shown you how doing enough of your everyday activities can keep you fit. But if you can't – or don't want to – make your working day more active you might like to do a simple, properly planned set of exercises (see the next two topics). Or you might like to increase your activity level by taking up a sport, in which case *In the swing* in this chapter will help you choose what to do. As long as you choose the right form of exercise, begin slowly and work up gradually day by day, week by week, you'll gain all the benefits without straining yourself.

What's in it for you?

What is the truth about exercise?

Should you be more active? Or might you just as well watch TV?

Nearly every week some expert makes a new claim about the benefits of exercise, only to be shouted down the following week by another expert saying that it can be bad for you.

In this topic we try to sort out some of the confusion. Many people decide to become more active because they hope to ward off heart disease and to live longer. You may feel that since being more active won't do you any harm and might do you some good you may as well give it a try.

In fact there is little hard scientific evidence that taking up exercise ensures any long term benefits because it is so difficult to measure or prove. Many factors such as where you work and what you eat affect your health and it is almost impossible to isolate the effects of these from the effects of exercise.

So we have concentrated mainly on the short term benefits such as an increased feeling of well being. You know very soon whether or not you are getting these! The following quiz will help you to see what you might get out of becoming more active. Then we suggest exercises and activities which will help you to achieve these benefits. And in *In the swing* we help you to choose and take up a suitable sport or activity.

Becoming more active can help you to:	Already achieved	Benefit desired	See text
1 work harder for longer without tiring too quickly			A
2 have more energy for everyday tasks			A
3 improve muscle strength for lifting, pushing, etc			A
4 bend down and stretch up for things more easily			A
5 be more agile and graceful			A, B
6 trim your figure by toning up your muscles			B
7 lose some weight			B, C
8 keep your body feeling young			B, C
9 ward off heart disease			C
10 have a feeling of well-being			C
11 beat the stress in your working life			C, D
12 relax and feel refreshed			D
13 meet people and socialise			D
14 enjoy yourself			D

Becoming more active

Place a tick by the benefits (above right) which you already get from any activity. Then place another tick by those which you would like to get out of becoming more active. Doing this will help you to decide which sport or exercise you might like to take up.

Most probably you ticked several items throughout the list. If so, you see becoming more active as a way to improve every aspect of your health and well being. This approach is the best although many people take up exercise in the hope of improving one particular aspect of their health. (But, in fact, the great thing about exercise is that it's almost impossible to improve one part of your health without affecting the other aspects for the better.) Some people hope to improve their physical fitness or work capacity, what they look like, their general health, or simply to relax and enjoy themselves through recreation. Enjoyment is important. You may want to gain the benefits at the top of the list, but unless you also get those at the bottom of the list, you are unlikely to continue with your chosen activity.

A – Physical fitness and work capacity

If you have several ticks between 1 and 5 you are concerned with your physical fitness and ability to work hard. This is definitely something you can achieve by becoming more active. It's probably one of the main benefits of exercise. Being physically fit means that you can work hard for a long time without becoming exhausted. It is a very useful ability and shouldn't be thought of as necessary only for sportsmen or manual labourers. Anyone who wants to be able to cope with the demands of life without undue stress and strain needs to be fit. If you are a parent, busy with energetic, growing children, being fit can be very important to you. Physical fitness has three elements – being supple, being strong and having staying power or stamina.

Suppleness is the ability to move freely, including bending, twisting and turning of the head, body, arms and legs. So you need exercises which move your joints.

Strength means that your muscles are strong and powerful and can lift and push heavy objects easily. For strength you need exercises which make your muscles work against some resistance, for example, against gravity in lifting, water in swimming, a pedal in cycling.

Stamina is the ability to delay the onset of tiredness and to continue doing an activity which uses up a lot of energy.

In *Getting and keeping fit* you can read more about how to improve your suppleness, strength and stamina.

B – Looks and figure

If you have ticks between 5 and 8 you are concerned with your looks and figure. Exercise can help you trim your figure by toning your muscles. But you are more likely to be successful if you combine your efforts with a change in your diet. (You can find out how to do this in the second half of this chapter.) Exercises which

improve the strength and flexibility of muscles will help to tighten flabby spare tyres and improve posture. Combined with a reducing diet (see *Overweight?*, Chapter 4) exercise can help you to lose weight. Though, of course, if you develop large muscles you may actually gain weight!

Vigorous activities such as swimming or cycling can improve your looks by giving your complexion a healthy glow and making your eyes sparkle. Other

exercises which depend on good co-ordination, for example, racquet games, can help make you more agile and graceful. Many people find that these benefits combine to give them an increased sense of well-being and confidence which in turn can improve personal appearance.

C – General health and well-being

If your ticks fall between 7 and 11 you are concerned with your general health and well-being. The majority of doctors now agree that exercise can make an important contribution to health and well-being. When normal people who have led inactive lives start to become more active they get tired and out of breath very quickly. But after only one or two weeks of regular exercise they begin to get less tired and report an increased sense of well-being.

In addition to feeling better physically they also get a mental lift. Other areas of their lives, such as personal relationships, seem to improve. A survey of bus conductors and bus drivers showed that the conductors were much less likely than the drivers to get heart disease. A similar survey of civil servants found that the ones who undertook some form of vigorous activity suffered much less from heart disease than their less active colleagues. And those who did have a heart attack were much more likely to make a full recovery if they had been active before the event.

These surveys suggest that taking part in some form of regular, vigorous activity helps to protect the individual from heart disease. Also by providing a means of relaxation and recreation, exercise can reduce stress, one of the major factors thought to cause heart disease.

D – Relaxation and social life

If you have ticks between 11 and 14 you are concerned with enjoying your leisure time. Gentle rhythmic exercises such as walking, swimming and cycling are very good ways of releasing the tension caused by the stresses and strains of everyday life. If this is one of the benefits you would like to gain from being more active, make sure you choose an activity which you enjoy and not one which puts you under even more strain than ever. Competitive sports can easily increase your nervous tension. Many people find that the increased vitality achieved through regular exercise sessions enables them to carry out their daily tasks with less stress and strain than usual.

For others sudden bursts of exercise are a means of satisfying aggressive drives without doing any harm. Other psychological benefits which have been observed in studies of exercise are increased self-confidence and self-awareness and, in the elderly, improved recall. Increased self-confidence probably comes from the pleasure of learning a new skill or improving an old one. Many people also report sleeping better at night if exercising regularly.

All these factors combine to form a calmness and psychological strength in the face of stress which cannot be measured but which is recognised as a great bonus of leisure activities. In fact doctors should perhaps be advising us to take exercise rather than tranquillisers!

Today many people take up activities largely for the purpose of meeting others and enjoying themselves. Rugby, football, tennis and keep-fit classes are well known for providing an active social life. Nowadays you can meet people through almost any activity. Even jogging, sometimes thought of as a loner's pursuit, has many clubs and there is also a National Jogging Association to support it.

What exercise cannot do for you

Though active pastimes can bring many benefits – both long and short term, they cannot solve all your health problems.

Exercise can help you lose weight but you will need to go on a diet as well (see Chapter 4, *Overweight?*).

Recreational sports and relaxation exercises may help deal with stress but they cannot get to the root of your problems or remove what causes the stress. The *Work and health* and *Stress and emotions* chapters may help you to do this.

Being slimmer and more supple may help you to feel more desirable and so improve your sex life, but how you feel about your body may be only part of the problem. Reading the chapter on *Your sex life* may help you sort this out.

Exercise won't change you from being inward-looking to outgoing, but it can give you the opportunity to meet new people with interests like yours. And self confidence gained from learning new skills can help you when making friends. Chapter 2, *Person to person* is all about personal relationships.

How do you feel about exercise?

By now you have probably decided what being more active has to offer you. But you may feel that, at the moment, taking vigorous exercise sounds altogether too energetic! In that case why not just try some simple warming-up exercises? These five mobility exercises done on only three days a week will help you become more supple. Even if you don't want to develop strength and stamina you probably do want to keep your body on the move as long as possible! Most people find that even these simple exercises make them feel good.

Exercise schedule

Exercises for mobility and suppleness
Mobility exercises should be done at an unhurried, relaxing tempo. Increased range should be coaxed, not forced. Breathing should be free and easy, to fit the rhythm of the movement. About 10 or 12 repetitions is enough for each exercise and there is no need to increase this number or the speed of the movement. Progress is achieved by gently increasing the range of the movement or, when you are mobile, by maintaining this level of flexibility.

1 Arm swinging

Start	Feet wide astride, arms hanging loosely by your sides.
Movement	Raise both arms forward, upwards, backwards and sideways in a circular motion, brushing your ears with your arms as you go past.

2 Side bends

Start	Feet wide apart, hands on hips.
Movement	Bend first to the left and then to the right, keeping the head at right angles to the trunk.

3 Trunk, knee and hip bends

Start	Stand 18″ behind the back of a chair, with hands resting lightly on the back.
Movement	Raise the left knee and bring the forehead down to meet it. Repeat with the right knee. Do not rush. This must be a long, strong movement. NB When you are used to this exercise, you can dispense with the chair and work from the standing position. The supporting leg can be bent.

4 Head, arms and trunk rotating

Start	Feet wide astride, hands and arms reaching directly forwards at shoulder level.
Movement	Turn the head, arms and shoulders round to the left as far as you can go, bending the right arm across the chest, then repeat the movement to the right. Keep the hips and legs still throughout.

5 Alternate ankle reach

Start	Feet wide apart, both palms on the front of the upper left thigh.
Movement	Relax the trunk forwards as you slide both hands down the front of the left leg. Return to upright position, then repeat on the right. **Those suffering from any back trouble must not try to reach beyond their knees.**

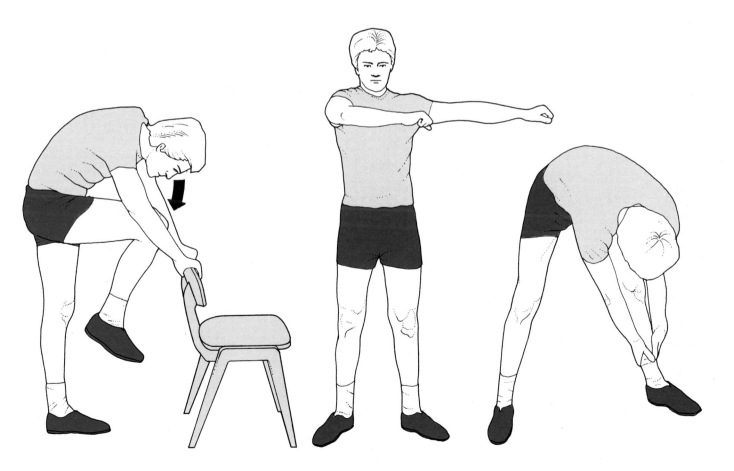

Getting and keeping fit

In this topic we look at what you can do to become really physically fit. This means you have to make more effort.

So why should you bother? Because being really fit will enable you to:
○ work physically harder and faster for longer, so that everyday chores seem easier.
○ meet the ordinary demands of everyday life and still have energy left over for unexpected demands and sudden stresses.
○ take part in sport and games without becoming exhausted.
○ keep your joints mobile and your body supple so that you can bend and stretch without causing strain.
○ keep your body in good working order and so ward off aches and pains.
○ feel healthier and more alive.
○ enjoy life more.
○ perhaps protect your body from heart disease.

Some of these benefits can be proven scientifically. Some are just based on claims made by fit people. (See *What's in it for you?*)

What does being fit involve?

You need to know what's involved in getting fit and how you can go about doing so. A person who is really physically fit is supple, strong and has stamina.

Suppleness is flexibility, the ability to bend, and stretch, twist and turn at will. The more mobile you are the less likely you are to suffer from aches and pains brought on by stiffness. You can keep your body supple by regularly exerting all of it. If you don't use it enough, it will become stiff and this is not because it is getting older. Being supple lets you stretch up to reach shelves or squat down to pick things up.

Strength is extra muscle power, used for those unexpected heavy jobs like pushing a car. To push a car a short way you need sheer strength, to push it half a mile you need stamina too! You can improve your strength by regularly increasing the amount of effort required of your muscles. Any exercise for stamina will also increase your strength. Strength

in your muscles is what enables you to lift things up.

Stamina is staying power, endurance, the ability to work harder for longer. You can improve your stamina by exercising the large groups of muscles in your arms, legs and trunk. When you are fit these muscles are so well trained that they can do a great deal of work without putting strain on the heart. The best exercises for this are walking, running (jogging), swimming and cycling. Though you exercise your limbs it is your heart and lungs that benefit.

How fit are you?

The best way to test fitness is by exercises involving continuous rhythmic movement of large muscle groups such as those of the arms, legs and trunk. But if you are very unfit, it's pointless to test fitness by this method. So for a rough guide to your fitness level answer the questions in the following quiz truthfully.

Before you try the fitness test

Many people in this country are unfit. Being unfit means not even being able to meet the ordinary demands of life. If you've recently done any of the ordinary activities mentioned in this quiz, has it been a terrible effort? If you've not done a particular activity in our quiz just lately, for example, digging the garden, don't dash off and do it just for the sake of answering the quiz!

✔ for Yes   ✘ for No

□ I can feel my heart thumping after climbing a few flights of stairs
□ I am left gasping for breath even if I run only a short distance
□ It is a terrible effort to bend and tie my shoelace
□ I ache all over after digging only a small patch of the garden
□ I am tired out after doing only an hour or two of housework
□ I am tired out after mowing the lawn with a hand-mower
□ I am tired out after carrying two bags of shopping for $\frac{1}{4}$ mile
□ I avoid physical effort if I possibly can

If you are over 20 and below 50 years of age, not pregnant and generally in good health, a tick in any of these boxes probably means you would benefit from more exercise. It would at least help you perform these ordinary tasks without effort!

If you put a cross for each activity you have done recently you are probably already fairly fit and can try the following simple fitness test. It will give you an indication of your general physical condition and can be done at home. But first read 'Sensible precautions' in the box below.

Sensible precautions In a recent report the Royal College of Physicians and the British Cardiac Society advised that, 'Most people do not need a medical examination before starting an exercise programme. There are no risks in regular rhythmic exercise as long as the programme begins gently and only gradually increases in vigour'.

However, before taking vigorous exercise you should consult your doctor if:

1 you have ever suffered from heart disease or high blood pressure.

2 you have chest trouble, like bronchitis or asthma or pains in the chest and heart.

3 you often feel faint or have spells of severe dizziness.

4 you have trouble with bone or joint problems such as arthritis.

5 you are recovering from a recent operation or illness.

6 you are worried whether exercise may affect your health in other ways.

Fitness test

Walk briskly up and down a flight of 15 steps, three times. If you are at all fit you should be able to do this and hold a normal conversation without becoming breathless. If you become breathless after doing only one flight of steps do not continue with this test.

How to get fit

To help you get fit we have included a simple exercise programme for you to follow. Carried out regularly it should bring you the benefits of being fit in about eight weeks. But you may begin to feel healthier and more alive very soon after starting.

The programme starts gently with the mobility (suppleness) exercises we showed on pages 68 and 69. These warm up your muscles. It then goes on to the exercises we show in this topic which strengthen your muscles and increase your stamina. **Always start any exercise session with the mobility exercises.**

The Health Education Council and Scottish Health Education Unit can provide you with booklets and posters on how to keep fit. If an exercise routine does not interest you but you would still like to get really fit, try jogging, swimming or cycling or a team game or competitive sport.

For swimming, cycling and jogging you don't need to be fit before you start but take it very gently to begin with. Swim widths not lengths. Cycle on the flat not up hills. Walk first then break into a jog for a short while. As you get fitter, you can increase the time you spend, the distance you cover, and the speed you go at, to make your chosen exercise tougher and more beneficial.

It is usually better to exercise longer before you exercise faster. To begin with always allow one day's rest between training sessions. Only when you are stronger should you train every day. As with exercise programmes there are many books telling you how to get fit by swimming, cycling and jogging (see What next?).

Don't overdo it

If you are very unfit or only moderately fit at the start of your exercise programme, it is very easy to exercise too hard and exhaust yourself. **To stop this happening never exercise beyond the point when you can hold a nearly normal conversation.** If you get very breathless and uncomfortable you will spoil your enjoyment and may put yourself off taking any more exercise. So remember, don't punish yourself, gently does it.

How to monitor your fitness

After a very short while you should begin to feel better, so you will know your efforts are doing you good! You can repeat the 'How fit are you?' quiz and 'Fitness test' at regular intervals. **When, and only when, you have been doing your chosen exercise programme for at least eight weeks, you could try the following test.**

Jog gently and easily for one mile. A trained man aged between 35 and 45 should be able to cover one mile on the flat in ten minutes without undue breathlessness or other discomfort. During the test and immediately afterwards he should be able to carry on an ordinary conversation. But the time taken to cover the distance depends on age and sex. See the guide below.

Age	Men	Women
Under 45	10 mins	12 mins
46–50	11 mins	13 mins
51–55	12 mins	14 mins
56–60	13 mins	15 mins

There is a more complex way of monitoring your fitness level using your pulse as a guide. If you want to use this method you will find it described in some of the books included in What next? We do not use it in this basic exercise programme for the following reasons. It relies on your exercising until your pulse rate reaches a certain level and then resting. Some people have difficulty finding and taking their pulse. Because of this there can be a delay between stopping exercise and counting the pulse.

This delay can mean that you get an incorrectly low pulse count and then you think you have not been exercising hard enough. This can encourage you to over-exercise. However if you are supervised by someone else in a keep-fit class it can be a very good monitor of fitness.

The exercise schedule

Try to do three exercise sessions per week, each lasting 15–20 minutes. Always start each session with the five mobility exercises on pages 68 and 69. You don't need to increase the number of times you repeat the mobility exercises. But the strength exercises on this page progress from eight or 10 to 20 or 30 at each stage. Heart and lung (stamina) exercises are regulated by stopping as soon as you begin to get out of breath. Do not start them until you can manage stages a and b strength exercises easily.

Stage a
Press-ups against wall.
Thigh raising seated in chair.
Squats behind chair back.
Stage b
Press-ups on table top.
Straight leg raising in chair.
Squats without a chair.
Stage c
Jogging, swimming, cycling or other chosen activity.

Exercises for strength

How to use the strength exercises
Start at the first stage of each exercise (on right) and do 8 to 10 of each in turn. Gradually increase this number to 20 or 30. When you can do this comfortably, progress to the second stage of the exercise and again work up from eight to 10 or 20 to 30. It is a good idea to do the leg exercises in groups of five, resting briefly between each group. *Do not be in a hurry to progress.* Wait until you can do the full number of repetitions at the first stage comfortably. Heroics are not only silly, they can be dangerous.

Exercises for stamina

Choose between jogging, swimming or cycling and aim to exercise for 10 minutes with pauses for breath until you can do it without getting out of breath. After a month you can begin to improve you fitness by increasing the duration of the exercise and by this time you'll certainly be feeling full of life.

1 Progressive press-ups

The standard press-up done on the floor is an excellent exercise for the chest, arm and shoulder muscles, but it is far too strenuous for unfit or overweight people. We advise an easier stand-up version.

1a Stand with hands on wall 12 inches apart at shoulder height, arms straight. Stand on your toes, then bend the arms until the chest and chin touch the wall. Return to the starting position – arms straight.

1b Hands 10 or 12 inches apart on a table (be sure it is safe). Bend arms, keeping body straight, until chest touches table, then return to start position.

2 Abdominal exercises

These exercises, which will flatten your tummy muscles, are very worthwhile. But the tummy muscles can be strained if you start too enthusiastically, so the exercises are progressive.

2a Sit on the front part of a chair, legs straight, heels on floor. Lean back and grip the sides of the seat for support. Bend the knees and bring the fronts of your thighs up to squeeze gently against the body.

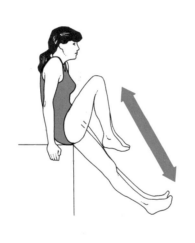

2b Once you find it easy to do this exercise with your knees bent try doing it with your legs held straight. You will find this more difficult.

3 Leg exercises

These are based on squatting. As you do a squat, you will soon become aware of weakness in the legs. This is because unfit adults seldom bend their knees beyond that needed to climb stairs or sit down.

3a Stand 18 inches behind a chair with your hands on the back. Squat down keeping the feet flat on the floor (women may stand on their toes at this point).

Straighten both legs and come up on the toes, then return to the squat position.

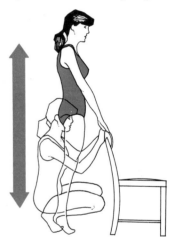

3b Once you can do this easily while using the chair as a support get rid of the chair and do it this time with your hands on your hips.

In the swing

Want to be more active? Tempted to try our exercise programme? This topic will help you keep it up.

Making changes

It's easy to have lots of grand ideas about the changes you will make but not so easy to put them into practice. Unless you are very unusual this is where you could use some help. In this topic we aim to help you bring your decisions about exercise together and begin to make one or two changes to your life.

It is best to start off with small changes introduced one by one and to be sure these work before you start anything bigger. Lots of little changes will eventually add up to a big change in your lifestyle. But if you have introduced these small changes slowly they will be much easier to maintain than one big change. The effort needed to maintain a big change, sprung on yourself out of the blue, is greater than that required to maintain small well-planned changes. So you can give yourself a head start by treating yourself gently and not expecting too much too soon.

Another way to help yourself make changes is to take advantage of good opportunities for change. Good opportunities for change occur when you start a new job, move to a new area, go on holiday or change your life in some other way. They make it easier for you to make other changes in your lifestyle without surprising or upsetting those around you and they are often the times when you feel that everything is going well and you could achieve almost anything.

They may set you on a new track almost without your realising something has happened and they really can take the sweat out of trying to change.

So making the most of these times can help you make your changes. You cannot always predict or plan them, but some good opportunities for change, such as going on holiday, or getting married, are usually planned in advance! On these occasions you can decide beforehand what changes you want to make to your lifestyle.

Planning for change

This is why planning for change is so important. If you have been working out how best you can include exercise in your lifestyle and have been trying out your programme, you will be ready to take advantage of any good opportunities that occur. With a little effort you will have your programme well established before opportunities for change have passed.

Your plan

Take a look back over the other topics in this chapter and review the changes you have decided to make. Make a list as you go along, like the one shown below left. The example shows you the decisions that Jean, one of our students, made after reading this chapter.

Review of your decisions	Jean's comments
1 Look back to page 64 to the 'How active are you?' quiz. How much time did you spend on D type activities each day?	*Only a few minutes. Want to be more active but don't think I can do this without proper exercise programme or some sort of sport*
2 Look back to page 66 to the 'What's in it for you?' quiz. Which benefits of exercise would you like to get? ○ Physical fitness and work capacity? ○ Looks and figure? ○ General health and well being? ○ Relaxation and social life?	*Would like to be more supple and improve my figure*
3 Look back to page 70 to the 'How fit are you?' quiz. How many of the common activities do you find tire you out? How did you get on with the 'Walking up stairs' test?	*Answered yes to three questions. Haven't done the stairs test yet because I live in a flat and I don't want the neighbours to think I've gone mad! Will try when I next go to my Mum's*

Which activity for you?

The chart on the right will help you choose the best activity for you if you want to get the benefits of exercise by taking part in a sport or game. The symbols show how good the activity is for helping you develop stamina, strength or suppleness. Three ★★★ means the activity is a very good one. One ★ means the activity has little or no effect. For example, swimming has ★★★ in all three columns and is therefore an excellent activity for all round fitness. In contrast fishing has only one ★ in each column. This means that fishing won't help you improve your suppleness or strength or

stamina. (But it can be a good hobby – many people find it enjoyable and relaxing.)

You now need to look back at section two of the chart on the previous page. If you chose physical fitness and work capacity or general health and well being look down the three columns for stamina, suppleness and strength on the next page and put a tick in column one for those activities which score high for all three and which you think you would like to try.

1 If you chose the benefits of looks and figure you particularly need an exercise which scores high for suppleness.
2 If you chose recreation and social life

you will need to fill in column two according to your interests. Whether or not an activity is relaxing or enjoyable or good for your social life is very much a matter of opinion. Some activities such as stair climbing are obviously not social activities. Team games such as cricket or football involve mixing with other people. Some are in-between such as running: it's a lonely pursuit but could easily be based in a jogging or athletics club and therefore have a good social life associated with it. In column two tick those activities which have the type of social life you enjoy.

In the third column you should put a tick if you can afford to take up your

chosen activities. You need to consider such things as:
○ do you need to travel? If so how much does it cost?
○ do you need to buy equipment such as racquets and balls? Could you hire them? (For example at a leisure centre.)
○ do you need to pay to use a court or a swimming pool?
○ do you need lessons? If so, can you get them more cheaply at a group price?

Cost may be your biggest deciding factor. Sometimes affording your chosen activity may mean changing your priorities. For example, if you decide you would like to go swimming this may mean paying a bus fare and an entry fee.

It may sound a lot, but when you compare it with the price of cigarettes or beer it is not so very much. Put a tick by those you can easily afford and a ? where the cost, although not unmanageable, would be on the high side.

Finally, in column four you need to consider whether you can fit the activity easily into your way of life.
○ Does it take up a lot of time? How much free time have you got?
○ If you need to travel, is the journey reasonably easy?
○ Do you need a partner? Or a team?
○ Is it seasonal? Or can you play indoors in winter?
Put a tick in column four against those

of your chosen activities which are easy to fit in to your life.

By now you are probably left with only one or two activities that you could take up. If you find you don't have even one left then either you don't really want to take up any kind of recreation or you have been too severe in your judgements. You may like to try going through the chart again. If you have several activities you would like to take up you can either take them all up at once (if you have the time and energy and can afford it!) or, if you really cannot choose, aim to do a different activity each season. This variety will benefit you physically and probably socially too.

	Stamina	Strength	Suppleness	1	2	3	4
1 Badminton	★★	★★	★★				
2 Billiards/Snooker	★	★	★				
3 Climbing stairs	★★	★★	★				
4 Cricket	★	★	★★				
5 Cycling	★★★	★★	★				
6 Dancing (Ballroom)	★★	★	★				
7 Dancing (Disco)	★★	★★	★★★				
8 Darts	★	★	★				
9 Digging in garden	★	★★★	★				
10 Driving	★	★	★				
11 Fishing	★	★	★				
12 Football (Soccer)	★★	★★	★★				
13 Golf	★	★	★★				
14 Keep-fit classes	★★	★★	★★★				
15 Housework	★	★★	★★				
16 Jogging on spot	★★	★	★				
17 Judo/Karate	★	★★	★★				
18 Mowing lawn	★	★★	★				
19 Rugby	★★	★★	★★				
20 Running	★★★	★★	★				
21 Squash	★★	★★	★★★				
22 Swimming	★★★	★★★	★★★				
23 Table tennis	★	★	★★				
24 Tennis	★★	★★	★★				
25 Walking briskly (over 1 hour)	★★	★	★				
26 Washing/polishing car	★	★★	★★				

Getting started

When you take up a new activity it's a good idea to think about any possible snags in advance so that you can plan how to deal with them. In this chart we have listed some of the common problems people find when they start something new. We have filled in Jean's comments about the keep-fit exercise classes she decided to take up. Think about how these problems would affect your chosen activity and make your own list of how you would tackle them. If you can't find a solution you may need to consider a different activity.

Now what do I do?

If you are only taking up an activity to improve your suppleness you can start straight away. Keep-fit, swimming and walking are examples of this type of activity. When you take up activities to improve your muscular strength and stamina it is a good idea to get fit before you begin. You can do this by following the exercise plan in *Getting and keeping fit.* To go on to advanced training for strength and stamina you will probably need to join a club. To find out about these clubs and other sports facilities ask at your local library, college or contact the Sports Council (see *What next?*).

If there isn't a local team or club practising the sport you want to try you might decide to start one yourself. First try to get your friends interested. You can advertise for other people in your local paper or post office. If there are at least ten of you interested you may be able to persuade your local authority to provide you with an evening class and tutor for the activity. Alternatively you can start your own club. The following case study may give you some ideas.

Residents of a small village with no recreation facilities, not even a village hall, decided that they wanted some sort of exercise for winter evenings. Jogging did not appeal because of the winter weather. After some thought it was realised that the local school assembly hall was big enough to take a badminton court. So they decided to form a badminton club. They asked the headmaster if they could hire the hall one night a week.

At first he was hesitant because he had to get permission from the local education authority. It meant painting lines on the floor, and he was concerned about damage to the lights from shuttlecocks. However, when these problems were fully discussed, he consented. Subscription money was used to buy a net and shuttlecocks, paint lines on the floor and hire the hall one night a week. It was decided that members would have to provide their own racquets.

At first the club opened for two hours once a week. But its popularity grew so rapidly that soon a second night's hire was arranged. And not long after that the hours increased from two to three both evenings so that a junior club could be started. Today the club is thriving.

Problem	Jean's comments
You find it hard to do or you are not very good at it	*I know exercising can be hard at first. You have to stick with it for a while to get the benefits. Anyone can do it though, it's not competitive*
You can't always find the time	*Sometimes I have to miss my classes. But I've bought a book and a record so I can do the exercises on my own*
Your partner or family resents your doing it	*Peter refused to do it with me. He doesn't mind me going to the classes though*
It clashes with your work	*I do the housework before I go out and put a stew in the oven for Peter's lunch*
It makes you ache too much or gives you a headache	*I ached a little at first. If you ache too much it means you have overdone it. Still, it wore off and I took it more gently after that*
You mind if your friends laugh at you and you don't like putting yourself on display	*Peter laughed at first but now he sees how much more relaxed I am he thinks it's great. At first I used to shut him out and lock the door when I practised at home*
You get downhearted if your progress is slow	*I'm still not as supple as I would like to be and sometimes I think I'll just give up. But everyone says it takes time*
You get bored by it	*I could get bored if I didn't vary my exercises. Playing different records to exercise by helps*
It becomes impractical because of the weather or cost or travel, etc	*Luckily I can walk to my classes. If the weather is really bad I do miss them*
Your special difficulties	*I'd love a leotard instead of my jeans but can't afford it*

Eating well

Is modern food really as bad for our health as experts are always telling us?

Unfortunately much of the information we are presented with seems to conflict. A few years ago we believed butter was good for us but now we are told that, if we eat too much, it may help to cause heart attacks. We used to be advised to cut down on bread and potatoes because they are fattening but now we are told to eat more of them instead.

Some of the foods we eat are blamed for playing a part in a whole range of disorders including heart disease, obesity, cancer, gall stones, strokes and diabetes. Changes in lifestyle affect our nutritional needs. So what do we need to know about the food we eat?

Today …

Less food

We have smaller appetites – because we use up less energy. We are definitely eating less than we used to, but our appetites haven't dropped quite as much as they should have done. Of course, as we shall see in *Patterns of eating* in Chapter 4, there are many reasons for eating that have nothing to do with hunger.

But more calories

We are eating a smaller quantity of food but the food we do eat is richer in calories. (Calories are the unit in which the energy content of food is measured.)

Energy rich food

As we become better off we change to energy rich foods. We eat more meat, cheese and chocolate.

Hidden calories

We eat more convenience foods which we may not realise are high in calories. Cakes, biscuits and pastry are rich in fat as well as sugar. Sugar is added to many prepared foods – for example baked beans – to make them tastier. (See 'Labels' section in the next topic.)

Alcohol

We drink more alcohol today. But many people do not realise that alcohol is high in calories. Alcohol is not thought of as a food – but many of us get a high proportion of our calories out of a bottle.

A new balance

Although we are eating less, we are not eating less of *all* foods. We have cut down on some types of food but maintained or increased our consumption of others. For example in the last 25 years we have halved the amount of bread and potatoes we eat but we go on eating the same amounts, or more, of the richer, highly flavoured foods, such as meat, cheese, eggs and butter. To look at it another way, we are eating thinner slices of bread but spreading them more thickly with butter.

The traditional meal pattern of 'meat, filler and veg' is becoming that of meat and a vegetable and no filler. (See the activity on the next page.) Although we are eating less packet sugar and jams than we used to we are eating more sugar in convenience foods.

The end result of this, from the nutritional point of view, is that the average British diet is proportionately higher in fat and sugar than it used to be. This trend is true for all rich countries.

More obesity

Our appetite, although lower, is not exactly matched to our need for food. This, together with the larger proportion of energy rich (high calorie) food we eat, is making many of us overweight. Of course, there is more to the story of obesity than this. *Patterns of eating* and *Overweight?* in Chapter 4 look at the problem in more detail.

Rich man poor man

The chart (right) helps you compare the diet of people in poorer countries with our own in Britain, a relatively rich country. Too much money can be the cause of an unbalanced diet just as too little money

Changing times

Compared with 50 years ago …

1a We now have labour saving machinery to do much of our work for us. Cars and public transport mean we walk less. Central heating warms us so we don't have to keep active to keep warm

2a Modern technology has progressed so far that we can now have almost any food we like, at any time of the year, usually at a reasonable price. Canning, freezing and drying of foods has taken away our dependence on the seasons for our food supply

3a Many of us now have fridges and freezers in which to store food. Convenience foods, in which most of the preparation and some of the cooking is done for us, are easily available

4a We live busy lives. We may have to rush off to work or school in the mornings. During the week our family may seldom all meet up. And when we want to eat, we want to eat fast!

So now …

1b We use less energy and therefore need to eat less

2b We have a much wider range of foods from which to choose what we will eat

3b We don't have to spend so much time shopping and preparing and cooking meals

4b Fewer of us eat breakfast – certainly not the large traditional cooked breakfasts. Proper family meals may be restricted to weekends. We eat many more sweets

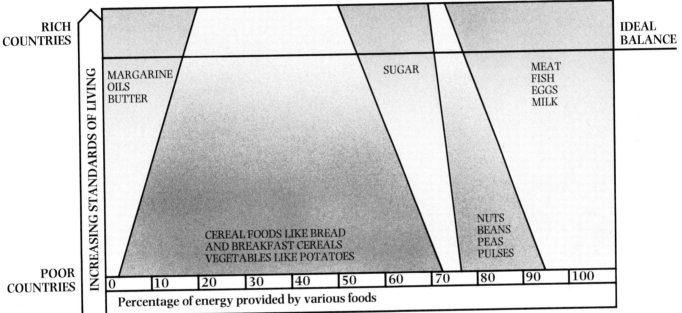

RICH COUNTRIES

IDEAL BALANCE

INCREASING STANDARDS OF LIVING

MARGARINE
OILS
BUTTER

SUGAR

MEAT
FISH
EGGS
MILK

NUTS
BEANS
PEAS
PULSES

CEREAL FOODS LIKE BREAD
AND BREAKFAST CEREALS
VEGETABLES LIKE POTATOES

POOR COUNTRIES

0   10   20   30   40   50   60   70   80   90   100

Percentage of energy provided by various foods

can. Although there is no such thing as a 'perfect' diet for everybody there is a general need for balance as indicated on the chart.

As you can see, the richer the country the higher the proportion of sugar, meat, egg, milk and fats in the population's diet but the lower the proportion of cereals, vegetables and fruit. If we compare our health with the health of people in poor countries we find there are many differences. In this country heart disease, obesity, diabetes, tooth decay, mental stress and cancer are much more common than in poor countries. But in these poorer countries children often die of starvation. Infectious diseases and illnesses caused by a deficiency of vitamins are more common in poorer countries. Of course, not all of these problems are directly caused by the unbalanced diets. A balanced diet is only part of what goes to make up a healthy lifestyle.

So what should we do?

The advice of most experts is that, in our diets, we should:

○ reduce the amount of fat we eat.

○ increase the amount of fibre.

○ cut out added sugar where possible.

This is what we should do in order to eat the best possible diet for our health. But eating to stay healthy is not the only reason for eating.

We often eat when we don't really need food or when we don't even particularly feel like eating or we eat even although we know the food is bad for us. Why do we do this? Because the social and emotional reasons for eating may be more important than anything else.

This is why making changes in our diet is never as easy as it sounds. Good advice to *just* cut down on this or that ignores the enormous importance of food in our lives.

The topics on diet in this chapter and *Patterns of eating* and *Overweight?* in Chapter 4 help you to take a wider view of the importance of food in your life. They will help you decide what changes you can reasonably make – and how to plan to make them.

Feelings about food

Having another look at what we eat is not important just for protection against disease. As well as keeping you in good physical shape a sensible diet plays an important part in your general feeling of well-being.

What do you choose to eat?

This activity will help you look at the balance of your diet – and how varied it is. The traditional way we plan meals is to choose 'meat and two vegetables'.

The 'meat' may often be fish or eggs and of the 'vegetables' one will be a 'filler' such as potatoes, or a substitute such as rice or pasta.

The chart below divides foods into these three main groups plus drinks and extras. Some foods, for example shepherd's pie which contains both meat and potato, or pizza, or stew will fit into two groups.

Go through the list and cross out all those you never or hardly ever eat. Then go through again and circle the ones you eat often. Add any others which you eat.

Most of us manage to grow and keep healthy without making a big issue of choosing between foods. This is because nearly everyone does choose a variety of different foods to eat through the day. You have probably found that you have circled some foods from each of the five groups.

Main
How many of these did you circle? Most people tick several in this column because they do pay attention to varying the main part of a meal.

Fruit/vegetables
These add fibre to our diet. They are also an important source of vitamins. But they don't all contain the same vitamins or the same amounts. So it is important to eat a variety of fruits and vegetables. The more ticks you have in this section the better. Cooking, particularly boiling for a long time, can destroy many of the vitamins. Check those you circled in the list and mark those you sometimes, or always, eat raw with an asterisk (*).

Fillers
You may have been surprised that we are encouraging you to eat fillers. The ideal meal today is often seen as main and vegetables and no filler. So many slimming diets recommend cutting out fillers that they are commonly thought to be bad for you. (A good slimming diet would be to eat a small amount of a well-balanced diet.)

'Fillers' fill us up so we don't feel hungry and then tempted to eat more of other probably energy rich foods. After all, two potatoes may seem a lot but a cube of cheese on a crispbread doesn't. However, the potatoes may better satisfy your hunger whereas the cheese and biscuit may leave you still feeling rather empty. And you will have eaten far more calories with the cheese!

Many of these fillers – particularly those made from whole-meal flour or cereals, like rice and porridge, or beans or potatoes provide us with fibre. (see p 90.)

These three groups, main, fruit/veg and fillers, provide a rough guide to eating a well-balanced diet. If each meal or snack were planned to include a food from each of these three groups they would provide the basis of a reasonable diet.

Drinks
You need drinks to quench your thirst. However, some, such as alcohol and sugary squashes and fizzy drinks, provide a lot of calories you may not need. Water is the only liquid you need – you don't have to sweeten it.

Extras
The 'extras' group are what they say – extra! They can be important for adding flavour but many of them are rich in fat and sugar.

Main	Fruit/Veg	Filler	Drinks
tinned fish	cabbage	bread	milk
bacon	cucumber	breakfast cereals	fizzy drinks
chicken	celery	buns	squash
fresh fish	carrots	rolls	wine
ham	lettuce	crispbreads	soup
beefburgers	mushrooms	crackers	fruit juice
roast beef	peas	biscuits	water
sausages	onions	toast	spirits
lamb chops	spinach	cake	chocolate
fish fingers	turnip	spaghetti	**Extras**
liver	tomato	baked beans	crisps
kidney	cauliflower	crisps	butter
luncheon meat	broccoli	rice	margarine
mince	apples	porridge oats	cream
stew	oranges	potatoes	lard
eggs	pears	chips	dripping
cheese	bananas	popcorn	ghee
meat pie	grapefruit	cornish pasty	sugar
cornish pasty	plums	meat pie	jam/marmalade
shepherd's pie	yams	shepherd's pie	ice cream
milk	sweet potato	pizza	sweets
pizza	plantain (green bananas)	ice cream	chocolate
pork chops	cassava	ravioli	tomato sauce
lentils	lentils	pastries	salt and pepper
baked beans	peppers	suet puddings	sweet and sour sauce
yogurt	fruit juice	instant whip	

Eating out

Next time you're out and about in town, look at the menus outside various cafés and restaurants.

Try and decide which dishes appeal to you most. Which cafés and restaurants would you most like to eat in? Is there one that you wouldn't consider eating in? Why? If you had to eat in each of them what would you choose?

Your answers should help you consider:
○ would you eat special dishes if you were out celebrating and could choose where to go?

○ how adventurous are you about trying new foods?

We will look at the significance of this in the next topic.

Your favourite foods

Many of us prefer our favourite dishes to new unfamiliar ones. Experts' advice is often ignored if they ask people to alter their diet so that they have to give up their old favourites and change to something they don't fancy. It would help if we only fancied what is nutritionally good for us! But what exactly is it that makes a particular dish so appealing?

Write down three of your favourite dishes and try to describe them in short sentences.

Think of: *colour* (drab, bright, etc), *smell* (sharp, tangy, etc), *how it feels* (smooth, rough, clinging, etc), *how it tastes* (savoury, sweet, sour, etc) and of course *cost* (pricey, cheap, good value for money, etc).

Favourite dishes

1
2
3

Now decide which kind of food or drink you think best fits the following descriptions.

Most enjoyable

Most attractive to look at

Most easily eaten day after day

Most revolting

Most romantic

Most fun

Simplest to make

You would most like to try

Try making this activity a bit more fun by asking your family or friends what they think.

When we think about the importance of food to health, we often forget that our own decisions about what to eat are affected by many things, including our likes and dislikes.

Some of these influences on our choices may conflict. For example bacon and eggs for breakfast is a fatty meal which is not good for our health but it is also an important symbol of British tradition and culture which many people would hate to give up.

83

How do we choose what we eat?

How much choice do you really have about the food you eat?

We have to make all sorts of choices. This topic looks first of all at the practical considerations and the constraints which affect what you choose and of which you may not be fully aware.

Next you are asked to look at your whole pattern of eating during the day. What kind of meals do you eat and when and where do you eat them? How do you choose what kinds of food and how much of them does your body need?

Finally, another area of choice is between fresh and processed foods. When it comes to processed foods are you sure you can tell from the label exactly what it is you are choosing to buy?

Practical considerations

Some of the factors which influence food choice are obvious, such as price and whether your nearest shops stock the sort of foods you want to buy. *Feelings about food* in the last topic should have helped you look at the kind of food you are used to eating. How adventurous are you with food? Do you like to try new foods or do you prefer to stick with what is familiar? Or maybe you are somewhere in-between, prepared to try some new dishes but drawing the line at others? Of course your choice may be limited by what other members of your family like to eat.

If you enjoy cooking you probably prefer to try out new recipes using fresh ingredients. On the other hand if time is short or you don't like cooking you probably buy more convenience foods, where a food manufacturer has done much of the preparation for you. Or you cook foods like eggs and chips which require little effort to prepare.

You may also be influenced by what you have read about diet and health and so are making a conscious effort to lose weight, eat less sugar or to eat vegetable fats instead of animal fats.

Unseen constraints?

You probably automatically take these practical considerations into account when you choose what to eat. However,

there are also a number of other constraints of which you may be unaware. What lies behind your likes and dislikes and what you feel is 'right' to eat?

Family and friends?

Many of our food habits are influenced by what we learnt as children. Such as the importance of 'proper' meals rather than snacks. Or a liking for a dish which was a family favourite. We may have learned to hate things too! Such as liver and green vegetables because we were made to eat them as children.

Friends can also have a strong influence. Most people like to conform to some extent to what other people do in case they are made to feel odd. How much you are influenced will also depend on how self-confident you are and whether or not you enjoy being 'different' or the 'same' as other people.

The presence or absence of other people may also affect the sort of meal eaten. A young man taking a girl out for a candle-lit dinner would be unlikely to order fish and chips. A person on their own might eat cheese and biscuits for lunch but would cook a meal if someone else were present.

What's 'right' and 'wrong'?

Some people are forbidden to eat certain foods by their religions, for example Jews and Muslims are forbidden to eat pork and certain foods have to be prepared in a special way. Others feel that it is wrong to kill animals for food and so are vegetarian. Whilst neither of these situations may apply to you many of us do have strong feelings about what is 'right' and 'wrong' about foods. For example many people hate to waste food and would eat up leftovers they do not even want rather than throw them away. Likewise some people feel that no 'proper' meal is complete without meat and so they will spend more than they might like to on it. It's odd that they will go without vegetables if the price of them is slightly above what they would normally expect to pay.

Advertising

How much do advertisements of different kinds influence us in buying foods? This is

a difficult question to answer but if the manufacturers of foodstuffs didn't think it worthwhile they wouldn't spend so much money advertising their food. We look at this further in Chapter 8.

Your eating habits

There isn't one 'right' pattern of eating. You certainly don't *have* to have three meals a day. Nor do you *have* to have breakfast. Our pattern of eating is probably largely determined by the work we have to do and with whom we eat.

Here's how two people describe their eating habits:

Jean Evans, age 33
'With a big family, I don't get much time to eat. I do sit down for coffee and biscuits as I miss breakfast. The rest of the time I snatch food between housework and taking care of the baby. I don't enjoy my evening meal as I'm so tired and I know there is still washing up to be done.'

Bob Jones, age 36
'I do get off to a good start each day with a proper cooked breakfast. At lunch I'll eat whatever the pub where I stop for lunch is serving with the beer. I'm pretty tired when I get home after driving around all day so I like to have my supper on a tray in front of the TV. I watch and doze until about 11.00 pm. When I take the dog for a walk that perks me up a bit so I usually have some cheese and biscuits with a cup of tea before I go to bed.'

Can you write a similar sketch of your eating habits? Describe a usual week day. It should help you discover the main pressures which determine when and what you eat. Is it how busy you are? How tired you are? How much you can afford to spend? The choice available at where you have to eat? What you fancy? What someone prepares for you? Would your description of a typical Sunday be different? If you need to change what you eat you may find it easier if you can fit it into your usual pattern. For example, eating less of what you *do* like may be easier than changing to less fattening foods that you *don't* fancy.

What does the body need?

Food not only provides the energy we need but also supplies the body with:
○ basic materials for growth and repair of tissues. These include protein and minerals like calcium and iron.
○ small amounts of vitamins and some minerals which are essential for various body functions.
○ fibre which is necessary for the healthy functioning of the digestive system.

Eating a variety of foods is the best way of making sure that we get enough of all these things.

How much do we need?

We are each of us different and so will have slightly different needs. There are some general rules and advice but we have to work out what is best for *us*. So we may need to weigh ourselves occasionally, or watch out for our clothes getting tighter, to check that we aren't eating more than we need. In theory our appetites will increase or decrease as our energy needs increase or decrease. For example, if we do a lot of energetic work

we feel more hungry. However, this only works if we only eat when we are really hungry. And we mustn't eat so fast that by the time we get the message that we're 'full up' we have already overloaded our stomachs. Eating sugary foods which are high in calories but low in bulk upsets the hungry/full-up signalling system. And of course we eat for many other reasons, nothing to do with hunger.

We need to balance the energy we take in – our food – against the energy we use up in our activities during the day. If you rush around all day you are likely to use more energy than if you sit down most of the time.

Some of us know that we put on weight easily whilst others remain stick-thin however much they eat. Some experts now think that weight gain is connected more with inefficient body burn-up of what we eat rather than the amount we eat in the first place. But it still means that many people have to diet, perhaps even harder, to compensate. It's all too easy for 'fatties' to feel, 'It's not fair – he can eat whatever he likes but I can't'. Well it isn't fair and it can be rotten to have to watch your weight all the time. But if you do let yourself get overweight you have the worries of knowing you are risking your health as well as probably not liking the way that you look.

Are you sure you know what you're eating?

When you buy fresh food you can see clearly, if you look, what condition it is in. But with any food that has been processed or prepacked it's not so easy – unless you learn how to interpret the information on the label.

The information on packs is strictly controlled by law and must indicate 'the true nature of the food'. But subtle differences in the wording on the label can be completely missed by the shopper. For example, if a yogurt carton has a 'fruity' picture on the lid then it will contain a reasonable quantity of *real* fruit. If, on the other hand, it is only fruit *flavoured* with no real fruit, then the pack will be plain.

When it comes to canned meat, the variations in the wording can make enormous differences to the quantity of meat in a can!

Ingredients have to be listed in order of quantity. So whatever there is most of will be listed first and the further down the list an ingredient is, the less there will be of it in the pack. Not all prepared foods have to have their ingredients listed as yet, but the law may change so that foods like bread will have to be labelled.

This chart appeared in *Which?*, June 1977

If a food is called:	the minimum amount of meat is
potted meat, chopped meat, minced meat	90%
(canned) savoury minced meat	85%
meat with gravy, salami, frankfurter	75%
meat spread, meat paste, paté	70%
pork sausages, pork sausage meat	65%
sliced meat with gravy	60%
meat with vegetable and gravy, sausages (not pork)	50%
meat with vegetable and sauce	40%

Processed v fresh

Many people believe that a processed food that has been canned, dried, frozen or preserved is not as good as fresh food. They consider that it has less nutrient value.

Some nutrient value is certainly lost during processing. But this is usually small and indeed may be less than what is lost if the fresh food lies around in the shops a few days or is boiled or stewed for a long time. It is perfectly possible to live healthily if you eat only processed foods. As long as you have a varied diet the nutrients which may be missing from one food are made up for by an abundance of them in another food.

Being able to choose from a wide range of processed food enables you to add more variety to your diet. It's only if you restrict your diet to a few kinds of food that you need to worry about whether the processing has reduced its nutrient value.

Many people are worried that chemicals added to processed food may be harmful. Chemical preservatives provide protection against food-poisoning bacteria and dangerous moulds. However, some chemicals are not added to protect us so much as to make the food more attractive.

Looking at labels

The ingredients list on labels may surprise you. Look at these three labels: the name of the food has been removed so that they show only the ingredients.

1 Skimmed milk, milk sugar, raspberry, skimmed milk solids, stabiliser, colour, flavouring

2 Beef, pork, potato, starch, skimmed milk powder, salt, emulsifying salts, spices, sodium nitrate, ascorbic acid

3 Beans, tomatoes, sugar, salt, edible starch, spices, flavouring

Write down what you think each food is. Check with the list at the bottom of the page (upside down). Did any of the ingredients surprise you? Sometimes extra information just confuses you.

1 Fruit yogurt, 2 Hot dogs in brine, 3 Baked beans in tomato sauce.

Striking a balance

Because times have changed modern man needs a different diet from that which was suitable fifty years ago.

Eating food that is best for our health may have to be balanced against such practicalities as can we afford it? Is it available in our local shops? Do we fancy it? And does it fit in with our work and family life? A balance often has to be struck between what we feel we ought to do and what best fits in to our life-style. It's much easier to make small adjustments to our existing eating habits rather than try to adopt a completely new pattern of eating.

Best for our health?

The link between food and health is a complex one. Research has suggested a link between various aspects of western diet and certain disorders, eg high fat intake and heart disease, low fibre diet and cancer of the bowel, high sugar intake and dental decay.

Today's killer diseases do not fall into a simple pattern of 'one disease, one cause, one cure'. It is unlikely that diseases like coronary heart disease or the common cancers are caused by just one factor such as too much fat or too little fibre. A range of other risk factors that also affect our health are known. These include cigarette smoking, social class, stress, obesity, lack of exercise and individual susceptibility (which may well be inherited).

Let's look at this in relation to heart attacks. Some people are more likely to be at risk from a heart attack than others. For example, if you are male, middle-aged, have a close relative who had coronary heart disease, smoke, are overweight, take little exercise, eat a lot of fatty foods and have raised blood pressure then you have a pretty good chance of having a heart attack well before you retire.

Roughly speaking, if you are in one of these 'risk categories' you are twice as likely as the average man to have a heart attack. With two risk factors – you are about four times as likely, with three risk factors, eight times as likely. So eliminating any one of the risk factors will help a lot.

However, if you want to do everything possible to reduce the risk of a heart attack, you need to give up smoking, take enough exercise, keep your weight down, cut down on fatty foods, and reduce the stress in your life. You may decide, of course, that you don't want to go as far as this because you feel you wouldn't enjoy life if you had to make so many changes.

Despite the fact that there may be many factors working together to affect our health many experts advise us purely along the lines of their own special interests. Advice about just one of the

factors instead of looking at all points of view can seriously distort the picture.

For example, a low-fibre diet has been linked with an increased likelihood of developing cancer of the bowel. This has led to a lot of publicity about eating more fibre. Advertising has urged people to dose themselves with bran. Unfortunately we may be completely missing the point. A high-fibre diet as eaten by people in the developing world is very different from a western diet in all sorts of ways. As the chart on page 90 shows these high-fibre diets are also low in fats, animal protein and sugar, and rich in starch.

Just adding bran to our high fat and protein diet isn't enough, we need to alter the balance of our diet. **It is the whole balance of the diet which matters.**

One perfect diet?

It would be untrue to suggest that there is one perfect diet which can be recommended to everyone to keep them as healthy as possible. This is because each person has different energy needs, different susceptibility to certain disorders and different eating habits. We don't yet know enough to be able to give each person an individual 'blueprint' for health. However enough is known to be able to suggest a wise pattern of eating which at best will prevent disease and at worst can do no harm. The chart on the next page sums up what is now considered to be the best advice for balance in your diet.

You need to strike a balance

You can work out what would be best for your health. Look through the chart on the next page and decide what you *should* change. But bear in mind what kinds of food you like to eat (p 82–83), what you can afford and what is available. Then you can decide what changes you can reasonably hope to make.

Next you need to plan, in advance, how you will introduce these changes. And how you will keep them up, so that you learn new patterns of eating. (See p 92–93 in this chapter and p 100–101 in Chapter 4.)

Target – eat less fats

Why?
Cholesterol is the main constituent of fatty deposits in arteries and of gallstones. Excess amounts are made in the body when high fat foods are eaten. Particularly food rich in 'saturated' fat mainly found in animal foods. Other fats in the diet – called 'poly-unsaturated' fats – tend to reduce cholesterol in the body. This type of fat is found in many foods, particularly in corn oil, sunflower seed oil and soya oil. (NB some vegetable oils and margarines are, in fact, rich in saturated fat.)

As far as general health is concerned it is more important to reduce the total amount of all fats rather than just to swap animal fats for special vegetable oils or margarine

By how much?
We get more than 40% of the calories we need from fats. It would be better to reduce fats to 30–35%. This is difficult to calculate. You almost certainly need to cut down if you often do one or more of these things. Eat fried food. Put butter or margarine on cooked vegetables. Spread butter thickly on your bread. Eat a lot of the foods listed in the next column. Provided you keep the total amount low you do not need to cut out completely your favourite butter, cream or fried food. If you are not prepared to cut down on the total amount of fat in your diet you should change to special vegetable oils and low fat spreads

Watch these foods
Fat is a major part of: cakes, pastries, biscuits and chocolates, sausages, salami, pork, lamb, cheese, cream, butter and margarine, cooking oils and fat.

If you love the taste of butter, really savour it on a plain slice of bread and butter.

Change your cooking habits by
○ Grilling instead of frying
○ Using non-stick pans
○ Using recipes which use less fat
○ Using skimmed (low fat) milk instead of ordinary milk in recipes

Target – eat less sugar

Why?
A high sugar diet encourages dental decay. Sweet foods can spoil the appetite for more nourishing foods. Sugar only provides energy which is also provided by, for example, potatoes and wholemeal bread. Because we become addicted to sweet things we are tempted to overeat and so may put on weight

By how much?
Most people get one fifth of their energy needs (calories) from sugar. About half of this is from the use of packet sugar and jams. The other half might be thought of as 'hidden sugar' which is added to many manufactured foods. *We do not need any sugar at all*

Watch these foods
Sugar is the major part of sweets, soft drinks, cakes, biscuits, puddings and jams. It is also added to many manufactured foods like tomato ketchup, tinned fruit, ice cream and frozen foods. Reading the label will tell you which have sugar added to them. If you have a sweet tooth you could have an occasional treat, eg, jam on your bread or a piece of chocolate

Target – eat more fibre

Why?
There are probably a dozen different kinds of fibres, all with different roles to play. Therefore cereal foods *and* fruit and vegetables are equally important. Extra bran is not the same as 'high fibre diet' and is only good for helping constipation. 'High fibre diets', which may offer protection from a number of digestive ailments, are also low in fat and animal protein

By how much?
You can't really eat too much when it is a natural part of food. You could eat too much bran – but you would be hard put to swallow it. You are probably eating enough if you have regular bulky, but not hard, bowel movements

Watch these foods
Eat more of the bulky foods listed in 'fillers' *and* a variety of fruit and vegetables
○ Eat breakfast cereals made from the whole grain
○ Try brown rice or wholemeal pasta
○ Eat wholemeal or brown bread
○ Eat the skins of old potatoes as well as new ones

Target – eat more filler foods

Why?
These foods are generally good sources of fibre. They also provide starch which, if fats and sugar are reduced, will fill the 'energy gap' ie, provide the calories we need. These foods are also good sources of proteins and several minerals and vitamins and fibre

By how much?
We have halved our consumption of bread and potatoes in the last 25 years and rich, fatty foods are now a larger part of our diet. Starchy, filler foods should be included in every meal. A sandwich makes a better snack than a chocolate bar

Watch these foods
Eat more breakfast cereals (not sugared ones), wholemeal bread, potatoes, rice and pasta. Watch out that you don't use recipes that use a lot of oil, cream or butter. Dishes such as pizza, curries and spaghetti contain about the right balance of 'main', veg and filler. If you are slimming remember the ideal is to eat less of a well-balanced diet rather than a one-sided crash diet

Target – eat more fruit and vegetables

Why?
These supply vitamins, and minerals, as well as fibre. Because they all contain a lot of water, they provide a lot of bulk on the plate without an extra load of calories

By how much?
Try to have some fruit or vegetables at least three times a day

Watch these foods
Eat more of a variety of fruit and vegetables, including root vegetables such as potatoes and carrots

Salt

Some people are sensitive to salt and may develop high blood pressure if they have a very salty diet. In the hopes that triggering off this sensitivity can be avoided it is now recommended that babies under one year should not have salt added to their food. But no one needs added salt. There is sufficient already in the food we eat. Think before you automatically sprinkle salt on your plate. And keep a check on how many salted nuts and crisps and other salty foods you eat.

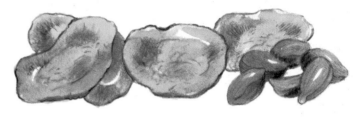

Alcohol

May be enjoyable but it provides a lot of calories. If you are watching your weight you need to watch out for these – sometimes forgotten – calories. On the other hand a small amount of alcohol improves your appetite. This can be an advantage for old people who have lost interest in food.

Protein

The proportion of protein in the diet of people from 'poor' and 'rich' countries is about equal but the source is different. In a rich country the protein will be mainly from animal sources. In a poor country it will be from vegetable sources. Protein from a mixture of vegetable foods – lentils, peas, beans of various sorts and bread – can provide as good a source of protein as that from meat. It's cheaper too!

In Britain the average diet provides twice as much protein as we actually need, so getting enough protein is never a problem for people in normal health.

The food on your plate

What do the targets on p90 mean in terms of food on your plate? These pictures are all of balanced meals illustrating the pattern of 'mains, filler and veg' which is a good principle to bear in mind when planning both meals and snacks. (See pp 82–83.)

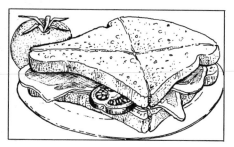

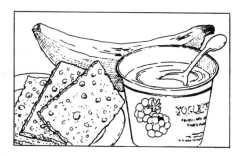

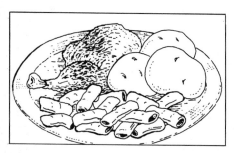

'Mains'	A variety of these would provide:
meat*	iron, calcium
cheese*	and other
milk*	minerals,
eggs*	protein, B
poultry	vitamins
fish	
beans and	
other pulses	
nuts*	

Don't forget these contain fat!

Fillers	
bread	protein, B
rice	vitamins some
pasta	iron and
potatoes	calcium, fibre
breakfast	(particularly if
cereals	whole grain
	cereals are
	eaten and the
	skins are left on
	potatoes). New
	potatoes are
	also a good
	source of vitamin C

Vegetables or fruit	
green	vitamin C,
vegetables	folic acid (a B
yellow/red	vitamin
vegetables	important for
fruit juices	blood),
citrus fruits	minerals, fibre,
soft fruits (eg,	water
plums, pears)	

Changing your diet – You can do it

Making changes isn't easy. It's best to realise this from the start so that you don't get downhearted and give up if you don't have instant success. It can be an advantage to make changes slowly because then the changes can be gradually and naturally fitted in to suit your own style of living. New habits need to be learnt, and old habits have got to be 'unlearnt'. This always takes time and it is one reason why people who go on 'crash' diets put all their weight back on.

Planning your changes

As a result of reading the other topics on nutrition, what have you decided you would like to change? Take time to look back and make a written list for yourself. As we look at the factors which can help or hinder you in making changes in your diet we will add comments from Sally (35) who planned to make changes for herself, her husband Tom (41) and her 16-year-old daughter, Ann.

Forewarned is forearmed

Old ideas about food are just one of the difficulties you may come across when trying to change your diet. There are others which may hinder your progress if you cannot find ways around them. Look at the list of common difficulties which occur (on right). Sally has filled in what she did to solve these problems. In your space put down how you will tackle these problems if they happen to you.

Talk it over

One of the best ways to begin to get round any problem is to talk about it. Sally needed to discuss the effect her changes would have on the family with her husband, Tom and daughter, Anne. If Sally doesn't have the support of at least one member of her family, changing the family diet to suit herself might cause a lot of resentment. You can find out more about how to discuss your needs in Chapter 2, *Person to person.*

Start with small steps

Don't try to change everything at once. Small steps added together will eventually give you a big change. When aiming for a more balanced diet gradually introduce one food you don't eat enough of. Let it replace one food you eat too often.

Sally was always eating pies and sweet puddings after her meals. The first week she started eating a piece of fruit or a yoghurt at midday instead of her usual custard tart. The second week she started eating fruit in the evening as well. This seemingly small change eventually made a lot of difference to the balance of Sally's diet. Gone was one main source of fat and sugar. Replaced by a good source of fibre, vitamins and minerals.

In order to cut down your fat intake try to start with something you won't miss too much. When Sally made sandwiches she started buttering only one piece of bread instead of two and added a few slices of tomato to moisten the sandwich. Gradually she hopes to stop frying so much at home but her husband doesn't like the idea of this. However he hasn't noticed the difference between grilled and fried bacon and tomatoes.

Increasing the fibre in your diet may not mean giving up anything else or eating extra. Try to replace a low fibre food with a high fibre substitute. Sally started making her sandwiches with whole-meal bread and filling them with salad instead of jam or sandwich spread. When she made pastry she used half wholemeal flour and cut down a little on the fat. Instead of toast and jam for breakfast she started to eat wholegrain cereal or toast and a savoury spread.

If you aim to cut down on sugar you could start this in several small ways. Sally started by substituting low calorie drinks and squashes for the usual sugary kind. This wasn't any hardship so she then cut down on sugar in her tea.

Maintaining your change

Once you have started to change your diet it's very important to keep it up. You can do this by praising yourself and rewarding yourself with small treats – preferably not food rewards. Also by getting help from other people. *What will you change?* in Chapter 4 tells you more about giving yourself small rewards to reinforce your new behaviour.

Support from others is very important too. Sally didn't feel she could succeed without her daughter's help. The support and approval of our friends and family can help us through the hard times of changing. Self-help groups can also help us to keep going. Groups such as Weight-watchers have proved to be particularly successful in supporting women who are trying to lose weight. See Chapter 4, *Breaking old patterns.*

Will this be a problem?	Sally's solution	What will you do?
Do you need support and encouragement from someone or else you can't keep going?	*Ann is keen to change her diet too so she will help. Husband Tom feels outvoted!*	
Will you need to cook and eat different meals from usual?	*I do all my own shopping and cooking so I organise the meals. But Tom misses the cakes and chips*	
Will the food cost more?	*Because I buy less processed and packed food and more fruit and veg the cost is about the same*	
Is the food readily available?	*Fortunately my supermarket sells the foods I need. Otherwise it would mean special weekly trips to the nearest big town*	
What will the effect be on the rest of your family?	*Ann is pleased. Tom gets fed up sometimes but I tell him it will be worth it*	
What will the effect be on your work and social life?	*It makes visiting friends awkward. I have to explain to them so they don't think I'm rude*	
Do you often have to eat away from home?	*Doesn't apply to me but I make my daughter fresh sandwiches instead of her stodgy school lunch*	

Breaking old patterns

Why do so many people overeat, drink too much, smoke or rely on 'pills' to keep them going?

Patterns of living

Many people use food, drink, cigarettes or pills to help them cope, in the short term, with stress and worry. But as long term measures they don't really help you cope and they do damage your health. The stress itself may have been produced by personal problems and this book tries to offer more effective ways of handling these. Perhaps it is social circumstances that make life difficult. But unfortunately it is much harder to improve housing and working conditions than it is to deal with personal worries.

It is also difficult to change the kind of foods which are produced, advertised and sold in the shops. Our society certainly does not make changing your ways easy. Persuading you to drink more, eat more 'junk' food and smoke more is big business. The Government gets high revenue from the sales of tobacco and alcohol – even though a different government department then has to spend as much on providing treatment for tobacco and alcohol related illnesses.

Large profits are made by the sale of junk foods (which have little goodness in them), white flour and refined sugar. These factors all make it difficult, particularly for people on a low income, to eat well and keep their weight down.

Of course not all poor patterns of living are ways of trying to cope with problems. They may have been picked up – without thinking about them – when you were a child. Or, if they were learnt as a way of coping, the original stress may have gone but the pattern remains as a habit. So far we have avoided calling these patterns habits. This is because most people think of habits as bad and that the person who has the habit should take the blame for what he does. Habits may be 'bad' in that they are damaging and difficult to change – but that may be nothing to do with the character of the person concerned. When people *do* want to change they have the problem that, whatever the reasons were for starting in the first place, habits, once learnt, are extremely difficult to break.

Learning new patterns

Most people know what they want to change – or feel they ought to change. They also know why they want to change. The damage caused by smoking, drinking or eating too much is well known.

What holds people back? They don't believe they can change, and to admit it may be too painful, because it makes them seem weak-willed. So they may swing the other way and maintain they don't want to change.

Have you decided that you do want to change?
You may have decided to try to change even though you cannot do much, at the moment, about your underlying problems.

Or perhaps you want to 'break the habit' whilst also tackling the underlying problem?

Or you may no longer have any problems but realise you are still left with a 'bad' habit!

You can change

It will need careful planning and you may need the help of your family or friends or workmates.

But it would be foolish of us to tell you that it is easy. Those of you for whom it is easy will already have got on and made the changes. But many of us have tried and failed in the past. We know it isn't easy and our confidence has been damaged by the failure. But that was probably because we did not make a good enough plan.

You can succeed and once you start to succeed you have the extra reward and satisfaction of knowing you can control what you do and what happens to you.

This chapter can help you work out what your present pattern of eating, smoking, drinking and pill-taking is. It will help you think about why you need to behave that way. This chapter then deals with the steps you need to follow to help yourself to change. You will be able to devise a personal plan for the changes that you want to make.

Patterns of eating

If only we ate just to keep alive!

If only it was physically impossible to eat more than we need!

Why else do we eat?

The giving and accepting of food can carry many messages.

We celebrate by throwing a party, going out for a meal or having a special meal at home. Many religions have special feast days of celebration or times of fasting, giving up food as a signal of self-denial.

When we entertain we may feel we are judged by the lavishness of the food we serve. If we are the guests we know we are expected to eat a lot and praise the cook! On all sorts of social occasions we expect to give or be given food.

A gift of food can say 'Thank you' or 'I love you'. If the food is an outward sign of the cook's love then it can seem vitally important to eat it. Refusing to eat is seen as rebellion or even as not loving the giver. The trigger for a parent's battering of a child may be the child's frustrating refusal to eat.

We punish people by withholding food. The child is sent to bed without his supper. The prisoner is put on bread and water.

We often reward ourselves with small treats of foods. Many people still go on trying to cheer themselves up with such a 'treat' when they are anxious or depressed. And, of course, it does make us feel better for a while.

When you start keeping a diary of what you eat you should be able to work out the importance for you of these social and emotional reasons for eating.

Keeping a diary

Knowing where and when you are eating – as well as what – will also help you work out why you're eating. Once you know why you are eating you can begin to choose. 'Do I need to eat or could I do something else instead?'

Keep a diary of your eating habits for four days, including a weekend. It may seem a bit of a bore but it will be surprising what it tells you about yourself. Make four pages like the one opposite – one for each day. One section has been filled in to give you a better idea of what kind of

notes to make. Fill in your diary each time you have something to eat.

At the end of each day look down each column and see what it tells you about your eating habits. The following questions should help you work out the important points for you.

○ **What time?** Is there a definite time of the day when you are likely to eat extra snacks? Is it when you get home from work? Or the time between the children's tea and supper time? Or after supper while you watch TV?

○ **How long?** Do you prolong mealtimes with extra helpings? Or sit around nibbling extras? Or never have definite mealtimes but snack off and on all day?

○ **Where?** All over the house while you're doing housework? Whenever you watch TV? In bed?

○ **Who with?** Do you eat a lot at special family meals? Or when you go back to see your mother? Or when you are visiting friends?

○ **What mood?** When you feel like celebrating? Or are depressed? Or tired and distracted?

○ **Were you hungry?** Some people find this difficult to answer. They no longer know what they feel like when they are hungry because they keep themselves topped up.

Are you convinced you feel hungry about every thirty minutes? If so, are you looking at TV or magazine adverts for food? Or can you smell cooking? Or are you doing something with which you always have something to eat?

Write down your own comments so that you build up a clear picture of your particular pattern of eating. After reading the next topic you may decide that you want to change this pattern. We shall refer back to this diary to help you spot your difficult times and make definite plans to handle them better.

Poor patterns of eating

Overweight?

Eating more than your body needs to keep going will result in excess weight. The charts on the next two pages will give you

an idea of how much weight you need to lose.

If you want to lose weight you will need to change your pattern of eating. Before you can do that you need to know your present pattern of eating. Whatever the reasons for your over-eating it is probably, by now, a well-established habit.

You may hardly think about it. So you may need to keep a detailed diary for a few days to become aware of just what you are doing.

Binge and fast?

You may be the right weight – but do you binge and fast? One day you eat everything you can find and perhaps end up being sick. Then you feel rotten and punish yourself by fasting. You may feel particularly 'good' about yourself when you are fasting. Then you start to binge again.

You feel out of control. Maybe you think that life, or you, is so horrible that you might as well stuff yourself. You like food but you hate yourself for being so weak and bingeing. Not only are you eating a poorly balanced diet (see Chapter 3) but you are undermining your self-esteem every time you do it (see Chapter 2). Keeping a diary should help you begin to get in control of your eating.

Underweight?

Some people never put on weight however much they eat. It's perfectly OK to be a little underweight. You may not like the way you look but it isn't medically harmful.

But if you are one of the few people who is seriously underweight (check the charts on the next pages) you should discuss this with your own doctor. He or she will be able to tell if you have anorexia nervosa which may have been preceded by 'a binge and fast' pattern of eating. There are often complex reasons for this. However, paying attention to your existing pattern of eating and learning more useful eating habits usually plays an essential part in the overcoming of this serious problem.

Overweight?

If you eat more food than your body can use the excess food is stored as fat.

How much should you weigh?

Work out your present weight for height on the chart. A metric scale has been included here in case you prefer to measure in metres (m) and kilograms (kg). Draw a line up from your weight on the weight scale. Then draw another line across from your height on the height scale. Mark an X where your two lines cross.

As long as your weight falls somewhere in the 'suitable' range (the lighter grey band on the chart) you don't need to worry about the effect of your weight on your health. It is not going to damage your health or shorten your life. If your X lies in the darker grey band you are carrying extra weight which, although it is unlikely to affect your health seriously, may make you feel unattractive. At this weight your doctor would rate you as fat – and most people would also themselves feel they would like to be slimmer.

If your X falls to the right of the darker grey band then, medically, you would be labelled as 'obese'. Of course your doctor may not call you obese to your face! But your health is now definitely at risk. (To be one stone overweight may be just as risky as smoking 10 + cigarettes a day.)

Damage to your health
Extra weight puts a strain on the weight-bearing joints, especially the hips and knees. You also tire more easily and become breathless. Large amounts of sugar are thought to be bad for your heart. Also large quantities of animal fats and dairy products may silt up the arteries and this increases the risk of a heart attack. Should you ever need an operation, thick layers of fat may make it more difficult to do.

Besides being harmful, being fat can make you lonely! Some people do seem to be 'fat and jolly' but other seemingly 'jolly fatties' are just playing the clown. They make fun of themselves rather than wait for someone else to do it. But it hurts inside. Many fat people are extremely sensitive to what others think of them.

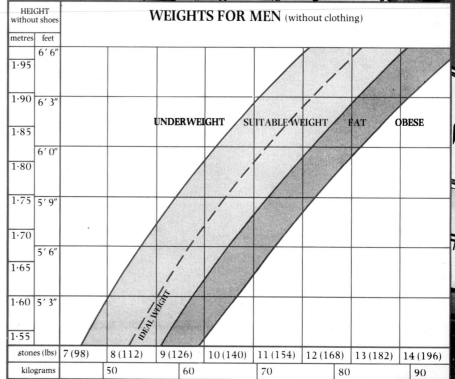

HEIGHT without shoes		WEIGHTS FOR MEN (without clothing)								
metres	feet									
	6' 6"									
1·95										
1·90	6' 3"			UNDERWEIGHT	SUITABLE WEIGHT	FAT	OBESE			
1·85										
	6' 0"									
1·80										
1·75	5' 9"									
1·70										
	5' 6"									
1·65										
1·60	5' 3"	IDEAL WEIGHT								
1·55										
stones (lbs)		7 (98)	8 (112)	9 (126)	10 (140)	11 (154)	12 (168)	13 (182)	14 (196)	
kilograms			50		60		70		80	90

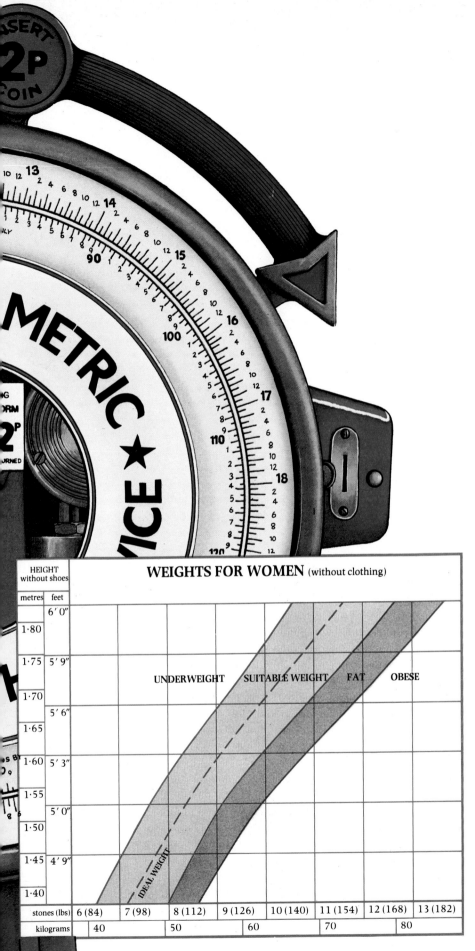

HEIGHT without shoes		WEIGHTS FOR WOMEN (without clothing)							
metres	feet								
	6' 0"								
1·80									
1·75	5' 9"								
1·70		UNDERWEIGHT	SUITABLE WEIGHT	FAT	OBESE				
	5' 6"								
1·65									
1·60	5' 3"								
1·55									
	5' 0"								
1·50									
1·45	4' 9"								
1·40									
stones (lbs)		6 (84)	7 (98)	8 (112)	9 (126)	10 (140)	11 (154)	12 (168)	13 (182)
kilograms		40		50		60		70	80

IDEAL WEIGHT

They may gradually become so embarrassed that they stop meeting other people and become isolated and lonely. This loneliness may make them eat even more, for comfort.

How did you learn?

Fat people have learnt poor patterns of eating. Unlike most slim people, fat people don't just eat because they are hungry. Their eating is triggered off by other signals.

Children can learn to eat for the wrong reasons. As you read through this list tick the ones which are true for you.

☐ **Early overfeeding** Fat adults are likely to have been fat babies, though not all fat babies become fat adults.

☐ **Everyone else ate too much** If the adults in the family eat huge meals or snack all day, the children learn to do likewise.

☐ **TV adverts** which promote junk foods or very sweet foods can teach you to value the wrong kind of foods.

☐ **Your family** could only afford the cheaper starchy or sugary foods. Most adults prefer the kind of food they got used to having as a child.

☐ **Food is used as a reward** for being good or doing well.

☐ **Food is given instead of love or attention.** Busy or distracted parents may find it easier to give food instead of taking time off to hug and play with a baby.

☐ **Food is used as a consolation** 'Have a sweetie to make it better' is a common response to a child's fall or bump.

☐ **Denial of food** can be used as a punishment. 'No supper for you, you naughty boy.'

☐ **'Eat up to please Mummy'** You get a good feeling when you please someone. You can go on getting that good feeling after eating, long after you've given up doing it for Mummy.

What can you do?

If you are overweight then you are eating more food than you need. Here are three ways you could learn to eat less.

A *Learn better eating habits* You need to keep a diary of your pattern of eating as we describe on page 97, then concentrate on *when* and *how* and *why* you eat. You may need to plan to eat only at certain times and places.

B *Count calories* The energy which food supplies to the body is measured as calories (or *joules* in the metric system). All foods can supply some energy to the body. Special charts exist to show the calorie content of most foods and the daily calorie needs of different people. If you add up the calories in all the food you eat each day, you can keep a check on your intake and make sure that your body takes in fewer calories than it needs to keep going. (Most people will lose weight if their food contains no more than 1,000 calories each day.) This way your body has to supply the extra calories (energy) needed by 'burning up' some of your stored fat.

C *Cut down on energy-rich foods*

The STOP	Eat as little as possible of high calorie foods
CAUTION	Be careful about how much medium calorie food you eat
GO System	Eat as much as you like of low calorie foods

STOP Sugar, sweets, chocolate, cakes, pastries, pies, biscuits, heavy puddings, honey, syrup, treacle, jam, marmalade, fruit tinned in syrup, dried fruit, cream, butter, margarine, lard, cooking oil, fat on meat, salad dressing, salad cream or mayonnaise, chips, crisps, peanuts, sweet aperitifs, spirits and liqueurs, most soft drinks and mixers

CAUTION Fatty meats (like bacon or salami), sausages, liver pate, eggs, milk, oily fish (like herring, mackerel, sardines, tuna, salmon), cheese (except cottage cheese), thick creamy soups, nuts, bread (eat wholemeal or brown rather than white), cereals, rice, pasta (like spaghetti and macaroni), potatoes, savouries, ready made-up dishes, wines, beer and cider

GO Fresh fruit, salads, green and root vegetables, white fish, seafood, poultry, game, kidney, heart, brain, cottage cheese, yoghurt (natural), skimmed milk, bran, consommé and clear soups, herbs and spices, low-calorie soft drinks, coffee and tea (without milk), saccharin, water

If you want to try **B** you will need to read a magazine or book for slimmers which will explain how to keep an exact check on what you are eating (See *What Next?*). You may find slimming easier if you join a special support group for slimmers.

However you lose weight you need to plan how to keep it off. Many people find that they can lose weight quite easily. But as soon as they stop dieting it all goes back on again. **Learning better eating habits will help you to keep slim.**

Learning better eating habits

Look back at your patterns of eating diary and tick any of these statements that are true for you.

1 Can't resist temptation

(Check columns 4 and 7 of your diary)
□ At home, do you eat your favourite foods if they are in the house?
□ At friends' houses, are you unable to refuse the food they offer?
□ In restaurants, do you give in when it's all there to choose from?

2 Eating twice over

(Check columns 1 and 7 of your diary)
☐ Do you eat a tea with the children and then have a big supper with your partner later on at night?
☐ Do you eat a large meal with your workmates at midday and then another when you get home at night?
☐ Do you have a bedtime snack even though you had a good supper earlier?

3 Snacking

(Check columns 1, 4 and 6 of your diary)
☐ Do you snack off and on throughout the day?
☐ Do you snack when preparing meals?
☐ Do you snack when watching TV?

4 Tension eating

(Check columns 8 and 9 of your diary)
☐ Do you eat a bar of chocolate (or whatever) when you get stuck or bored at work?
☐ Do you eat as soon as you get home to help yourself unwind?
☐ Do you eat more when lonely, or anxious, or after you've had a quarrel?

What often happens is that you feel tense and eat to relieve this tension. Then you feel fed up because you have eaten an extra snack. So now you feel tense again and may find yourself eating to relieve it. Fat people do not have more worries and stress than slim people. But they cope with the tension differently. They overeat!

5 'Empty' habits

(Check column 6 of your diary)
You may have once eaten for a particular reason (eg, stress) – but now you no longer have the reason you find you still have the habit.
☐ When you were busy, did you eat at the same time as you read a book, did the housework or travelled to work?
☐ While you were driving, or watching TV or were in bed at night did you eat to help you relax?

While you were doing these things your mind made a link between what you were doing and eating. So even if, for example, you no longer feel tense when you watch TV or drive a car you still get a 'trigger signal' to start eating. You have learnt another poor eating habit. Look back at column 6 and check if your extra eating could be explained in this way.

6 Hidden overeating

(Check column 10 of your diary)
☐ Do you drink alcohol?
☐ Do you eat cheese and chocolate?
☐ Are you liberal with relishes?

☐ Do you eat fatty meats, cream or fried food?
You may think 'I didn't eat much of that' but it may have been loaded with calories.

Now you have checked through your diary, make a list of the important parts of your pattern of eating that you need to change. You may feel you still don't know where and how to start, but *Changing your ways?*, pages 114–121 in this chapter, can help you. It takes you step by step through the planning stages.

Preparing for change

A *Where and when you eat*
Look down columns 4, 5 and 6 in your patterns of eating diary. Are you eating all over your home or at work? Do you sometimes eat standing up? Or whilst doing other things? All of these situations may trigger off eating. Try to eat in just one place at home – and one at work. Sit down at a table and don't read or watch TV. You will gradually weaken your wide range of eating triggers and only want to eat in the 'proper place'.

B *When you do eat*
1 Taste every mouthful Practise with a bar of chocolate. Eat one piece very slowly, rolling it around your mouth. Enjoy every moment. Do you want another piece? Yes? Then eat another piece. You may want to eat the whole bar tasting it slowly. That's fine! At this early stage you are practising tasting. When you do this regularly with your food you will find you enjoy it more but gradually want less.
2 Eat slowly Check column 2 of your diary. How long do you spend over a meal? Take small forkfuls. Chew the food well and enjoy its taste. Put your knife and fork down between forkfuls. Keep checking – do you still feel hungry?
3 Leave some If you feel you have had enough, *leave the rest*. Never mind what your mother told you. You are in control of your eating now.
4 Assert yourself Check column 4 and 7 of your diary for danger spots. Don't let friends or waiters load your plate or press you to second helpings. Say that eating too much would spoil the pleasure of what you've had already. You may like to re-read the topics in Chapter 2 that help you to assert yourself.
5 Know what you are eating Watch out so that you don't have whole meals of high calorie food. *What next?* suggests where to find out more about this.
6 Plan ahead Try and eat less the day before a large meal you know you can't avoid or know you won't be able to resist.

Smoking may damage your health

Almost 50% of adults in Britain smoke.

Yet almost all are aware that smoking may lead to disease and death.

Statistics about how many smokers become ill or die early don't seem to mean anything to individuals who smoke. But if a close friend or relative is seriously ill, or the smoker develops a smoking-related illness, then a smoker is much more likely to give up.

The 'lift' you get from smoking is instant because it takes only $7\frac{1}{2}$ seconds from the first draw on a cigarette for the nicotine to reach the brain. Every cigarette you smoke gives you an immediate reward. The ill-effects may take many years to show up. No-one wants to know that every cigarette also shortens your life by $5\frac{1}{2}$ minutes.

The fact that many smokers are dependent on nicotine doesn't seem to fit a smoker's image of himself. Many refuse to believe it. If you don't believe you might be dependent why not put it to the test? Don't smoke tomorrow! Your dependency may have become so bad that you develop a painful craving for cigarettes if you try to stop smoking. However, this passes off after two or three weeks if you keep off cigarettes.

What does smoking do?

Smoking helps you to concentrate and be more alert. You may feel less tired and less bored. If you are feeling tense it will help you become calm and more relaxed.
Smoking harms you in many ways. The tubes to the lungs become narrower and breathing is more difficult. Thick mucus

builds up which has to be coughed up as phlegm. The smoker is more likely to get colds and sinus trouble and takes longer to recover. Chronic bronchitis today is almost entirely caused by smoking.

Nicotine, which gives you a lift, is also a powerful poison. It speeds up the heart rate and puts extra strain on the heart. It makes the blood clot more easily and raises blood pressure. Carbon monoxide, a poisonous gas in the smoke, makes any existing heart trouble worse. It prevents haemoglobin, the red pigment in blood, from carrying vitally needed oxygen around the body. The heart muscle which needs a good supply of oxygen is particularly likely to suffer. Smokers are twice as likely as non-smokers to have a heart attack.

The tars in tobacco smoke can trigger off cancers. Smokers are ten times more likely to get lung cancer than non-smokers. Other cancers triggered off by smoking affect the mouth, throat, oesophagus (food-pipe) and bladder.

Smoking while pregnant can harm the baby in the womb. Nicotine narrows the blood vessels carrying food and oxygen to the baby. The blood can carry less oxygen anyway because of carbon monoxide.

Your smoking affects others who have to breathe in your smoke. 'Passive' smokers are also more likely to get respiratory infections. This is particularly the case for small children, since early childhood respiratory infections may leave them with damaged lungs.

Your choice

Need to keep on?

The aim of this book is to help you decide what you can do to improve your health. We know that 50% of smokers would like to give up and so we have put the emphasis in these four pages on helping people give up. However, some people feel very strongly that smoking is the best thing for them. Here is a list of the reasons they give. Tick any with which you would agree. Maybe you too do not want to give up?

☐ If I stopped smoking I might not be able to concentrate on my work

☐ If I stopped smoking I might batter my children

☐ If I stopped smoking I might have a nervous breakdown

☐ Living as long as possible is not the most important thing in life to me

☐ No-one would be really upset if I got badly ill or died

☐ I don't believe that any of these horrible things would happen to me

☐ I don't care if my smoking upsets others

☐ There isn't anything else I would rather do with the money

☐ I pay my NHS contributions and have a right to medical treatment even if I did bring it on myself

☐ I think I would have trouble keeping my weight down if I stopped smoking

Smoker's diary

I think I usually smoke ___ cigarettes a day

| | HOW MANY | | | |
When you smoked	Fri	Sat	Sun	Mon
First thing – in bed				
Getting up				
At breakfast				
Travelling to work				
Starting work				
When a problem came up				
Answering the phone				
In the loo				
At tea/coffee break				
With a meal (except breakfast)				
After a meal				
Waiting to meet someone				
Over a drink				
While driving				
While reading				
Doing the housework				
At the shops				
At the pub				
Watching TV				
Last thing at night				
After making love				
Other times*				
TOTAL SMOKED				

*Write in your own 'special' times

Will you give up?

Stop smoking for good and

Cut by half your chance of dying before you are 65

Save enough money each year for a holiday abroad

Become fitter

Lose your smoker's cough

Be more attractive: no smelly breath or stained fingers

Rid yourself of the mess and smell of tobacco where you live

Stop children from smoking because they copy you

Recover your lost senses of taste and smell

Be proud of yourself for breaking the habit

but you must also

Go without a pleasure that you will miss

Expect to feel uneasy and find concentration hard sometimes

Resist eating more

Feel tense and irritable for a while

Gains outweigh losses for most people. What about you?

This list is taken from a Quit Smoking poster, which also suggests that 'it is hard to stop but it helps if you can talk to people who are having the same problems. Join a quit smoking group and share the difficulties with others.' *What next?* suggests how you can find such a group if you feel that you would find it easier to stop if you have others' support.

Before you stop

It seems to be easier for most people to stop if they set themselves a definite date for quitting smoking. Allow two or three weeks to plan how to make stopping smoking as easy as possible for yourself.

Make yourself a diary like the one on this page and keep it for four days, starting on a Friday. You need to know your usual pattern of smoking before you can learn to change it. So while you are keeping the diary just keep to your usual pattern of smoking.

When asked how much they smoked most people's guesses were far too low. Before you start to keep your diary make a note of how many cigarettes you *think* you smoke a day.

Which are the vital 'smokes'?

You now need to keep a new kind of diary – for just one day. Choose either a week-day or a week-end day, whichever you smoke more heavily on. Smoke whenever you want to. Don't try to cut down. Carry a notebook or a piece of paper around with you and note down for each cigarette you smoke the exact time, where you were and how much you wanted to smoke.

Score		
3	if you were desperate for a smoke
2	keen
1	just fancied it
0	didn't realise you were lighting up

For example:

Time	Where	Importance?
8.25	On the train to work – everyone else was smoking	2
9.05	At work – thinking about the day ahead	3
9.50	On the telephone	0

You will need this information to work through our chart on the next page.

Want to give up?

You need to make yourself a personal plan. First answer the questions on the following page to find out what kind of a smoker you are. For those sections in which you score 10 or more read across the page and use our guide to make some definite written plans for yourself. Score high in them all? Read section 5, on craving, first.

Do you feel like this?	Your smoking type	What's in it for you?
For each statement score as follows: 1 – never, 2 – seldom, 3 – occasionally, 4 – frequently, 5 – always		
a Smoking a cigarette is pleasant and relaxing **b** I want a cigarette most when I am comfortable and relaxed **c** I find cigarettes pleasurable TOTAL: ___	**1 Pleasure/Relaxation**	Most people score highly on this section. Provided you *don't* also score highly on 4, 5 or 6 you are not dependent on the nicotine and should be able to give up fairly easily
a Handling a cigarette is part of the enjoyment **b** Part of the enjoyment of smoking comes from the steps I take to light up **c** When I smoke, part of the enjoyment is watching the smoke as I exhale it TOTAL: ___	**2 Handling**	Fiddling with things is a common way of coping with worries. Everyone has these comfort habits. But if fiddling for you means lighting a cigarette, you should try to find a substitute
a I light up when I feel angry about something **b** When I feel uncomfortable or upset I light up **c** I smoke when I feel blue or want to take my mind off worries TOTAL: ___	**3 Tension**	The more anxious you are, the more you smoke. But smoking keys you up more, it doesn't really reduce tension. Your heartbeat, in fact, speeds up which may of course direct your attention from what was making you tense
a I smoke in order to keep myself from slowing down **b** I smoke to stimulate me; to perk myself up **c** I smoke to give myself a lift TOTAL: ___	**4 Stimulation**	Nicotine does stimulate heart beat and concentration, but by now your body is used to a regular supply and so you need it to feel your 'normal' self. When you give up you won't feel so alert or able to concentrate for a while. It takes three or four weeks to get over this
a If I run out of cigarettes it is almost unbearable **b** I am very much aware when I'm not smoking **c** I get a real gnawing hunger for a cigarette when I haven't smoked for a while TOTAL: ___	**5 Craving**	Do you ever ☐ Drive around late at night looking for a cigarette machine? ☐ Stop work to dash to the shops before closing? ☐ Borrow change to make sure you have the right coins for a vending machine? The craving has got the better of you and you'll have to work hard to beat it
a I smoke automatically without really being aware of it **b** I light up without realising I still have one burning in the ashtray **c** I've found a cigarette in my mouth and not remembered putting it there TOTAL: ___	**6 Habit**	You may keep yourself so well supplied that you don't have to go long without a cigarette. You may not realise you have a craving for cigarettes. Try keeping yourself in short supply. If smoking really is only a habit you won't feel desperate!

Giving up

Substitutes

Using your smoker's diary

If you kept a diary, as suggested on the previous page, you can go back to this and tailor your plans to your particular pattern of smoking

In the two or three weeks before you quit for good, try making smoking less pleasurable:
○ go and sit somewhere uncomfortable and cold to smoke
○ smoke two or three cigarettes quickly and inhale deeply. It feels horrible

Make an effort and choose to do something else to fill the gap. You should be able to find something else enjoyable to do. In the car, sing along to the radio instead of smoking. Put a record on to relax at home. Carry around something to read when you might smoke

Did you find you smoked most at coffee and tea breaks, after a meal, with a drink after work, after supper or after you've made love? These are the key times for which you need to plan definite substitutes for smoking

Handling something else will probably do the trick. But you need to *plan* to have things to fiddle with

Do something else with your hands! Keep some scrap paper handy so you can doodle. Fiddle with coins, pencils, paper clips, key rings, jewellery, worrybeads, or special 'executive toys'. Play with a plastic cigarette

Go through each situation that's linked with smoking for you and plan to do something different. While you're on the phone, shuffle your papers; fiddle with your pen in meetings. Twiddle the lemon in your drink instead of lighting up

To reduce tension in other ways:
○ learn a quick relaxation technique and use it!
○ keep a supply of crunchy foods to bite (carrots are better than hard sweets)
○ when possible go for a brisk walk instead of smoking a cigarette
○ ask your doctor for a short course of tranquillisers while you give up

Try exercises to get rid of anger or frustration. Arm swinging or shadow boxing is effective. Take a brisk walk if you have the time. Learn relaxation exercises (see Chapter 6) so that you can 'let go' instead. Chew something – but watch out! You may substitute eating for smoking

Are there some things that always make you feel tense? After you've seen your boss? Or an irritating neighbour has called? Plan to run up and down stairs or crunch a hard sweet instead. But as a long term solution learn how to handle your feelings better (see Chapters 2 and 6)

○ Try waiting until you feel too ill to smoke, then give up at once and completely. You may not need so much 'stimulation' while you're unwell.
○ Your life will seem dull and you may feel less alert at first, so use the money you save to buy yourself 'rewards'

Buck yourself up with some exercises or a brisk walk, or with a cup of tea or coffee. Turn on your radio to pop music programmes and dance for three or four minutes

Look at your diary to find the times when you felt most in need of something to buck you up. Plan to do something else instead: make a cup of tea or put the radio or a record on. If you are swamped by pressures at work take time out for a few minutes relaxation (see Chapter 6)

○ Don't attempt to give up until you get a smoking related illness such as a painful cough, breathlessness or heart complaint
○ Work out really powerful rewards or make a contract to give up for someone you love

Giving up will be horrible but you will feel so much better once you do manage to stop that you are unlikely to want to smoke again. You may have started smoking very heavily when you had a lot of problems. You may need to get help for these problems rather than risk going back to smoking or substituting alcohol or pills

Because the nicotine level in your blood is low you will feel a real craving for the first cigarette of the day. But don't be tempted to give up slowly by cutting down instead of cutting out. It prolongs the agony. During the withdrawal symptoms keep reminding yourself that you knew you would feel like this and that you are proud of yourself for giving up

Before you quit for good make yourself aware of when you want to light up so that you don't later on find yourself smoking without realising it.
○ Keep your pack in a different pocket, leave your lighter in another room
○ Watch for trigger events like using the telephone or a cup of coffee, when you tend to light up automatically

You don't need to replace this kind of habit. Watch out you don't start popping sweets into your mouth unnoticed instead!

Keeping the diary going may help you give up! Having to make a note each time you smoke makes you aware of what a hold the habit has on you

Drinking

A little alcohol can make life more enjoyable.

A lot of alcohol can ruin it. How much do you drink?

We enjoy alcohol for the good things it can do for us. But it is sometimes difficult to know where to draw the line. It's something we have to work out in advance rather than leaving it until we've had a few drinks. That's because alcohol clouds our judgement whilst making us believe that we are thinking more clearly than usual!

Patterns of drinking

The way we were brought up and the society in which we live usually determine what we consider to be an acceptable pattern of drinking.

It's possible to make a good guess at what a person's pattern of drinking is likely to be if you know their sex, nationality, occupation and religion. Statistics do show that patterns of drinking are related to these four factors.

For example, publicans are seven times more likely to die of cirrhosis of the liver (damage caused by excess alcohol) than the average man. (Actors are five times, and doctors three times more likely.)

Scottish people are four times more likely than the English to have a serious drinking problem.

Statistics like these apply to large groups, not individuals within them. The statistics tell us that if we looked at a large number of publicans we would find more heavy drinkers than if we looked at the same number of people who weren't publicans. Any one particular publican, of course, may be very careful about what he drinks. So you can't say of any one person, 'Well, he's a publican, so he's bound to drink too much' or 'What can you expect – he's a Scot'. Neither should you excuse your own excesses by saying 'Well I'm a Scot who runs a pub – so I don't stand a chance!'

However these four factors (sex, nationality, occupation and religion) often shape our ideas, without our being fully aware of it, about what, for us, is a suitable pattern of drinking. If you want to be able to choose your pattern of drinking freely for yourself, you will need to look at what you have already learnt about when it's OK or not OK to drink.

Is it OK – for someone like you?

Please note, this is not a list of good and bad reasons to drink! Fill in column 1 first by ticking whichever of the statements is sometimes or always OK for you. This will help you build up a picture of when, where and why you think it is appropriate for you to have a drink. Then fill in columns 2 and 3, trying to decide from your family or your friends' point of view when it's OK for you to drink.

It's OK for someone like me to …	I think it's OK	Your family think it's OK for you	Your friends think it's OK for you
1 Go out to a pub for a drink at night			
2 Go for a drink after work			
3 Go for a drink in the lunch hour			
4 Pop out for a drink as soon as the pub opens			
5 Have a drink in the morning before starting work			
6 Keep alcohol at work			
7 Drink over a working lunch			
8 Have wine with a meal			
9 Have a night-cap			
10 Have a couple of drinks to unwind when I get in after work			
11 Drink on my own			
12 Have a drink to pass the time: on a train			
while waiting for a bus or a train			
while waiting for my partner to come home			
13 Buy rounds of drinks in a pub			
14 Have a drink when I am depressed			
bored			
frustrated			
angry			
15 Drink before I go to a party or meet someone new, so I won't feel ill at ease or shy when I get there			
16 Celebrate with a drink when I win something			
collect my pay packet			
get a job			
get promotion			
get engaged			
get married			
have a birthday			
have a baby			
finish watching a match			
finish playing a game			
17 Offer visitors a drink			
18 Drink while I watch TV			
19 Throw a drinks party			
20 Drink more at weekends – because I don't have to go to work			

If you have many statements which you have ticked for yourself only (that is, you have put ticks in column 1 but not 2 or 3) you may already be rather worried by your pattern of drinking. Neither your family nor friends agree that it's OK for you to drink at these times!

Marriage problems are all too likely if your partner would not support your pattern of drinking, but your friends will.

If you decide you want to cut down on alcohol it will be times when you and your family and friends would expect you to have a drink that may prove especially difficult for you.

Heavy drinking

So the way you were brought up and how you live play a large part in determining the pattern of your drinking.

But what makes it likely that so many people will end up drinking too much? In 1979 it was estimated that there were at least 300,000 people in Britain with a serious drinking problem.

The pressures on you that may lead to heavier drinking could be linked with:

What you think others expect of you
Advertising can add to this kind of pressure. So you drink
○ to prove you're one of the boys
○ to prove a woman can hold her drink as well as a man
○ to keep up with the Jones's. After all, the adverts assure you that everyone else is doing it
○ to make your life as exciting as the adverts promise you it will be

What you feel alcohol can do for you
So you drink
○ because you feel you deserve a reward
○ to cheer yourself up, to console yourself and forget your problems
○ to fill in empty hours

It does seem likely that people slip into heavier drinking patterns without noticing it – and this is why you may find it interesting to work out your 'drinking score' and keep the diary we suggest in this topic. They would help you to become more aware of what you are drinking.

107

Your drinking score

Use this list to work out at the end of each day how many drinking points you have scored. Make a chart like the one shown below – with a line drawn down at 4 to mark the moderate limit and another at 8 for the upper limit. Each day mark in your drinking score and add any notes to explain why you were drinking that day. Fill the chart in for one week.

How to score – drinking points

1 pt beer	2 points
1 small sherry (Martini, Dubonnet, Wincarnis etc.)	1 point
1 small whisky (gin, vodka, rum etc.)	1 point
1 small glass of wine	1 point
1 standard bottle of wine	8 points
1 one litre bottle of wine	10 points
1 bottle of sherry	12 points
½ bottle of spirits	15 points
1 bottle of spirits	30 points

Below is Tom's chart. He works as a carpenter with a building firm and only drinks beer. His workmates consider him to be 'not much of a drinker'. And yet on two days he went over the recommended upper limit of safe drinking. On two days his drinking points score was in the caution zone.

If your own scores fall more than twice a week into the caution zone we suggest you keep a detailed diary for a week, as on page 109, so that you can choose the times when you could cut down on drinking by planning to do something else instead.

If your scores reach the stop zone at all we suggest you keep a detailed diary *and* consider seeking help from someone for your problem. See *What next?*

Drinker's diary

Try to keep your own diary (like Jenny's diary on p. 109) to find out when, where and why you drink.

Start on any day. Write in the day of the week and the date. See 'How to score' (left) to work out the total drinking points for each day.

Keep up the diary for a week if you can. Don't skip a day, for example the works outing, just because it wasn't a typical day. If you can only keep it up for a few days then fill it in for Friday to Sunday.

See how Jenny filled in her diary on the first day. Jenny is married but doesn't have any children. She works on a magazine. Her husband is a civil servant. On a double income they can afford to keep plenty of drink in the house. But Jenny was a bit worried by her score on the first day . . .

1 Look back at your diary and circle any time you drank 'alone'.

2 Also circle any 'no food' with your drink.

3 Tick √ any times when, for you, quite the best thing to do at that moment was to have a drink.

If you score between 4 to 8 on more than two days you should start to plan to cut back your drink. If you score more than 8 on most days you will probably need professional help with your problem.

Weekly drinking pattern – Tom's Chart

	Go			Caution			Stop					
	Moderate limit This amount is probably doing you good – provided you don't have trouble sticking to it			**Upper limit** You need to keep an eye on what you drink			**Over the top** You need to cut down					

	1	2	3	4	5	6	7	8	9	10	11	12	Notes
MON	🍺	🍺	🍺	🍺	🍺	🍺	🍺	🍺					*After work – at home feeling depressed*
TUES	🍺	🍺	🍺	🍺									*Just a drink at lunchtime*
WED	🍺	🍺	🍺	🍺	🍺	🍺	🍺	🍺					*Darts match at pub*
THU	🍺	🍺	🍺										*Just a lunchtime drink*
FRI	🍺	🍺	🍺	🍺	🍺	🍺	🍺						*After work at pub – Seven rounds of beer*
SAT	🍺	🍺	🍺	🍺	🍺	🍺	🍺	🍺	🍺	🍺			*Saturday night round at Clare and Mike's*
SUN	🍺	🍺	🍺										*Sunday lunch drinks at pub*

DRINKER'S DIARY

When?	Where?	Who with?	Why?	What?	How much?	+Food?	*Drinking points
Monday – February 12th							
12.40 Lunch-time	Bar at work	2 work-mates	To be friendly	Lager	1½ pints	(No)	3
6.15 Before supper	At home	(Alone)	Dead beat ✔	Large gin & tonic	1	(No)	2
7.45 Supper	At home	Husband	Usually do	White wine	¼ bottle	Supper	2
11.45 Nightcap	In bed	Husband	Helps to sleep	Brandy	1	(No)	1
*see 'How to score' – on page 108						TOTAL	8

We shall refer back to your diary in the rest of this topic and you may need to come back to it after you have read to the end of the chapter.

What's behind your drinking habits?

Ask yourself: Did you think the limits we suggested were ridiculously low or were they reasonable?

Your diary Look back at how you filled in 'Is it OK?' to see if heavy drinking is accepted in your circle of family and friends. If so it will be difficult for you to avoid drinking at times when you feel it is expected of you. *But* do you really want to go on drinking heavily and damage your health and possibly break up your marriage and family life just because you're caught in the old ways?

What can you do? This topic should help you to change how you see yourself as a drinker. How about this?

'People like me – keep an eye on their drinking so that they can enjoy it without letting it damage their health or upset their relationship with their family and friends, or cause problems at work.'

Social pressures?

Ask yourself Were there times when you only drank because your drinking companions expected you to? Social pressures often make people drink more than they want to.

Your diary For example – Jenny drank a pint and a half on Monday lunchtime because there were three people there and she felt she must buy her round. Tom, in the pub after work on Friday, felt he would be thought mean if he didn't buy his round. He felt he had to stay for the full set of beer rounds because if he said he wanted to go home they would think he was 'hen-pecked' by his wife.

What can you do? Maybe you need to learn how to refuse a drink without offending people too much? Choose a situation from your diary when you would really have liked to refuse a drink and practise what you might say. You could try:
A true, good reason:
'I have to drive home.'
'I'm taking antibiotics (or sleeping tablets or cough medicine) and mustn't drink as well.'
Inventing a reason:
'My doctor says he thinks I may be getting an ulcer and wants me to lay off for three months.'
Using a good insult:
'I know when to stop.'
'I want to be able to make love when I get home tonight.'
Admitting you just don't want another
'I've had just the right amount; any more and I'll regret it tomorrow.'

Emotional pressures

Ask yourself if you *sometimes* or *often* drink to cheer yourself up? Pass the time when you are bored? Help you unwind? Escape feeling angry or fed up?

Check column 3 in your diary and also look back to 'Is it OK?' on the previous page – to see if you have any ticks for questions 2, 10, 12 or 14.

Your diary If you almost always drink when you are bored, depressed, angry, etc, then you need to think about what it is that's making you feel that way and what you might usefully do instead of having a drink. Also, drinking on your own when you feel like this is one of the ways that really serious drinking problems are known to build up.

What can you do? If you have just got in to the habit of drinking at these times you need to *plan* what you will do instead. Carry around something you can read or do when you're bored or need to fill in time. It's usually possible to lift yourself out of a passing mood of depression by taking some brisk exercise. It's a good way to work off anger too.

If you are drinking because of serious emotional problems, the best thing to do is to talk about the problems with someone you can trust. Chapters 2 and 6 should help you to look at what may be behind this kind of drinking. They also suggest who you could talk to, to get some help.

Changing your ways?

The topics on pages 114–121 will help you make a definite plan for changing your drinking habits. Don't forget that you need to decide in advance how much you will drink. Alcohol clouds your judgement whilst making you feel that you are thinking more clearly!

Deciding in advance avoids another problem. If you wait till you *feel* as if you have had enough it may be too late as there may be two or three drinks waiting in your stomach to get in to your blood stream where they will make you feel worse and do damage to your body.

Pills for problems?

Advertisements tell us 'You don't have to learn how to cope with problems – just take a pill'.

We learn as children to take our medicine because it will do us good. So we grow up believing that medicines will always be good for us. We may learn, too, that we should not show our feelings – or, better still, we should not even have them! Grief, anxiety, and patches of depression are a natural part of everyone's life. But today many of us feel we must take a pill to mask these feelings.

Doctors are under pressure from the drug companies who tell them there *is* a pill for every problem. Patients also put pressure on doctors to prescribe them pills. The combination of pressures leads to the prescribing of pills as an easy way out. Even if we can't get prescribed pills from a doctor there are plenty of medicines in the chemist's shop offering us relief from our problems.

But you do need to ask yourself:
○ should you make yourself feel full of energy when your body is tired and needs sleep?
○ is it a good idea to calm yourself down when danger signals of stress are warning you to change the way you live?

Your body and mind are trying to tell you something. Tune in, not switch off!

Pills for a crisis? Perhaps – Yes. Pills every day against life's ordinary problems? Definitely – No. Because after a while you get to feel you couldn't manage without them.

Pills for your problems?

Make your own list on a separate sheet of paper. Put the three questions shown at the top of page 111 on your own sheet.

1 Fill in column 1. Try to remember what medicines (we mean liquid medicines, tablets or pills) you have taken in the last three years, when you have felt upset, worried, anxious, depressed, couldn't sleep, needed to calm down, vaguely under the weather but not really ill, or in need of a pick-me-up or a tonic. If you don't know the name just write 'sleeping pills', or tranquillisers. But see the checklists (right) in case they jog your memory.

2 Fill in column 2. Write down why you or your doctor felt you needed the medicine.
3 Fill in column 3. Mark each medicine as follows:
   a Did you ask the doctor for that kind of medicine? If Yes mark △
   b Did he prescribe that particular kind of medicine without you asking for it? If Yes mark □

Checklist A: pills a doctor might prescribe

For anxiety (mild tranquillisers)	For depression (anti-depressants)	Sleeping tablets
eg	eg	eg
Valium	Nardil	Soneryl
Librium	Tryptizol	Sodium Amytal
Tacitin	Tofranil	Nembutal
Atacax	Anafranil	Seconal
Integrin	Impramine	Welldorm
Sernid		Mogadon
Nobrium		Oblivon
		Dalmane

Checklist B: pills you might buy at the chemist

Cough linctus – because you know it helps you sleep?
Travel sickness pills – because you know they help you sleep?
Aspirins, Disprins etc. – because you find they help you to sleep or because you take them if you feel a bit under-the-weather?
Tonics or tonic wines – to buck you up?
Glucose tablets or Glucosade – to help you feel more energetic?

c Did you buy the medicine from the chemists without prescription? If Yes mark *
d Was the medicine given to you by a relative or friend? If Yes,

   (1) Did they get it without a prescription? If Yes mark † or

   (2) Was it prescribed for them by a doctor. If Yes mark ‡

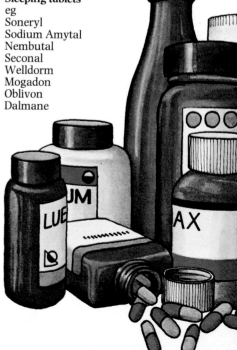

What did I take? For how long?	Why did I need it?	How did I get it?
Valium (last 5 weeks)	*My mother is staying with us – she's too old to change and I'm upset*	□
Sleeping pills (last November for 3 weeks) – don't remember their name	*Away from home on a training course – very noisy place*	‡
Valium (last Spring for about 2½ months)	*Felt very jumpy after I'd given up smoking*	△

Getting pills ... from your doctor

How open are you with your doctor? Or, perhaps, how open will he let you be? Look at column 3. Did you –

a Mark mostly △ because you asked for pills? Is this because you think you know what you needed. Does your doctor agree and give them to you? Or does he disagree but give them to you to 'keep the peace'?

b Mark mostly □? If every time you go with a symptom that might be caused by worry or anxiety and your doctor prescribes pills, he may be taking the easy way out.

Do you think this may be because –
○ he's too busy?
○ he thinks that almost all problems *are* best treated with a pill?
○ he thinks you wouldn't agree to talking about your underlying problems?
○ he doesn't have the necessary skills to help you?
○ he doesn't know who to send you to for help?
○ you don't give him the chance to ask you the right questions?

If your doctor goes on prescribing like this then we think you may need to be the one to ask, 'I keep getting pills for my problems. I wonder if I ought to be seeking other help for them instead?'

Getting pills ... from the chemist

Did you mark any *? When taking cough linctus or travel sickness tablets some people find that they make them go to sleep. They may buy them for this purpose another time. You should not do this. It's not what the medicine was made for and you may get other unpleasant side effects.

Some people take aspirin or similar pain killing tablets whenever they feel a bit under the weather. If you take more than four in any one day – or two or more, for more than three days – just because you have a vague feeling of being unwell then you should see your doctor.

Getting pills ... from friends and relations

a Did you mark any †? If so go back and read the previous section, 'From the chemists'.

b Did you mark any ‡? Prescription drugs must be prescribed for the person who is taking them at the time he or she needs them. Don't take other people's.
Someone else's medicine may, for example:
○ harm your baby if you are pregnant,
○ interact badly with other medicines you already take,
○ make another illness or problem you have worse.

Your problem needs your doctor's advice

You may need to be more open with your doctor. Some people find this very difficult.

It may help if you work out what you want to say in advance. Try saying:
I feel ...
Use your own words: eg, worried, on edge, jumpy, like screaming
I think it might be tied up with ...
eg, quarrels with my teenage daughter, trying to do a paid job and running a home, being made redundant
Do you think I need something to ...
help me stop worrying, buck me up, help me to sleep, give me more energy?

Read more about this in *Talking to Your doctor*, Chapter 8, pages 226–229.

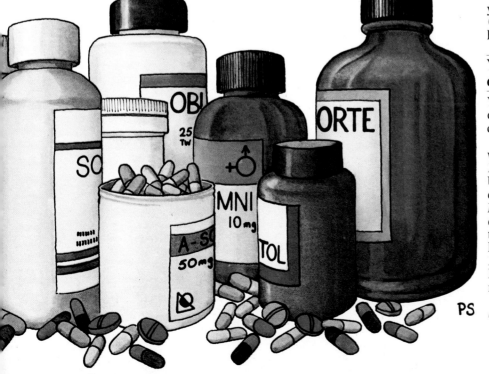

Sleeping problems

There are some good reasons for using sleeping pills for a short while. But on any one night in England and Wales, three and a half million people take sleeping pills! Many of them don't need to take them.

The trouble is it is easy to get into the habit of taking sleeping pills. Once you believe you can't sleep without one then you will genuinely have difficulty getting to sleep.

If you do take sleeping pills suggest to your doctor that you give up the pills and learn how to sleep properly (see opposite). He should be delighted to help you gradually get off the pills.

Enough sleep

1 Do you feel alert throughout most of the day but tired out by bedtime? (Boredom or lack of food or a heavy meal can make you feel tired – don't count these times.) YES/NO

If YES, then regardless of how many hours you are sleeping, *you are getting enough sleep.*

If NO, then you don't have enough sleep. So look at the following questions.
2a Are your nights interrupted by crying babies, sick relatives, or low flying planes etc? YES/NO
2b Do aches and pains make it difficult to drop off or stay asleep? YES/NO
2c Do you do shift work so that you have to keep changing your pattern of sleep? YES/NO
2d If you wake very early in the morning and feel tired but can't get back to sleep, it may be a sign of mild depression. Might this be true for you? YES/NO

If you answer YES to any of these questions in section 2, you need to get help for these underlying problems. There's little point in trying to improve your sleeping habits – except in so far as they help you to make best use of the little time you do have to sleep.

If you answered NO to all of them, then you may find that an extra 30 to 60 minutes sleep a night will be enough. We suggest you 'teach yourself to sleep' (see right).

Coping without pills?

We are not giving advice as to whether or not you have been prescribed the right medicine. You may have done absolutely the right thing taking certain pills at a particular time. Don't worry. We are not trying to say you should never take pills for problems. What we are suggesting is that maybe you need to look at the alternatives. This will help you to be more aware in future of what choices you have.

There can be times when taking pills can seem a lot easier than trying to find out and face the cause of the problem.

Look back at your list. Could you have coped with these problems in other ways? It *can* become a habit to take a pill if life isn't going smoothly.

Anxiety and depression

Tranquillisers and anti-depressants are the most commonly prescribed drugs today. For some people some of the time they are the best treatment. But they don't remove the cause of anxiety, although they can make you care less about it. The trouble is that if you no longer feel anxious, you may think you needn't bother to solve your problem or get to the bottom of an anxiety at all (Chapter 6, *Stress and emotions*, looks at this in more detail).

Really we have a choice. We can take a pill to mask painful feelings. Or we can face them so that, by living through these painful experiences, we can cope better with similar experiences in the future.

Teach yourself to sleep

Ask yourself	Is the answer 'No'?	You might say 'But …'
Do you go to bed at the same time every night?	While you are learning new habits be strict about this. Go to bed at the same time each night. Don't choose too early a bed-time. You know what time you need to get up. Seven and a half hours sleep is plenty to aim for	'I don't want to live such a boring regular life.' You don't need to once you've got your sleeping cycle well established
Once you are in bed and want to go to sleep are you usually asleep within 20 minutes?	○ If you don't have trouble getting to sleep it doesn't matter what you do when you go to bed. But if you are starting to learn new habits don't watch TV, read or eat or listen to the radio. Try to link going to bed with going to sleep	'I can only get to sleep after I've read for an hour, or listened to some records or made love.' That's fine if you don't mind having to do it! But you have taught yourself to go to sleep that way. You *can* learn a new habit if you want to
	○ Do relaxation exercises when you are in bed (see p.156)	'I've had insomnia for years – I start to worry about getting to sleep as soon as I get into the bedroom.' You may need to take drastic action and teach yourself to sleep in another room or change your room around as much as possible. Once you have learnt to sleep well you will be able to do it anywhere
	○ Practise thought control so that worrying ideas don't distract you. Counting sheep is OK. But it's better to imagine you're on a tropical beach dozing in the sun. If you only picture the scene before you go to sleep, you can reach a point where it will trigger sleep within two or three minutes. It may help to repeat certain words as you breathe (see meditation on p.159)	
Are you able to un-wind gradually during the evening?	Emotional problems and physical tenseness make getting to sleep difficult	'Exercise will wake me up!' Only temporarily – exercise really does ease emotional and physical tension (see Chapter 6). After that it's easy to relax and go to sleep
	○ Divert your mind from your problems. (In any case it's easier to think clearly about them in the morning.) You need to find out what works for you. Playing chess or doing a crossword will help some people but would make others more tense. Watching TV helps many people – but don't fall asleep in front of it!	'I always have a nightcap before I go to bed.' Alcohol can sometimes help you get off to sleep, but it can also cause restless, unsatisfactory sleep
	○ Some exercise before bed (a short walk or dancing to a record) helps most people	'I'm so desperate for sleep that I need that nap in front of the TV.' In the short term you will need to feel worse in order to end up better!
	○ Traditional hot milky drinks can help. Don't drink tea or coffee or alcohol within two hours of going to bed. Too much to drink may also mean you will need to get up in the night to go to the toilet	However tired you are – don't go to bed until it's the time you decided on. In the mornings get up at the right time however little sleep you had or however much you now feel able to sleep. Your aim is a new pattern of sleep. You may have to lose a little sleep while you are learning it

Changing your ways?

You can do it if you really want to ...

This chapter should help you choose what patterns in your life, if any, you would like to change. Your friends can help you. Self-help groups may help you. But you must be the one to commit yourself to bringing about a change and keeping it up once you have changed. We've given you some help already. The remaining topics in this chapter help you understand more about the problems you may encounter and more about how to overcome them. After all, you *can* do it if you really want to.

Changing what you do?

○ Should you try to change the way you feel? And rely on this changing the way you behave?

○ Can you try changing what you do in the hope that this will alter how you feel?

○ Should you work on both at once?

Knowing why ...
Some experts would argue that, unless you know why you behave the way you do, you are unlikely to be able to make yourself behave differently. They would say that once you understand your underlying problem you won't need to go on behaving as you do. Tackling underlying problems (if you know you have them and can get help to do so) is always worthwhile. We urge you to do this in many other topics in this book, and *What next?* suggests how to get help.

... but still can't change?
Knowing why we feel and behave as we do doesn't always enable us to change. It can even be used as an excuse not to change. We can say, for example, 'What can you expect? With my troubled childhood and difficult job it's no wonder I can't stop smoking. Even though I know it's ruining my health.'

Don't know how to change?
You can end up really wanting to change but lacking the skills to help you to do so. We get set in our ways and breaking the old patterns and learning new ones isn't as easy as it sounds. Perhaps in some cases the underlying problem has long since disappeared but the way we behave has carried on as a habit.

Never mind the feelings?

Other experts would suggest you concentrate only on the skills you need to help yourself to change. They can present plenty of evidence to show that changing what you do *can* alter how you feel. This chapter has concentrated on what's called behaviour modification – learning different ways to behave. This is because we think that, whether or not you look at your underlying problems, it is often well worth while to learn the skills needed to change what you actually do.

Why is it difficult?

Because it's so easy to stay the way you are!

1 Short term rewards, long-term punishments

Unfortunately it often happens that a pleasant consequence follows immediately after the undesired action. For example, you probably feel 'good' within a few seconds of inhaling your cigarette smoke.

Ill health may come months or years afterwards. Chronic bronchitis may not develop till after ten years or more of smoking and lung cancer after 20 years of smoking.

Fattening food tastes delicious. You only realise later that you've put on weight.

2 Hidden pay-offs

However much you want to change what you do, there is nearly always a pay-off or reward for carrying on your present way of behaving.

Often the 'reward' is that what you are doing prevents you from facing something else that worries you. The obvious example is, 'If I drink enough I can forget my other problems'. Does this or any of the other following ideas suggest what's in it for you?

'While I'm so fat I can't be expected to … dash around or join in sports or be sexy.'

'If I got slim and people found me sexually attractive I would have to admit how anxious I feel about sex.'

'So long as I'm too anxious to go out I don't have to … visit my in-laws or face the boss at work or worry about what I look like.'

'I don't want to think about lung cancer because it will make me think about death. If I manage never to think about lung cancer, I don't feel worried about smoking.'

'I've tried before and failed – and I don't like being proved to be weak-willed.'

'If I don't even try to change I shan't have to put my self-control to the test. The worst thing to do would be to try and be seen to fail.'

The skills of self-control

These last two quotes reflect a common misunderstanding about self-control that may prevent many of us from even trying to change. Self-control does not involve 'gritting your teeth and bearing it' or 'keeping going with grim determination' or 'hanging on through sheer will-power'.

It is more useful to think of self-control as the ability to achieve the goals we set ourselves. Reaching these goals involves skills which can be learned.

Some people learn these skills, without thinking about them, as they grow up. But for most of us it helps if we look at and try to learn the skills of self-control. Then we can make good use of them when we need them.

If we want to change our ways we can learn how to work out a plan of action which will make it as easy as possible to reach our goal. We need to work out:

1 exactly what it is that we hope to achieve.

2 exactly where we stand at the beginning.

3 what steps we can take to move from where we are to where we want to be.

4 and then – have confidence in our ability to carry out the plan.

Your own worst enemy?

The rest of this chapter looks at how to put your plans into practice. But first you may need to find out where you tend to undermine your confidence in yourself. It seems that we often do just that without fully realising what we are doing. To stop this you need to learn to catch yourself at it – become aware of what you're doing. It will help, however silly it sounds, to tell yourself to stop thinking like that and start behaving more positively.

If you think like this:	Why not try telling yourself …
1 I'm dogged by bad luck 2 Things just happen to me	1, 2 Rubbish! There are lots of things I can control
3 I can't control how I react	3 I may not have been able to in the past – but now I'm learning how to
4 What can I expect with a background like mine?	4 I'm not shackled by my past. I can learn how to change
5 I've never succeeded. I don't expect to now	5 That was before I learned how to change
6 Whatever else, I must get people to like me	6 I shan't die if someone doesn't like me. I must do what I think is best
7 It must be my fault when something goes wrong	7 Wait a minute. Is there another explanation?
8 I can't resist temptation	8 I'm keeping a record to prove that I can

Wanting to change

'One of these days I'll do something about …'

Well, how might you complete this sentence? However they complete it many people would need to go on and add, 'but at the moment I'm too busy or too tired or too weak-willed to do anything about it.' Or even, 'although I know I ought to, I don't really want to change!'

Do you really want to change?

In this chapter we are concentrating on what you can do to change your personal habits. (This is only one way of changing what affects your health. Chapter 8, *A healthy community*, looks at how the attitudes of the society we live in, and the policies of our government, also affect our health.)

Turn back to page 15 in Chapter 1, which shows the steps you need to take in choosing and changing the way you live. By now you may be able to list some changes you would like to make. Now you need to choose which one you will tackle first, to be sure you are really committed to changing. Working out the ways to bring about this change, the possible snags and how to get extra support are looked at in the rest of this chapter.

Think about one of the things in your life you want to change. The following questions will help you decide if you really are committed to wanting to change and how likely you are to get off to a good start and keep it up.

1 As a child did your parents keep their promises to you? □
2 Can you work out a careful plan of how to change rather than just rush into it? □
3 Have you recently done so much of what you would like to change eg, smoking, eating chips, nagging, that you are 'sick to death' of it? □
4 Do you now feel guilty or worried about it? Or afraid of the consequences of what you have done? □
5 Are any of your friends trying to change the same thing? □

6 Will someone you are close to be really pleased when they hear what you intend to do? □
7 Will your partner, or boss, stop nagging or criticising you if you change? □

The more of these you can tick, the more likely you are to be firmly committed to changing.

Comments
Q.1 If parents keep their promises, this helps a child build up confidence in his or her own ability to carry out plans and keep promises. If you couldn't tick this question then you may feel that you can't make plans and keep promises. This may mean that you easily nag yourself and put yourself down by saying things to yourself like, 'That's just like you – you can't stick to anything!' You will need to watch out for this – you could be your own worst enemy when it comes to making changes.

Q.2 The six-point plan on pages 118–120 will help you, if you don't know how to make plans of action.

Q.3, 4 You may have to wait until you can tick one of these questions before you get the final spur to make you really want to change!

Q.5 Can you get friends to join in with you? Or find a self-help group in your neighbourhood? See *Self-help groups* on p.230–233, and *What next?* There are some changes like quitting smoking or losing weight that you are much more likely to succeed in if you do it with a group of people.

Q.6, 7 Friends and partners can help a great deal, as we suggest on the next page. They can also sabotage your plans, see page 121.

If you have several things you want to change, we suggest you go through this list for each one of them. Make a start with the one for which you get most ticks.

Rewarding yourself

In the next three pages we give you a six-point-plan to help you help yourself to change. **You can help yourself to behave in the new way by rewarding yourself for each step you take towards your new**

goal. You will need to use little rewards but often. For instance, have you read this far with the intention of really working out how to change something you do? That's good. Well done! Give yourself a reward!

Long term rewards like a holiday in Majorca if you lose three stones are too far off. You can lose heart and feel you'll never reach your goal. What keeps up your motivation and makes you feel good are small, frequent rewards. Don't start punishing yourself if you fail. You need to build up your self-confidence, not destroy it. Just start again *and* reward yourself for having the courage to do so!

What kind of a reward?

To make the plans we suggest in the next topic you will need to know what kind of rewards you like best! Over the next two or three days jot down on a piece of paper all the small and big pleasures in your life. If you can't think of many try pinning copies of your list in the bedroom, kitchen or office so that they remind you to be on the lookout for pleasures. Here is Joan's list. She wants to cut down on smoking and we follow her plans to do this on the next three pages.

Small pleasure

Having a cup of tea √	Doing a bit of gardening
Brushing my hair	Having a catnap
Eating a chocolate biscuit X	Cleaning my teeth
Stroking the cat √	Having a cigarette (but that's one of the things I'm trying to stop!) X
Coffee with Anne △	
Phoning Mum △	
Having a bath √	Buying small items of make-up √
Putting on perfume	Being kissed by Richard △
Rubbing on hand cream	Having my back massaged △
Reading a paper √	

Big pleasure

Buying a record	Making love △
Watching a favourite TV programme	Breakfast in bed △
	Drinks at the pub with Richard △
Buying clothes	Buying a rosebush

When you have made your list:
Mark △ any which need another person. They may have a special use in your plans.

Mark X any that might be bad for you if you did them too often. Joan marked the chocolate biscuits and cigarette with an X. From the remainder in your small pleasures list mark with a tick the five you like best.

As the days go by you may think of other pleasures to add to your list. Keep reminding yourself that pleasurable things are good for you! You should enjoy working out in the next topic how you can 'win' extra rewards as you succeed in each small step of your plans for changing.

Help yourself to change

A six point plan to help you succeed

This section takes you through the final steps of choosing and changing that we outlined in Chapter 1. As we go through this plan we follow Joan's ideas about how she can cut down on smoking and Harry's scheme to lose weight. You need to make a similar list for what you want to change. Take time to think about the details of your plan. The more carefully you plan the more likely the success.

1 Choosing to change

A Do you really want to change? You can find out how committed you are and which change you would like to make first by doing the quiz on the previous page. However if you doubt if this plan can work for something really hard, try it out first on a simple problem. That way you will gain the confidence to tackle a bigger problem.

B Choose something you can measure If you try to make vague, general changes, it will be difficult to know when you have succeeded. For example, 'feeling less anxious' is too general. But you could measure how many times you speak up in public, accept invitations to parties, or ask a girl to a dance or whatever else you would like to be able to do if only you weren't so anxious. If you want to change and 'be nice more often to my partner' you could measure how many times a day you complimented him or her or helped with something or listened to him or her for five minutes.

c Aim low Set yourself an easy goal to begin with. Once you reach your first target you can always set yourself another one. For example 'I will exercise vigorously for five minutes on at least three days.' Once you reach this standard reward yourself – and set a new one. And then another new one, and so on.

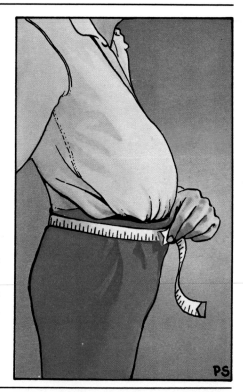

Joan	Harry
I am going to cut down on smoking (I just can't stop all at once).	I want to lose weight now I can't do up the trousers of my suit
A Scored 5 on the commitment quiz	A Scored 4 on the commitment quiz
B I will note down the time each day when I smoked my first cigarette	B I shall measure my waistline (rather than weigh myself)
C I will set mini targets, cut back one hour at a time	C Losing 3″ is a low target

2 Keeping a record

A Before you start to change The drinker's diary and chart on pp 108 and 109 in this chapter show how important a record can be for making yourself alert to just what you do get up to. The diaries in 'weight problems' and 'smoking' show that you need to note down where and when you eat or smoke.

B To see how you improve This way you can prove to yourself that you can change your ways. It can boost your morale and help you keep going to have a record of your success. You can brighten up your charts by giving yourself gold stars or whatever you like on particularly good days. (Be careful not to punish yourself on bad days. Just start again and try to do better the next day.)

Joan	Harry
A I will keep a smokers diary for a week before I try to change	A I know what my waist measures!
B I will write on the calendar in the kitchen the time I have my first smoke of the day. I'll make myself a chart to show how I improve too	B I'll measure my waist every Sunday morning with a piece of string. Each Sunday I'll cut off the extra bit I don't need now that I'm that much slimmer – and burn it!

3 Looking at the pattern of what you do

A Break the old pattern Alert yourself to what you're doing. For example, if you eat snacks without thinking about it, stick warning notices or pictures on the fridge and biscuit tin.

Set limits on when or where. For example, only have a drink when your partner is with you. Or, only eat when sitting up at a table.

Make it less pleasant. Make it a rule you will only smoke while sitting on a hard chair facing a blank wall.

B Make the new pattern easier For example, if you want to get to work on time, set everything ready the night before! Or, if you are dieting, don't keep any sweets or biscuits in the house.

Joan

A To make sure I don't smoke 'by accident' I will put the pack inside a tin with a difficult lid

I'm limiting my pattern by trying to start smoking a little later each day

B I'll drink orange juice for breakfast, it tastes a lot better if I don't smoke at the same time

Harry

A I'm going to stop myself wolfing down food without thinking when I come in at night by putting a warning notice on the kitchen door

The first week I'll cut out all potatoes. The next week add bread and the following week cake and biscuits, to the forbidden list. The fourth week I'll be brave and change to drinking halfs instead of pints

B I'll get my wife to serve out the meals on to my plate instead of serving myself

4 Help yourself to change

If something good happens just after you've done something then you are likely to repeat the action. You have linked it in your mind with a reward. This will make you more likely to want to do it again.

If something bad happens you link the action with what seems to be a punishment. So make an effort to remember this punishment when you are next tempted and you will be less likely to repeat it.

A What rewards you? If you haven't already done it, turn back and do the rewards activity on page 116. You need your own private list of rewards! Remember it has been proved that small rewards, given at once, make it easier to learn new habits.

B How can you earn rewards? Break your task of changing into very small steps. Plan to give yourself many instant, small rewards, so it makes it easy to earn them. (Keeping your record chart each day deserves a reward.) If you like you can try collecting points towards a bigger reward. In that case it is important to give yourself a visible token reward that you can 'trade in' for the real reward (like green shield stamps!). That way you have something to look at to remind yourself that you are steadily working towards your big reward. Otherwise you may get discouraged.

C Get your friends to help Rewards from friends can speed things up. A kiss from his wife every time he remembered to fasten his seat belt worked best for one man. Look back at your private list of rewards. Use those marked △ as extra rewards when you begin to find that changing is harder than you thought when you started.

D Punishments Watch out! These can be very tricky to use, particularly the punishment of nagging yourself. They can easily make you give up hope. Punishments from your friends may be tricky too. They may agree to confiscate your cigarettes if they catch you with them – and then you get angry with them for doing it. That way you may end up losing friends!

Sicken yourself. Chain smoking for 10 minutes or until you get sick or dizzy is sometimes used at the start of trying to give up smoking. Or eating chips until you are sick may put you off them for a long time (but add pounds to your weight!).

Joan

A The five 'rewards' that I ticked on my list were:
  having a cup of tea
  reading my favourite magazine
  having a bath
  stroking the cat
  buying make-up

B I'll have a cup of tea each time I fill in my chart

If I start to light up but then stub it out again I'll take five minutes off to read magazine

On the days I go a whole extra hour without smoking I will buy myself some make-up

C When I feel desperate I'll ring up or go and see Mum or Anne

D I'd feel silly punishing myself

Harry

A My five pleasures I ticked were:
  doing the crossword in the newspaper
  playing country & western records
  having a quick look at Penthouse
  a cigarette (I'm going to give those up next but I might as well enjoy them while I can)
  eating apples

B I'll take an apple to work and reward myself with it if I don't eat chips

I'll do the crossword when I get in at night instead of going into the kitchen and eating

Instead of taking a snack to bed with me I'll have a quick look at Penthouse magazine

C I'm not going to tell my friends, so I can't get them to help

D If my waist isn't any smaller when I measure it on a Sunday, I'll have a week with no beer at all

5 Remind yourself

A What you want to stop Impulse actions, on the spur of the moment, are the most difficult to stop. If you find yourself saying, 'I'm dying for a drink' and you gulp one down fast you might try sticking a picture of a drunk on your drinks cupboard.

B What you hope to achieve For example, if you have a photo of when you were slim put it on the table where you eat. Don't have one? Stick your face (from a photo) on to a picture of someone else's slim body!

C By talking to yourself No, it's not a sign of madness. It's a well-tried way of gaining extra control over what you do. Actually say the words, 'I want another drink? Why do I want to do that? Because I'm fed-up. What could I do instead? How about ringing Peter? I'll try that, Good!'

Joan	Harry
A I'll stick a label saying coffin nails on my cigarette case	A I'll leave my best trousers out in the bedroom as a silent reproach
B I'll put the Sun Silk girl advert on my dressing table mirror. She looks clean and fresh and full of life	B I'll put the advert that shows that slim bloke with the sexy girl on the inside of my wardrobe door
C I already talk to myself like that	C I'll try talking to myself when I'm choosing what to eat in the works canteen. That's where I'm in a hurry and not thinking and usually just grab a plate of food

6 Secret support

A Break the chain Make a break between wanting to do it – and actually doing it. Reward yourself at once for managing to do this. For example, although you feel anxious or panicky in certain situations you manage to stick it out for ten minutes or so before leaving. That's a good step forward so give yourself a reward. (Don't think about it in terms of 'I still had to leave' but instead 'I stayed for longer this time'.)

B Imagine you're doing it right For example – if you're trying to stop feeling anxious in public, try imagining you're speaking in a group and that it's going well. Or if you're cutting back on the amount you drink try imagining successfully refusing an offer of another drink. Do this when you are feeling relaxed and confident.

C Link the 'bad' action to something unpleasant You have to be tough to try this but it works well. You can't resist cream buns? Imagine you are picking one up, biting into it and it's full of … well, what would disgust you?

Joan	Harry
A I've already decided to do that by rewarding myself if I stub out a lighted cigarette. That's certainly breaking the chain if I stop between lighting up and actually smoking	A If I leave the chips on my plate after going in and taking some, I'll … (I'm not going to write that reward down where someone might see it)
B My day dream is about being fresh and clean and meeting Paul Newman!	B I'm going to rehearse asking for 'just a half' and not weakening if the others laugh
C As I inhale I'll tell myself it's a poisonous gas – well it is really	C My dog sicked up my left over chips last week. I'll think about that when I next see chips

We hope you found Joan and Harry's ideas interesting. You need to go through these six steps and work out your own plan. Don't forget to 'reward' yourself when you've made your plan!

Will your family and friends be upset?

Will changing your ways upset your family or workmates? Perhaps, in some way, they felt good about the way you used to behave. For example many of us feel good if our cooking is eaten with obvious relish. It's upsetting if our meals are picked at or refused. If you are dieting and other people cook for you you may need to talk this over together. It's not their love, just the fattening food, that you're turning down.

Maybe your partner feels good about buying chocolates for you as a present? You need to find other ways for the expression of this love. What would you like as a present instead? Choose something that it still feels good for your partner to give.

Maybe your boss feels good if he buys you a drink? What could you do about that?

We often break our good resolutions about changing our ways because we don't like to think we are hurting someone else's feelings. You may need to give top priority to explaining to your family and friends why you want to change your ways.

Will they undermine your plans?

One of the most difficult tasks is to work out how you can continue to go to the pub at lunchtimes or after work with your workmates because you like their company – but no longer want to drink so much. You may need to rehearse what you will say when you are pressed to 'have another' or jeered at for not being able to 'keep up with the boys'. Perhaps you need to plan to go somewhere or take up a hobby where there is no chance to drink.

Nagging can upset your plans too. If your partner shouts, 'That's right! Now I've upset you, go off and stuff yourself with chocolates' or 'I suppose you think your hard day at the office entitles you to just sit there and drink all evening', then you probably will do just that. *And* end up feeling rotten about yourself.

Will they support you?

If you take them into your confidence most people will support you as much as they can. They like to be asked to help. You will need to decide exactly how your family and friends can help you with your particular plan. They can help in three ways. Let's look at how Harry and Joan arranged to get support.

Setting a good example Harry's wife agreed not to eat snacks while watching TV because he found it almost unbearable to watch her eat when he was most tempted himself.

Making it easier to keep to your plan. Harry got his wife to serve the meal on to his plate in the kitchen so he wouldn't be tempted to take large or extra helpings from the serving dishes on the table. Joan got her friend Anne to phone her each morning for a few weeks at the time when she was most likely to weaken as she gradually put back the time of her first cigarette of the day.

Rewarding you Joan didn't suggest this to her husband but he did reward her by commenting when he kissed her on how much nicer she tasted now! Harry's wife rewarded him by noticing when he had been particularly good at refusing tempting food when they were out – and praising him for it on the way home.

Each of these steps towards changing your ways may seem small and unimportant. But you learnt your old pattern of behaviour in just the same way, by small, and probably unnoticed, steps. Learning a new pattern can give you a more healthy life.

Work and health

Work outside the home is central to many people's lives. It has a powerful effect on your health.

Work can affect your health in two major ways.

It can affect your mental health. As a source of pleasure, stimulation and satisfaction it can add to your well-being. As a source of boredom, monotony or stress it can lead to feelings of depression, worthlessness or anxiety.

It can affect your physical health. On the credit side, using your physical and mental abilities can help you stay fit. On the debit side, many modern work processes involve hazards that can lead to illness.

In this chapter we look at both these aspects of health and work. Our first topic *A satisfying job?* takes up the issue of how far you enjoy your work. At first glance this might seem to have little to do with health. But work that isn't enjoyable is often stressful. It takes its toll in days lost through minor illnesses, emotional problems and a general loss of that sense of well-being that is essential to a full, satisfying and healthy life. Finding a job that *is* satisfying isn't always easy but it can be worth looking at the possibilities of change. The second topic, *Want to change your job?*, suggests some ways of going about this. The next three topics are about some of the hazards to your health that you may encounter at work. *Stress at work* looks at the particular stresses that work can produce and ways you can counter them. *Health hazards at work* takes you through some of the risks you may be exposed to as a result of the industrial processes you work with. *Accidents* looks at how and why accidents happen at work and what should be done to prevent them. The final two topics deal with what can be done about health hazards at work. *Taking action* and *Rights and responsibilities* should help you to see what you can do to make your workplace a safer and healthier place.

Work can take up approximately a third of your life between leaving school and retirement, so it's worth taking a look at how it affects your health.

5

A satisfying job?

Do you have pride in your work? A feeling of fulfilment at the end of the day? Satisfaction in what you are doing?

Most people would like to be able to feel these things about their work but in many jobs it isn't easy. And the effects of dissatisfaction can be far-reaching.

Satisfaction and health

Satisfaction at work can come from many different aspects of a job. It's different for different people. In this topic we ask you to take a look at how satisfying *you* find your work and why. Satisfaction at work is important for your emotional health. If you're unhappy in your present job or have been unhappy in a previous job you may recall having some of the following reactions:

○ you become irritable with those around you – your workmates, family and friends.

○ you're more susceptible to minor illnesses such as colds.

○ your opinion of yourself drops. You have low self-esteem.

○ little things upset you.

○ life seems dreary and worthless.

○ you're easily depressed.

All these things *can* be the result of unsatisfying work so we'd like you to start this topic by taking a look at what's satisfying about your job.

Listed below are a number of reasons why you might enjoy your work. Circle the numbers of the ones that apply to you.

1 Good salary/wages

2 Good relationships with workmates

3 Good physical working conditions

4 Good relationship with supervisor or boss

5 Good firm to work for (ie, efficient, flexible, good fringe benefits, treats employees well)

6 Responsibility for your own work or work of others

7 Chance of advancement/promotion

8 Work itself (ie, you enjoy the particular thing you do for its own sake)

9 Recognition by other people for being good or successful at your job

10 Achievement of a goal (ie, solving a problem, making something new, seeing the results of what you've done)

Working conditions and relationships

Items 1–5 are about working conditions and work relationships. If these aren't good you are likely to feel angry or dissatisfied with your work. If they are right, (ie, you circled numbers in this section) you have some basic satisfaction with your job. However, you can have good fringe benefits, a comfortable office, pleasant relationships and a good wage and still feel bored and fed-up at work. You may feel that your talents are not being used. You may feel undervalued. You may feel frustrated. Something else may be lacking in your job.

Motivation

Items 6–10 are about motivation. They're about the factors that make you enjoy the work itself. Circling numbers in this section means that you enjoy what you're doing. The job makes sense. You feel it's worthwhile. You feel that you're getting somewhere. Satisfaction of this kind is usually more long-lasting than the first kind. Unfortunately, it's also less common. Why should this be so? In many jobs it seems to have something to do with the way work is organised.

How work is organised

In our society work is organised in such a way that few people are able to be in direct control of what they do. Most people have to sell their ability to work in exchange for wages. The contract is that they do whatever tasks are assigned them for a particular period of time. In return they get wages that will cover the necessities of life. In industry, particularly, they have little say over what they do or how they do it. Owners and managers have to ensure that, while they are at work, the workers produce more goods than equal the value of their wages. If they don't do this, the company won't make a profit and will go out of business.

One result of this is that management is always looking for ways of making workers more productive. One way of doing this is to use more machinery and automation. Another is to divide up tasks so that they become simpler and more straightforward. Workers become extensions of the machines they operate.

Automation

Automation always means that a minority of tasks become more skilled and the majority become less skilled. Complex machinery needs complex engineering skills to design and maintain it. But only a few of the workforce will be engineers.

Over the last century there has been a *decrease* overall in the number of skilled jobs available in industry and elsewhere. This means that for most people the possibilities of getting satisfaction from work itself are small. As one American manager disarmingly put it, 'We may have created too many dumb jobs for the number of dumb people to fill them.'

So how do people cope when the work itself isn't very fulfilling? Here are descriptions of how two people in this position got satisfaction from their jobs. They're taken from a book of interviews with American workers called *Working*, by Studs Terkel, and which you may find interesting to read. Although the examples are American you'll probably find that they still apply to you.

Coping

Dolores Dante, a waitress, got her satisfaction from turning her job into a piece of theatre:

'It would be very tiring if I had to say, "Would you like a cocktail?" and say that over and over. So I come out different for my own enjoyment. I would say, "What's exciting at the bar that I can offer?" I can't say "Do you want coffee?" Maybe I'll say, "Are you in the mood for coffee?" Or, "The coffee sounds exciting?" Just rephrase it enough to make it interesting for me. That would make them take an interest. It becomes theatrical and I feel like Mata Hari and it intoxicates me.'

Grace Clements, a factory worker, got her satisfaction by putting her energies into working for the union:

'Before the union came in, all I did was do my eight hours, collect my pay-check and go home, did my housework, took care of my daughter and went back to work. I had no outside interests. You just lived to live. Since I became active in the union, I've become active in politics, in the community, in legislative problems. That has given me more of an incentive for my life. I see others, I'm sad. They just come to work, do their work, go home, take care of their home, and come back to work. Their conversation is strictly about their family and meals. They live each day for itself and that's about it.'

Can you write a similar description about your job? Try asking friends or members of your family to write descriptions of their jobs too.

Compare what you write. Are the ways you get satisfaction from your job the same? Or are different things important to different people?

How satisfied are you?

Work takes up such a large part of your adult life that it's important to make sure that it's as satisfying as possible. This isn't always easy. You may not have much choice over where you work if work is hard to come by or you don't have many skills. If you're going to change anything, however, you do need to know what it is you like and dislike about work and the kinds of things you're looking for in a job.

In this activity we look in a bit more detail at the kinds of things that make people feel satisfied with their work. The list shown just below will help you clarify your ideas.

Place a tick against the items which you're satisfied with in your present job.

In my present job I'm satisfied with
☐ my wages/salary
☐ pension scheme
☐ bonuses
☐ the amount of overtime available
☐ the hours I work
☐ the place where I work
☐ the distance I have to travel
☐ the security of my job
☐ the size of the firm
☐ the products made or the services offered
☐ the relationships between workers and management
☐ the rules and regulations at work
☐ my relationship with my boss/supervisor
☐ the attitudes of the people I work with
☐ the number of people I work with
☐ my relationship with the people with whom I work.

What's important to you?

The next checklist has two columns for you to tick.

In the first column place a tick against any items that are important to you in a job.

In the second column place a tick against any items that are important to you and which your present job fulfils.

	1	2
I have to use my skills and judgement		
I have a lot of responsibility		
I have a lot of authority		
Work is challenging or difficult sometimes		
I work on my own		
I work with others		
I meet the public		
I do a variety of tasks		
Work involves me in learning something new		
I use my physical skills		
I use my mental skills		
I have to solve problems		
I'm respected by my workmates		
I'm respected by my boss/supervisor		
I'm recognised as having particular skills or expertise		
I feel I'm achieving something		
I feel I'm doing something useful for others		

Satisfied or not?

The first checklist is about your working conditions and relationships. It has 16 items. You'd be very lucky if you ticked all of them. That degree of satisfaction would be quite unusual. If you ticked less than half, however, this suggests that you have a significant amount of dissatisfaction with your job.

The second checklist is about aspects of the job itself that you might find fulfilling. What you should look at here is how far the ticks you placed in the second column match the ticks you placed in the first one. If you ticked the same items in both columns then clearly your present job *does* give you what you want. If, on the other hand, you have no ticks in the second column to match the ones you placed in the first, then clearly your job doesn't give you what you want.

How important is dissatisfaction?

If both checklists showed that you were dissatisfied with your job, what should you do? The first thing is to decide just how important this dissatisfaction is.

It might be that the only item you are satisfied with from the first list is your wages or salary. While this probably means that you're not very happy at work you may feel that a good wage outweighs the other disadvantages, at least for the time being.

It might be that the only item from the second list that is important to you and that your job fulfils is the fact that you have a lot of responsibility. If this is the most important thing for you it may outweigh the fact that you feel your abilities are unused in other areas. If, on the other hand, having responsibility is the least important of these items for you, then your dissatisfaction is really quite important.

Satisfaction at work is important to your health. People often think it's unrelated or under-estimate it. Yet, as we said at the beginning of this topic, people who are bored or unhappy in their jobs may:
○ get easily depressed.
○ have low self-esteem.
○ feel they're wasting their lives.
○ be more likely to have accidents at work.
○ take more days off sick for minor complaints.
○ take their frustration out on family or friends.

Making a change

As we've said throughout this book, making changes is never easy. In the area of work there can be an awful lot of things you can't control as an individual. You can't control the availability of work. You probably can't control the way it's organised. So if you want to change what you do at work you may need a lot of persistence and support from your family or friends.

If you are dissatisfied with your job and would like to make a change, the next topic suggests some things you might think about and tells you about organisations that could help. At times when unemployment is high, it may not be easy to find the kind of job you would like.

Want to change your job?

You have decided that you are dissatisfied with your job – what will you do next?

First of all, you could look at yourself and your family, if you have one, and consider how a change of job might affect both you and them.

The other thing you can do is to gather information about possible jobs, either vacancies for the same type of work as you are doing now or some other kind of job entirely.

If you decide to consider changing to something quite new, then you need to collect information about all possibilities open to you.

You might want to talk the idea over with someone, or even take tests to find out whether you are really suitable for the job you have in mind.

Questions to ask yourself

Resources
How much do you earn now?
Could you manage on less?
Do you really need to earn more?
Could you move house if you had to? Abroad?
If you have children, how would they be affected by a change of job and/or a move? Are your parents alive? Do they live near you, and what is their health like? Do other people have expectations about your career? Are these important to you? Do you have any family job traditions? Have you any useful contacts or special opportunities?
How do you travel to work? Does this affect what you do?

Coping with work
How much time have you had off work for sickness in the last year? In the last five years?
Do you suffer from any recurrent illnesses or allergies?
Do you have any hearing or visual difficulties? Are you colour blind?
When did you last have a medical?
Are your pulse, breathing rate and blood pressure normal?

Qualifications
What external examinations have you passed at school? At any further educational establishment?
What vocational or professional courses have you taken, with what results?
What job training have you completed?
What home study have you completed?

Job experience
What jobs have you held and for how long?

Filling in the answers to these questions should make you think a bit more about what you have to offer and how changing your job might affect you and other people around you.

Now that you have taken a little time to consider yourself and your circumstances, write down a list of points which you will have to bear in mind when you are considering a change of job.

Geoffrey Stevens went through these questions having decided that he was fed up with the job he was doing (he worked as a garage mechanic) and wanted to look at new kinds of work. He's married and has two children, both at school, who are fairly independent. He bought his home some time ago before prices got as high as they are now so the proportion of his income that he spends on mortgage repayments is lower than for many people. His wife Sheila has recently started work as a secretary again so the family income is now quite good.

He produced a list like this:

1 I don't want to move because both my parents and Sheila's live near and will look after the children during school holidays.

2 Job will have to be within cycling distance as Sheila needs the car to get to her job.

3 We could manage on a bit less money now Sheila's working. If I could get a grant would consider re-training.

4 My health is all right but I want a job where I can move around a bit and not be stuck at a desk all day.

5 Only 3 O-levels, but would hope that I can use my Open University degree (when I get it).

Geoffrey's next step is to investigate different jobs he is interested in. He has always liked the idea of working directly with people but isn't sure whether or not he'd be good at it. His eye has been caught by advertisements in the papers for mental nurses, and he writes off for information. He discovers that he could train as a registered mental nurse. The pay is better than for an ordinary nurse and the prospects are good as there is a shortage of mental nurses. As he's still a bit unsure of whether he'd enjoy working with the mentally ill he also gets in touch with the local hospital which is just down the road. They suggest that he becomes a voluntary helper with the patient's social club to get more of an idea of whether he is suited for this kind of work.

Geoffrey was perhaps luckier than most because his comfortable financial position allowed him the chance to re-train. But, even if this option isn't open to you, others are. So find out what could suit your circumstances.

Where can you get information?

If you simply want information about new jobs in your area, the local paper and the job centre should be able to help. The job centre may refer you to PER (Professional and Executive Recruitment). Remember that it is always worthwhile approaching firms you are interested in, even if they are not advertising for staff at the moment.

But if you want to browse through information about different jobs that you might consider taking or training for, you will have to spend some time in the reference section of your local library or in your local job centre. A list of books which tell you all about different jobs is given in *What next?*. One of the easiest to use is the *Choice of careers* series, published by the Careers and Occupational Information Centre of the Employment Service Agency.

How can you get advice?

Maybe you have spent some time in your local library looking at job descriptions, and you still have no idea what you would really like to do, or you have made a short list and cannot decide between them. So you could consider trying vocational guidance. There are two main sources of vocational guidance.
○ Through a government, or other public agency. This guidance is free.
○ Through a private vocational guidance agency – which will charge you a fee.

Free Vocational Guidance Agencies

Occupational Guidance Units Make an appointment through your job centre or direct. You usually fill in a questionnaire before you go and are interviewed for about one or one and a half hours. The unit should refer you to your job centre or PER for actual jobs. Some OGUs work directly with them.
Look them up in the local phone book, under Occupational Guidance Unit.
Careers service Used to cater only for school children, but now available for adults as well. You may fill in a questionnaire before you are interviewed, usually for less than an hour. It gives you information about training courses as well as jobs.
Look them up in the local phone book under careers service.
Services based in universities, colleges, polytechnics and adult education centres While these bodies have careers services for their full-time students to help them get jobs or some further form of training, more informal guidance services for adults have been set up over the last ten years. Because these informal services have been set up to meet local needs, they vary tremendously in the sort of information they offer, but in general

they can tell you what training courses are available as well as about classes in subjects which may be useful but will not necessarily help you to get a better job. These advice services have different names, like EGA (Educational Guidance for Adults) ERIC (Educational Resources Information Centre) and Education Shop.
Look for advertisements in libraries, job centres and even unexpected places such as launderettes, child welfare clinics, supermarkets and bingo halls.
Agencies where you pay
There are about twenty agencies in different parts of the country. Best known are probably the Tavistock Institute of Human Relations, the Vocational Guidance Association and the National Advisory Centre on Careers for Women, all in London. Some agencies advise you on the basis of a questionnaire filled in by you and one interview; others invite you to call back for more interviews (for which, of course, you pay).
Look up names in the phone book under Career or Vocational Guidance, ask for a list of their charges and find out how they work.

Want to change your job?

Follow the steps on this chart to see what you should do.

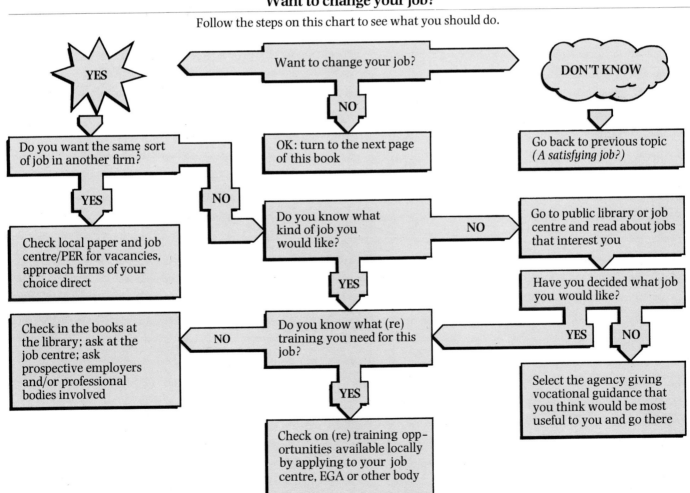

Stress at work

Stress at work can be the worst stress of all. And it can be the most difficult stress to beat.

In Chapter 6 we discuss what is meant by stress and how it is caused. Put simply, if too many or too few demands are made on someone this may cause them to suffer from stress. Most people have heard that an executive under stress can suffer from ulcers, heart attacks and other illnesses. Not many people realise that people in other occupations experience as much if not more stress in their working lives.

The effects of jet lag on big business or political decisions make news. The effects of shift work (which feels just like jet lag) on accident rates and home life hardly ever make the news. Yet the results of being under stress can be the same for any individual in any walk of life.

If you work in a non-manual job you are more likely to feel stressed by the people you work with than by your working environment. The typing pool dragon who is always nagging you or the boss who expects a little too much are probably more of a worry than the temperature of your office or the height of your chair. But if you work with your hands you are likely to be stressed by physical and chemical hazards as well as by your relationships with your workmates. It's hard to hold a sensible conversation when you're wearing ear protection all day long because of the machine shop noise. The following activity will help you identify the factors you find stressful in your work.

Causes of stress

Above is a list of common causes of stress at work. Look through and tick those which apply to you. Do you think your workmates feel the same or are you alone in your suffering? By getting others to check through the list you will probably find that you are not the only one stressed by certain aspects of your job.

Notice that the last five common causes of stress are all double edged. Responsibility, promotion, recognition, the job itself and achievement can cause stress both by their presence and their absence. As we have said before, either too many or too few demands on a person can cause stress.

	You	Work-mates
Money worries You're not sure your job is secure, you don't get paid enough and can't earn more		
Personality conflicts You don't get on well with some or all of your workmates, you're forced to work with people you don't like		
Pressure from the management You never seem to be able to satisfy your boss or supervisor, whatever you do		
Poor working conditions You have to put up with noise, vibration, poor lighting, heat, cold, poor ventilation, danger from physical or chemical hazards, fear of accidents, long hours, overtime, shiftwork, piecework		
Poor administration and company policy You get a lot of bother from inefficient administration, your hours are rigid, there are no fringe benefits, it's a bad firm to work for		

	You	Work-mates
Work load You have too much responsibility and/or too much work to do; or you have too little responsibility and/or not enough work to do		
Prospects There is no hope of promotion, or advancement; or you have been promoted too far too soon		
Recognition No-one appreciates what you do; or everyone is so enthusiastic that you're worried you won't be able to keep your standards up		
Satisfaction You don't like the job itself, it's boring, it doesn't give you any satisfaction; or you enjoy it so much you don't have any leisure time		
Goals You never achieve or finish anything or see the results of what you have done; or you are finishing things so fast you don't get a chance to admire and reflect on what you have done		

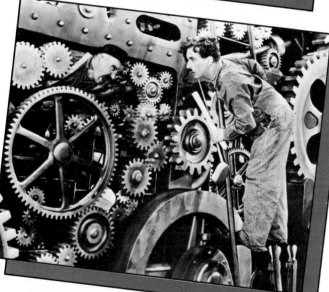

Where did you tick?

If you and your workmates felt stressed by the same things it might be worthwhile taking action to change things collectively rather than individually. The topic at the end of this chapter on *Rights and responsibilities* may help you get started. If you find you are alone in being stressed by your work it is possible that it's not the right job for you and that you ought to think about a change. The topic, *Want to change your job?*, may help you. Alternatively, you may decide you would like to control or counteract the stress in your job. The topic, *Managing stress*, in Chapter 6 suggests various activities which help you combat stress.

Signs of stress in your workplace

Organisations as well as individuals may show signs of stress. The early signs that an individual is under a lot of stress may be increasing nervousness, irritability, indecision, poor memory, tremors, reduced appetitte, loss of weight, irregular bowel movements, headache, backache, skin rashes, and insomnia. Sometimes these warning symptoms never appear and chronic stress can lead unexpectedly to more serious diseases such as asthma, stomach ulcers, high blood pressure, ulcerative colitis and coronary heart disease.

The signs that a workplace is under stress are:

- high turnover of labour.
- high absenteeism.
- high illness rates.
- high strike rates.
- high accident rates.

Are any or all of these common in your workplace?

Even if wages are high and conditions are good, a job which is basically boring and without satisfaction will not keep a steady workforce. People will leave or strike just to produce some change in the environment. If job satisfaction is low more people will have days off through illness. This isn't just skiving. Aches and pains and illnesses seem much worse when you spend all day bored and depressed. When a job is rewarding other troubles diminish.

Britain's industry loses far more days' productivity through backache than it does through strikes. It can be a silent way of protesting against stress. Even when all the measurable physical and chemical hazards of a workplace have been reduced to a minimum, accident rates may remain high. Stress of a different kind may increase the accident rate. Under continued stress alertness and dexterity deteriorate, making workers vulnerable in the presence of machinery or when handling dangerous chemicals.

Clumsiness, induced by stress, is often blamed on the individual. But it is not always possible for individuals to change the causes of stress on their own. They are the responsibility of those who design the working environment. It has been shown very clearly that if a job has satisfaction and meaning to those who do it, if there is pride in the work, the turnover rates, absenteeism, illness, strike and accident rates are all low.

Organising a solution

In a few places successful efforts have been made to improve job satisfaction. The best known of these is the experiment at the Volvo car plant in Sweden. Here the traditional production line typical of car factories since the days of Henry Ford has been abandoned.

Assembly work at Volvo is carried out by 25 construction teams each consisting of about 15 workers. Each team arranges its own work schedules in consultation with a foreman. Although the team does not make a whole car it is responsible for completing an entire process. This is the fundamental difference from ordinary production line work where each man completes just one operation over and over again. The result is that the Volvo workers have far greater interest and satisfaction in their work. Greater control of the tasks they do and a greater variety of tasks lead to a higher standard of work. There is less absenteeism and fewer strikes. People stay in the job longer.

So why aren't such methods more widely adopted? Some work processes lend themselves more easily and cheaply to re-organisation than others. Lack of imagination on the part of management can be another factor holding up changes that might be beneficial to everyone. However, it's worth considering why Volvo brought these changes in when they did.

They were introduced at a time of full employment in Sweden. Volvo were finding it hard to attract workers to the dull, repetitive work of the production line. There was a good chance that a change in work conditions could lead to a more stable work force, higher productivity and greater profitability. In the circumstances Volvo were prepared and able to take the risk. It paid off, as the work force stabilised and became more efficient.

The situation in Britain today is rather different. Re-organising an entire factory is an expensive business. In a period of economic stagnation, capital investment is unlikely to be put into something management feels is not fully tried or tested. It's too risky. In addition, in periods of high unemployment workers are two a penny. It may sound cynical but management don't need to improve working conditions in order to find employees. So better or more imaginative working conditions sink to the bottom of the list of priorities.

All this may not sound very hopeful as regards change. However, even if major changes aren't possible, perhaps minor ones could be carried out? What sort of changes would you make at work?

Health hazards at work

Many people work in places where every day they are exposed to hazards to their health.

At home you might be eating all the right foods. You don't smoke. You take plenty of exercise and get on well with family and friends. But what happens when you get to work? It's possible that you run risks to your health you wouldn't consider tolerating at home. In this topic we look at some of the hazards of work that can affect your physical health.

Spotting hazards is difficult

Some hazards may be obvious. Many are not. You may have got used to the presence of a hazard. You may not notice it any more; or you may not know it's there because you cannot see, hear, smell, taste, feel or touch it.

A machine or substance may only be safe if used in accordance with strict rules. But new machines and substances come into use every day.

The effects of a hazard on your health may be hard to detect. The effects may occur suddenly with no warning. Or creep on gradually over the years. You may have changed jobs by the time the effect on your health is noticeable. And neither you nor your doctor may link your illness with your past job.

Ask yourself

	YES	NO
Do an unusually high number of people in my type of work complain of similar symptoms or illnesses?		
Do many of the people in my type of work retire early through illness?		
Do people seem to take a lot of sick leave?		
Do new people starting at my workplace mention hazards I haven't noticed lately?		
Do people get extra payments for certain jobs?		
Do people living near my workplace complain that it's a health hazard, eg, it leaks fumes or radiation?		
Do people only work at my workplace for a short while and then leave to go elsewhere?		
Do my workmates and I often grumble about the working conditions?		

Look at the questions we ask on the left. If you've answered yes to even one of these questions it's possible that you're running some sort of risk to your health at work. We only have room here to say a little about common hazards and how they can affect your body. You'll need to identify the particular hazards in your workplace using this as a guide. The books and organisations mentioned in *What next?* should be a help too.

Your body under attack

Chemical and biological hazards get to your body in three main ways:

○ by being breathed in, eg, dust, some germs.

○ by coming into contact with your skin, eg, oils and acids.

○ by entering your mouth and digestive system, eg, eating contaminated food or licking dirty fingers.

Physical hazards do not necessarily have to enter your body – or touch it – to cause damage.

Physical hazards such as heat can affect your whole body or affect mainly certain points. Noise, for instance, damages your hearing.

Types of health hazards

Physical hazards to your health, like noise, vibration, abnormal temperatures and radiation, are often ignored or put up with but they can result in long lasting damage to your health.

Chemical hazards include the dusts, fumes, gases and vapours that you may be breathing in You may also be handling poisonous chemical liquids and solids. Some may explode or ignite. Some irritate skin and body linings.

Biological hazards exist wherever germs are, especially in dirty, over-crowded conditions, toilets and canteens. In some workplaces people work directly with germs, eg, hospitals and special research laboratories.

Psychological hazards at work like stress, boredom and overwork are common enough. They can have a rebound effect on your home-life. (The first few topics in this chapter looked at these problems.)

Accidents happen for lots of reasons. But they are more likely to occur if a health hazard is already present.

On the pages overleaf, we show some of the more common health hazards. At the end of each section describing a certain hazard, you'll see a few check-list statements to help you assess if you're being affected by that hazard. If you know a statement applies to you tick it ✔. If not put a cross ✗. If you're not sure put a question mark ?.

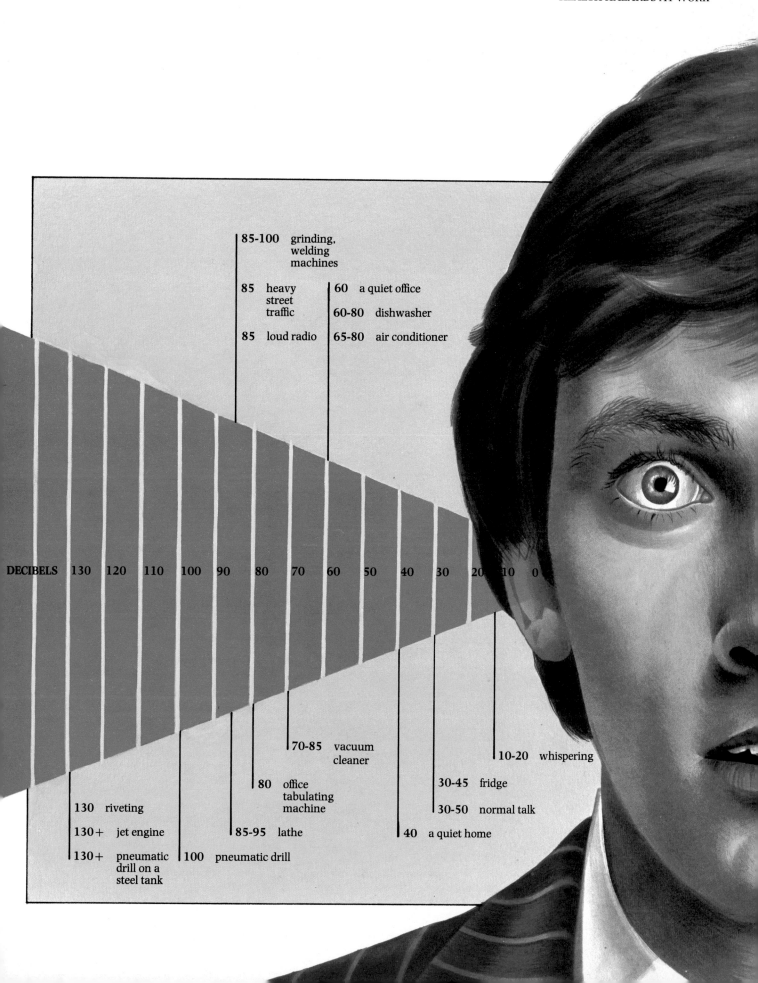

85-100   grinding,
         welding
         machines

85   heavy   60   a quiet office
     street
     traffic   60-80   dishwasher

85   loud radio   65-80   air conditioner

DECIBELS 130 120 110 100 90 80 70 60 50 40 30 20 10 0

70-85   vacuum
        cleaner
                                                    10-20   whispering

80   office   30-45   fridge
     tabulating
     machine   30-50   normal talk

130   riveting

130+   jet engine   85-95   lathe   40   a quiet home

130+   pneumatic   100   pneumatic drill
         drill on a
         steel tank

Noise

Noise can be annoying. Especially a noise that whines or varies in tone. Loud noises can be particularly disruptive, and damaging too. Noise can lower the efficiency of your work by hindering communication. It can muffle warning signals and cause accidents. Worst of all it can damage or destroy delicate mechanisms in your ear. A temporary hearing loss may result from exposure to an intense noise over only a very short time. A really intense noise could destroy hearing permanently. Regular exposure to loud noise over a long time leads to increasing deafness. In fact noise can accelerate the usual hearing loss that occurs as we get older. Some reports indicate that stress and circulatory problems are also caused by exposure to excessive noise.

☐ I cannot hear a match struck five feet away

☐ When I leave work everything outside seems very quiet

☐ I don't know what the noise levels are in my workplace

☐ I don't know if I should wear ear plugs or other protection

Lighting

If the lighting in your workplace is at too high or too low a level it can cause health problems. Poor lighting and glare put a strain on your eyes and create stress. Accidents and bad lighting go hand in hand. Stairs and corridors are the usual blackspots. Remember light bulbs lose brightness with age. Regulations do exist for the lighting of workplaces but these only give minimum requirements and are really out of date. An office, for example, should have ten times more light than a corridor.

Intense flashes of light such as those from arc welding and brightly glowing furnaces are dangerous. A condition known as arc eye is common in welders.

☐ I don't think the standard of lighting where I work has been examined by an expert lately

☐ I don't know when the light bulbs/fluorescent strips were last changed

☐ The level of lighting varies from one area to the next. Suddenly things go from light to dark or vice versa

☐ My workmates and I complain of frequent headaches

Ventilation and heating

A good standard of ventilation is very important in all workplaces, especially those that are dusty and smelly. Working in hot stuffy conditions can make you feel dizzy, sweaty or sick. In extremely hot places the body can lose its ability to control its own temperature.

Cold conditions can also be a health hazard to many workers. And not just for those who work on roads or farms, but for those in offices in winter too. Coldness makes you confused. You can't think properly.

Long term complaints like chest trouble and arthritis are more common in those who've worked regularly in cold conditions.

☐ My work is done sitting down in a temperature below 17°C, or above 20°C

☐ My work is done standing in a temperature below 15°C, or above 18°C

☐ I have to do heavy physical work in temperatures above 15°C

☐ There are no fans or a mechanical air exhaust system to clean the air

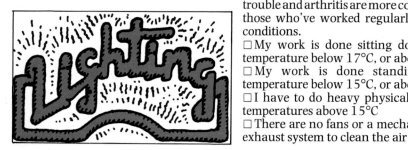

Overcrowding and cleanliness

Levels of crowding in a workplace and levels of cleanliness are important in maintaining the health of a workforce. When people are crowded together germs pass round very quickly. Flu can soon deplete numbers. Various industrial acts require that each person has a certain amount of space allocated to him. The space allotted is the amount estimated *after* having accounted for the space equipment and machinery takes up.

Overcrowding also places severe psychological pressures on people. If the cleanliness of the place is poor the problem is aggravated. Regulations exist to cover the number of toilets and washbasins that should be available. Often lockers and a place to dry wet clothes have to be provided. Obviously the hazard from spread of infection is greater in hospitals and laboratories doing research using germs.

☐ I've not seen a notice saying how many people should work in my area

☐ There's so much equipment and machinery that our floor space is minimal

☐ There's no 'Now wash your hands' notice in our washroom

☐ There's only cold water in the washroom

Vibration

The body is harmed whenever some part of it is in contact with a vibrating surface, eg, the handle of a power drill. But it is not just the part of the body directly in contact that can be damaged. People suffering from excess vibration become uneasy, tired and irritable. Even low level vibration can cause symptoms of motion sickness. Particular damage is done in the long term to the bones, which lose some of their substance. It accelerates the ageing effect on joints so they become stiff and worn. The control of blood flow in the fingers is damaged so that they become white, cold and numb or tingly. Coldness makes this condition, known as 'white finger', much worse. People who have poor circulation in their fingers should not work with vibrating machinery.

☐ I use a power vibrating machine regularly or for most of the day

☐ my fingers go white in the cold

☐ my fingers or joints are painful after using a vibrating machine

Radiation

Light is a form of 'radiation' – rays of high energy that enable us to see. There are also other forms of radiation such as ultraviolet, infra-red, microwave and the more dangerous X-rays and ionizing nuclear radiations (radioactivity). Apart from being found in sunlight, ultra violet energy is used in blueprinting, welding, laundry marking and for dial illuminations, amongst other things. It can cause sunburn symptoms and damage sensitive areas like the eyes.

Infra-red rays are given off by all heated bodies. So workers like welders and steelworkers are at risk to over-exposure which again can lead to damage to eyes. Microwaves are used in food ovens, some communication systems and in surgery. They may damage the eyes and testicles in particular.

Ionizing radiation is the most dangerous radiation if not properly controlled. (There are several types of ionizing radiation of which X-rays are one type.) It is not just used in hospitals but also in industries, like welding. Different types have different degrees of energy and different powers of penetration through bodies and solid objects. At one time there was little control on how often you had an X-ray at hospital. And children's feet could be measured in ordinary shoe shops by using simple X-ray machines. The serious effects of ionizing radiation were not appreciated until recently.

Radiation can affect people who receive small doses over a long time. Or people given a huge dose all at once. Radiation attacks living cells in the body, damaging or destroying them. As a result parts of the body may weaken or even die. Some types of cancer are associated with over-exposure to radiation, although controlled radiation is actually a useful treatment for killing off cancer cells in the body.

Radiation can cause damage to unborn children. People who live near buildings where machines give off high energy radiation, or that deal with nuclear waste, need to be aware of the possible hazard.

☐ I work near radiation machines but don't know how their effect on me is monitored

☐ I am not restricted from going near radiation sources

☐ In the last year I've had two or more X-rays of the same part of my body or three or more anywhere on my body

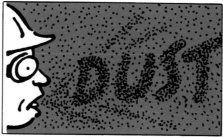

Dust

Many forms of industrial dust exist. Some can be highly dangerous, eg, a particular type of asbestos dust, or carry less, but still significant, risks. Whatever the nature of the dust it can affect your health. The most dangerous dusts are usually the ones so small that you cannot see them. In general the smaller a dust particle, the further it goes into your lungs and the more damage it causes. Bronchitis is very common amongst people who work in dusty conditions. Some cancers have been linked to exposure to certain dusts.

Common sources of dust are coal, silica and graphite. Less well known sources include wool, cotton, hay, fibreglass, talcum powder and detergents.

☐ I work all day in a dusty atmosphere with poor ventilation
☐ I have a chest complaint
☐ I cough and sneeze a lot
☐ My eyes get irritated with dust

Gases

Industrial gases can take up space in the atmosphere and prevent some of the oxygen we need from getting to us. This may lead to headaches and dizziness and sickness or tingling or numbness in limbs. Some of the gases irritate sensitive tissues of the eye and the linings of our breathing tubes. Damage results from either short exposure to a high concentration of gas or repeated low level exposure.

☐ I think the ventilation is bad
☐ My eyes feel sore and look red
☐ I don't know exactly what the gas cylinders at my workplace contain

Chemical solids and liquids

Many chemical solids including metals and liquids can be poisonous to your whole body. A solid particle or drop of liquid may enter the body or touch it. Fumes given off by the liquids and solids may be breathed in. Dizziness, sickness and collapse are common symptoms of chemical poisoning. Your skin is particularly susceptible to chemical damage. Some substances like petrol and paraffin dissolve the skin's natural oils and fats, making it flaky and sore.

Chemicals like acids, alkalis, glues and resins can irritate and burn skin. Mineral oils provoke a special type of acne and skin complaint. Some skin cancers have been associated with contact with a wide range of chemicals but, if treated early, are usually curable.

☐ I don't know what chemicals I come into contact with at work
☐ My skin touches chemicals directly – no barrier creams or gloves
☐ It's difficult to get to a wash basin to rinse contamination off

What did you discover?

Can you now take a clearer look at your workplace? This topic just aims to give you a general idea of the hazards you may face. You need to know in detail the special risks that exist in your own workplace.

Look back at how you have marked the checklist statements.

Were there any you put a tick ✔ by? Well it's pretty urgent to start finding out details of that hazard right away. Even if you only ticked one statement under a particular heading, do something now. The topic on *taking action* (p 142) and the information in *What next?* will help.

Were there any you put a cross ✘ by? OK! Are you sure? There are still things to do. Find out more about hazards you think you might come across in the future. See if your family and friends could be at risk at work.

Were there any you put a ? by? The first thing is to come to a definite decision on whether they apply to you or not. Don't leave it as unknown. Consult people who can give you more information.

Accidents at work

Most accidents at work are avoidable!

Unfortunately the set-up in many work-places often seems designed to encourage injury, not safety.

A worker's own personality, feelings or actions can make an accident more likely. But the root cause is usually the way in which the work is designed or organised.

Accident figures

It is impossible to say exactly how many accidents occur at work each day. Many accidents are not reported or notified to authorities. Accidents are usually 'notifiable' by law if:
○ the accident occurs on work premises.
○ a person is off work for more than three days because of an accident or
○ a person is killed in an accident.

This leaves an awful lot of accidents unreported and unaccounted for. But employers don't always comply with the law and give notice of the accidents they should. Statistics of accidents are very difficult to interpret.

Have you had an accident recently?

Can you think of an accident you were involved in at work? Major or minor. Let's look at what was behind it, using the three charts on this page and pages 140 and 141.

Chart A asks you to describe details of where you were and what you were doing at the time of the accident and what happened.

Chart B asks you to decide what factors in the way your work is organised and designed contributed to the accident.

Chart C asks you to decide what part your own actions and feelings played.

In each case we show how Sally, a secretary, and Tom, a crane driver described accidents they'd been involved in.

Well, did your accident happen in an office, shop, factory, on a building site, down a mine? Were you handling goods? Was machinery involved? Did you fall and injure yourself?

We've already said that official accident figures are difficult to interpret. But they certainly reveal some interesting general information. They show which types of work have more than their fair share of accidents, and the situations in which the accidents occurred.

For example, one-sixth of industrial accidents happen to construction workers – and one-third of fatalities. Miners run very high accident risks. Thousands of accidents happen every year even in comparatively safe shops and offices! It would be pointless to give long lists of statistics here but if you are keen to find out the figures for your particular type of work, *What next?* will tell you sources of further information.

Tom as a crane driver is especially likely to have an accident. His accident was typical for his work in that it involved a moving vehicle and a person being struck. An office accident like Sally's often seems to involve a fall and the handling of a load.

The following list shows typical accident situations. You can probably think of many more things to add to the list.

Chart A – What happened?

Read the 'Questions to ask yourself', then fill in your reply.

Questions to ask yourself	Sally's replies	Tom's replies	Your replies
Where was I when the accident happened?	In the corridor of the offices	In the cab of my crane on the building site	
What was I doing just before the accident?	Carrying a typewriter from one room to another	Starting crane up ready to move a large crate	
What happened?	The typewriter was very heavy. As I turned a corner I tripped over a packing case. It had been left in the corridor. I fell and twisted my ankle. The typewriter was damaged a bit too!	I pressed the wrong control. The crane swung in opposite direction from what we thought it would. I couldn't stop it. I shouted to a chap in the way, he couldn't hear me above the noise. The crate caught him on his head	

A typical accident might involve ...

Poor 'housekeeping' Accidents happen when:
○ gangways and corridors become cluttered.
○ waste is not cleared promptly.
○ tools are left lying about.
○ floors are slippery or worn.
Poor housekeeping frequently results in fire or falls.

Handlifting Accidents happen when:
○ the wrong lifting technique is used (you should bend your knees, and keep a straight back, but it's easy to forget).
○ too heavy a load is lifted.

Tools Accidents happen when:
○ tools are poorly designed or manufactured.
○ tools are worn.
○ the proper tool is not used for the job.

Machines Accidents happen when:
○ guards or safety devices are missing or not in the right position.
○ a machine is poorly designed or manufactured.
○ a machine is not cleaned or checked frequently.
○ a power machine is cleaned whilst on.
○ a machine is difficult to stop.
○ a machine is in an awkward place and difficult to get to.

Working overhead Accidents happen when:
○ loose materials are left lying about and likely to fall on people.
○ hard hats and protective boots are not worn.
○ a working area is not fenced off.

Electrical equipment Accidents can happen when:
○ cables trail over the floor.
○ plugs and wires are rarely checked or incorrectly connected.
○ the equipment is of a confusing design or not compatible with other equipment.

Cranes Accidents can happen when:
○ the controls of a crane vary from one make to another.
○ people get too near a crane's load.
○ a load is wrongly attached.
○ the crane driver is distracted.
○ the cab is difficult to get in and out of.

Entrances and exits Accidents can happen when:
○ fire exits are too few, blocked or difficult to find.
○ people take short cuts through factories.
○ temporary alterations are made to or near exits and entrances.

Ladders Accidents can happen when:
○ a ladder is defective or the wrong size.
○ slippery or heavy footwear is worn when climbing ladder.
○ a ladder is badly placed – in front of a door, for example!

Transport Accidents can happen when:
○ a driver is distracted.
○ a truck is badly loaded.
○ a vehicle goes too fast.
○ a vehicle has confusing or awkward controls.

Chart B – Workplace design

Here we look at how the design and organisation of your workplace contributed to your accident. Look at the statements in the first column. Put a tick by those which apply to your accident and a cross by those which don't. Add a comment if you like.

In my workplace there is/are:	Sally	Tom	You
a lack of protective clothing, equipment, methods	✔ no chairs to move typewriter on	✘	
no or few safety instructions	✔ there's the odd poster up but that's all	✔ not much	
failure to keep standards of temperature / lighting / noise / vibration reasonable	✔ corridor badly lit	✔ noise is awful, chap just couldn't hear me	
badly made or designed machines	✘	✘	
a shortage of trained people	✘	✘	
different types of machines that do same job but work differently	✔ I had to move typewriter to do piece of work in certain typeface. Didn't have that typewriter myself	✔ pressed button I thought was right. But it was different make of crane from others on site and controls were in different position	
injury records available showing where blackspots are	✔ I think injury records are kept but no-one's said what they reveal!	✘	
machines that are difficult to get to	✘	✔ Difficult to get in cab – no space to settle comfortably	
cluttered up rooms or corridors	✔ I fell over empty packing case in corridor	✘	
slippery floors or surfaces	✔ carpet's a bit worn	✘	
badly organised waste disposal and collection	✔ packing case should have been thrown out	✘	
poor fire exits or poorly marked exits	✘	✘	
machines that are not serviced properly	✘	✘	
irregular or odd working hours	✘	✘	
a policy to move a man from job to job or machine to machine	✔ we haven't all got the same make of typewriter, so if a letter has to be done in a certain typeface …	✔ don't stay on the same crane all the time. Can move from one make to another	

Chart C – Actions and feelings

Here we see how your actions and feelings contributed to the accident. Look at the statements in the first column. Place a tick by those which apply to your accident and a cross by those which don't. Add a comment if you like.

When the accident happened I was/had	Sally	Tom	You
tired	✔ I had a busy day	✔ up late last night	
feeling poorly	✘	✘	
poor sight/hearing	✘	✘	
little experience of job	✘	✘	
hungry	✔ yes, missed lunch	✘	
worried	✔ yes, promised to collect son early from nursery. Worried this last job would make me late	✘	
not using right gear	✔ should really put typewriter on chair with wheels to move it	✘	
not using protective gear	✘	✔ I used all protective gear but fellow who got hit didn't have his helmet on	
rushing	✔ yes	✘	
being careless	✘	✘	
affected by drugs	✔ take small dose of Valium every day	✘	
affected by drink	✘	✔ had a pint at lunch-time, but ate too	
being untidy	✘	✘	

In Sally and Tom's accidents there were several factors that made their accidents particularly likely to happen. Sally was rushing and anxious. She knew she should move a typewriter on a chair with wheels, not in her arms. But there were no chairs on wheels available, which wasn't her fault. And why did she have to move a typewriter in the first place? Because the office did not use a uniform typeface. Her own typewriter did not do the right type for the letter her boss requested. She wasn't allowed to use the right machine in someone else's room. And what about that empty packing case?

In Tom's case he was probably a bit sleepy from his late night out. The control panel on this crane was different from the one on the crane he usually operated. All too easy to press the wrong button.

Most safety at work education concentrates on the factors we mention in Chart C. These are the workers' personal habits, actions and feelings. Indeed it is vitally important for everyone to be aware of how their own actions and feelings can cause accidents. It's obvious that someone affected by drink or drugs is going to be less safe than he would have been. And someone who's forgotten their spectacles will not see their work so clearly. But current safety education often ignores the factors we mention in Chart B. That is how the organisation and the design of a workplace set the scene for accidents in the first place.

Engineers aim to design a machine so that it fulfils its function perfectly. But they may not pay much attention to the man who'll be operating it. This can lead to control panels that are difficult to read correctly at a glance; cramped seating space in front of the controls; awkwardly shaped machines, difficult to move.

A company which thinks of profit and nothing else at all may not spare the money to repair a leaky roof at once. And leaky roofs mean slippery floors. Slippery floors mean accidents.

Some people adapt well to working shift hours or irregular hours. They seem to be as efficient as ever. But some people find it very difficult. Their bodies are out of synch with themselves. And they are more likely to have accidents. If they can get work at regular hours instead, that's better. But their company's policy may not be able to give them this opportunity.

In the previous topic we looked at common hazards in the working environment. If the conditions are less than satisfactory, accidents are more likely. Research shows that the conditions in which people are most comfortable and work most efficiently are also those in which there are fewest accidents.

In the *Stress at work* topic we saw how a man under stress is more likely to have an accident. It seems that certain people are more prone to have accidents than others. But research has found it impossible to pick out these people. But we do know what sets the scene for accidents. The root cause is usually the design and organisation of the workplace.

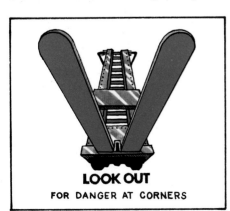

LOOK OUT
FOR DANGER AT CORNERS

DON'T BE SOFTHEADED
WEAR YOUR HAT—IT MAKES SENSE

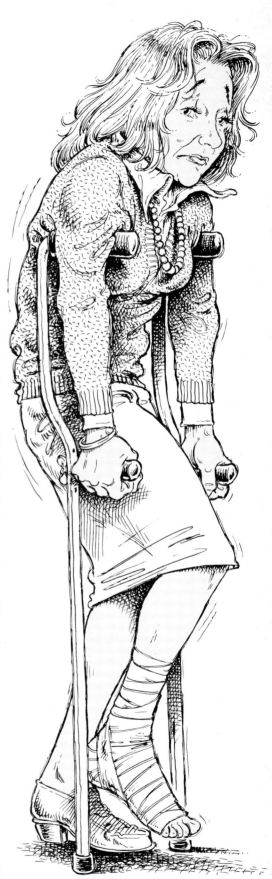

Taking action on health hazards

It's absolutely vital to take steps to make your workplace safe.

How will you go about it?

Some things you can do as an individual. Most often you will need the help of your workmates and may need to make demands or seek the co-operation of officials.

Where are you at risk?

Look back through the last two topics in this chapter. By now you should be able to pin point:

○ biological hazards in your workplace, like inadequate wash areas.

○ physical hazards in your workplace, like noise.

○ chemical hazards in your workplace, like dust and resins.

○ likely accidents in your workplace.

○ personal factors making you more prone to accidents.

○ factors in organisation and design of workplace that make accidents more likely.

Get a piece of paper and make a list of these.

Now what are you going to tackle first? Something personal – like poor eyesight? It's easy to start doing something about this straight away, as it is your individual problem. Or a small, seemingly uncomplicated hazard, like a slippery floor covering, or a long-term hazard like insufficient heating? Or a big but serious immediate problem like leaking chemical fumes?

Emma works in a bakery and confectioners. She made a list of hazards she faced (see chart below).

Make yourself a similar chart, about your work situation. If you have many hazards to cope with, choose three or four to start with.

By your action you can try to:

○ remove or reduce the health hazards.

○ protect yourself where it's impossible to remove the hazard.

○ establish how to reduce the effects of an accident should it occur.

We can give here a few general pointers for tackling these things.

Removing and reducing

Personal factors

○ Check your physical health – especially poor eyesight and hearing. Take steps to overcome this. See relevant person eg, doctor, optician. See topic in Chapter 8, *A healthy community*.

○ Keep concentration up and avoid lack of sleep and food. Look back to Chapter 3, *Looking after yourself*.

○ If you're ill, don't force yourself to work. You could cause an accident and damage yourself and your work-mates, or pass infectious illness around. See your doctor immediately.

○ If you're affected by pills or alcohol and it is a problem, see your doctor, and see topics on pills and alcohol in Chapter 4, *Breaking old patterns*.

○ If worry is affecting your work performance see topics in this chapter on stress at work, and Chapter 6, *Stress and emotions*.

○ List times of day when you think your habits most affect your work adversely and be aware of your actions at this time.

Work design factors

This area can be most difficult to change as you need the co-operation of management. But you do have rights, as we explain in the next topic, and you are also more likely to succeed if you organise collectively, preferably through your union.

You should be pressing for:

○ working areas and machines with good access.

○ quality machines and equipment, tested for performance.

○ adequate testing and checking, inspection and monitoring.

○ consistent design and layout of machines.

○ substitution of safer materials and machines for risky ones.

○ isolation of hazardous processes.

○ automatic and remote handling where possible.

○ good 'housekeeping'.

○ provision of more training and information.

○ adequate supervision of inexperienced workers.

○ special plans and precautions for when normal routine is interrupted by cleaning, repair and maintenance.

Accidents in general

○ Obtain injury record for workplace – through safety representatives or union representatives where they exist. Look for patterns, eg, a particular injury in a particular place and press management to concentrate on improving things there. Could you get blackspot warning notices put up in appropriate places around your factory?

○ Make a list of all machines in your workplace. Find out, from manufacturers if necessary, exact instructions for use and for maintenance. See if actual use and maintenance meets with specified requirements.

Hazard	When to act	By myself	With workmates
slippery floors	soon	yes, if I'm to remind myself not to run on them!	yes, if we're to get them treated so they're not slippery
uncleanliness from not wearing hair covering	as soon as possible. A customer has complained already	when we get hats I must remember to wear mine	yes, we'll have to ask the management together for hats – or complain to health people
too hot and ventilation is poor	when we can. It's not too bad in winter		the whole place needs new ventilation system. We'll have to fight for this together
lack of concentration till coffee time in morning	now	eat breakfast	

Chemical, physical and biological hazards

By seeking help and information find out what 'threshold limits' for physical hazards are, eg, level of noise it is safe to be exposed to and for how long. Compare with your situation. Similarly, check chemicals, how they should be handled and how they *are* handled and, above all, what they are. It is possible to obtain various meters and apparatus to check some hazards yourself (noise meter, dust concentration sampler). You can ask your local health and safety officer to call and check. If you know for sure that hazards in your workplace exceed advised limits you are in a good position to press for reduction or removal if possible.

Protection

Wherever possible the hazard should be removed or reduced. This is often more possible than it seems at first. However, all means of protection against the hazard should also be taken.

The method of protection might be applied to the sources of the hazard, eg, a guard to put on a dangerous machine or a room to be sound-proofed. Or protection might be given directly to the individual at risk, eg, ear muffs and shields. You should always be on the look out for more efficient and more up-to-date means of protecting yourself. Trade journals are sometimes a good source of information.

Protection devices sometimes produce their own problems. They may be bulky and cumbersome. A respirator may make talking difficult or create a sense of isolation and unease. A worker may use up his own energy more quickly if he's dressed in heavy gear and so tire more quickly. This effect can be serious if a worker has existing heart problems and he's subjected to extra stress. If a person's job contains such hazards that he needs protective gear he can't cope with, he'll seriously have to think of changing to a more suitable job.

Minimising effect of accidents

If an accident does happen, knowledge on the part of management and workforce on what do do can reduce the drastic consequences. So check what plans there are, for example, for fire-fighting, containing fumes and first-aid.

All work areas should have trained first-aid personnel who are regularly re-examined and undergo refresher courses. First-aid boxes with approved contents should be readily available. The chemical plant explosion at Flixborough in 1974 was a great disaster. There had been a lack of pre-planning for coping with the effects of a foreseeable hazard.

The provision of means to cope with accidents is the duty of management. You may need a joint effort from your workmates to obtain or improve these. Initiating action is as much your job as anyone else's.

Getting help

Help and information can be obtained from these people. Details appear in the next topic.

Rights and responsibilities
fellow workers
safety representatives
management
safety officer
works nurse/doctor
health and safety executive officers
Employment Medical Advisory Service officers

And from these places (see *What next?* for details):

British Safety Council/Royal Society for Prevention of Accidents – good source of information posters and leaflets though it tends to put all the emphasis on the worker

British Society for Social Responsibility in Science – a pressure and advice group

Claimant's Union – for advice if you're suffering from effects of a work-induced illness or accident

Libraries – for general books, an index of manufacturers

Manufacturing companies – if you're worried about the operation of a machine or substance you work with write directly to the manufacturers' concerned asking for details. Mark your letter 'Public Relations'

Department of Health and Social Security – produces booklets and gives advice

Rights and responsibilities

Everyone has a right to work without damaging his health. Everyone also has a responsibility to protect himself and his workmates.

Health and safety at work

In 1974 a new Act was passed to try and improve things. It's called the Health and Safety at Work Act. It extended the laws that were already in existence and made many new provisions.

This new Act has done a number of things.

It created an organised way of dealing with health and safety at work for *all* workers in *all* work places.

It placed a duty on employers to provide healthy and safe working conditions.

It placed a duty on employees to help protect themselves and workmates as far as is reasonable.

It created a special government body – the Health and Safety Commission – to plan health and safety matters and to coordinate its inspectors.

It recognised that the general public should be protected against working conditions that might affect them outside their immediate workplaces.

It encouraged cooperation between workers and management to improve health and safety at work.

The Act has many sections, dealing with hundreds of points. It is backed up by regulations applying to special instances or situations. For example:

○ particular hazards to health, eg, asbestos, dusts, and pesticides.
○ particular machinery, eg, wood-working machines, power presses.
○ particular industries, eg, shipbuilding, docks, foundries, construction.

Codes of practice exist too. They do not have the force of law. But they can be used by inspectors to encourage employers to bring conditions to higher standards than the law lays down.

What do you know about your rights and responsibilities?

Let's look at a few of the main areas that the law deals with. As you read through these areas, try and decide who has what rights and responsibilities.

Rights

By each area put:
A if you think a worker has a right in this area
B for the employer's right
C for the government's right
D for the general public's right

You are likely to put more than one letter for each area. If you can't decide, put the most likely letter. We've suggested letters for the first area.

Responsibility

By each area put:
a if you think a worker has a responsibility in this area
b for the employer's responsibility
c for the government's responsibility
d for the general public's responsibility

You might find it useful to do this activity with a friend at work. We have left enough room for more than one person to fill it in.

Area	Rights	Responsibilities
Area 1 Control, storage and use of dangerous substances. Protection against leakages within and outside workplace	AD	ab
Area 2 Co-operation between all those in a workplace to ensure health and safety measures are taken and kept		
Area 3 Provision of information to workers and the public about the exact nature of work and the machinery/substances involved		
Area 4 Provision of information on company's health and safety policy		
Area 5 Provision of protective clothing and equipment		
Area 6 Ensuring the actual building of a workplace is safe (apart from machinery etc)		
Area 7 Safe use of machinery		
Area 8 Design, manufacture and supply of machinery		
Area 9 Inspection of work places and enforcement of law		

Area 1 – Control, use and protection of dangerous substances

As you can see from the chart we thought this was mainly the responsibility of employers (**b**) and employees (**a**). The main rights were those of employees (**A**) and the general public (**D**). Many dangerous substances can be safe if they are used and treated properly. Employers should take responsibility to make sure all known means of keeping the substances safe are used. They also, by law, have to use the best means for dealing with a leakage if one occurs. Workers have the responsibility to handle dangerous substances correctly. Workers have a right to be protected whilst handling them. The general public has a right to be protected against the possibility of dangerous substances getting out of a workplace.

Area 2 – Cooperation in workplaces

We suggest that both employers and employees have rights and responsibilities in this area (**AB ab**). Employers have a duty to consult workers concerning joint planning and action on health and safety matters. Workers have a duty to cooperate in these matters. Recognised trade unions can appoint safety representatives in a workplace. The employers must set up safety committees if the safety representatives wish. The committee then keeps under review measures taken to protect workers.

The safety representative must act on behalf of his workmates. His name should be posted up for all to see. He has a right to see any company papers about health and safety. Special training is often arranged for these representatives.

Area 3 – Provision of information to workers and the general public

We suggest that this is mainly the responsibility of employers (**b**) possibly with government assistance (**c**). Workers (**A**) and the general public (**D**) have very definite and important rights in this area. Workers should know exactly what risks they are exposed to at work. They should, for example, know the full names of any chemicals they handle and what these chemicals can do. To get information about this you should first try asking your foreman, chargehand, immediate supervisor, or your trade union safety representative. Large companies have safety officers who should be able to give you information. The works nurse or doctor, or even your own doctor, may help.

Many health education units in local health authorities can now offer a range of advice and help on health and safety at work. Contact them if you are interested in organising talks, lectures, discussions or exhibitions about health and safety at work. The Government health and safety inspectors can be contacted by any worker for information. They have offices all over the country (see *What next?*). These inspectors can call on the Employment Medical Advisory Service to back up or help out regarding difficult information. The general public has a right to know details if leakage of substances outside a workplace occurs, eg, radiation from nuclear installations, polluted air, contaminated earth.

Area 4 – Provision of information on a company's health and safety policies

We suggest this is the responsibility of employers (**b**). Rights belong to workers (**A**), certain sections of the general public (**D**) and the government (**C**). Naturally workers have a right to hear about the policy of a company regarding health and safety. This is part of Area 2 cooperation. Directors of companies are required in their annual statements to say what they are doing in health and safety matters.

147

Area 5 – Provision of protective clothing and equipment

Fairly obviously, it's the responsibility of the employer (**b**). It is surprising that it's often the responsibility of workers too (**a**). An employer only has to provide protective clothing if the law says so. It's then a definite right (**A**) of the worker to have it.

But if the protective gear is only advised, then a worker may well have to buy and provide his own! Having got the protection gear it's naturally the responsibility of the worker to use it.

Area 6 – Ensuring the building is safe

This is a responsibility of the employer (**b**). He has to make sure the actual workplace building is safe. Workers (**A**) have a right to expect this. And so has the general public (**D**) if they enter it as visitors or walk past it.

Area 7 – Safe use of machinery

This is basically the responsibility of the worker (**a**). His workmates have a right (**A**) to expect him to use his machinery properly and so does the employer (**B**). Once trained, the worker should do all he can to make sure he and his workmates are safe.

The employer is responsible (**b**) for seeing that his employees are well-trained and know about the hazards and their consequences.

Area 8 – Design, manufacture and supply of machinery

The safety of the design and manufacture of a machine is the responsibility of those who made it – employers (**b**) and employees (**a**) in the company concerned. This is not always so straightforward, however. Safety standards are influenced by the need to remain competitive and may be the minimum rather than the maximum desirable. Workers (**A**) and employers (**B**) have a right to expect that goods designed, manufactured and supplied by other companies are up to standard. The designers and manufacturers are required to carry out research on their product. They have to test it thoroughly.

Area 9 – Inspection and enforcement of law

Basically inspection and enforcement is the responsibility of the government and its inspectors (**c**). Workers (**a**) have some responsibility too. Their safety representatives are allowed to, and should, inspect workplaces at least every three months and after any accident or major risk is identified. Workers (**A**) have a right to expect that their workplace is officially inspected.

The general public (**A**) has a right to expect that workplaces be inspected especially where a harmful substance may escape from it.

How does it work in practice?

The Health and Safety Commission is the government body responsible for developing health and safety policies. It appoints a Health and Safety Executive to carry out its policies and enforce the laws. The Executive is mainly composed of inspectors. Many inspectors deal with specialised areas, eg, just factories, or mines and quarries. Local authorities also have some health and safety responsibility, particularly regarding the law about offices, shops and railway premises.

Sanctions

Inspectors can compel employers to make remedies if they find a fault in health and safety conditions by:
○ giving out an improvement notice. This requires an employer to put things right in a given time.

○ giving out a prohibition notice if danger is imminent or if any employer doesn't act on an improvement notice. This asks the employer to stop the operation or process where there is danger.
○ arranging for fines or even imprisonment if an employer takes no action on the prohibition notice.

Finding out more about rights

You'll probably want to know about points special to your industry or workplace. As suggested in Area 3, the people to contact are:

○ chargehand / immediate supervisor trade union representative (for safety)
○ safety officer
○ works doctor or nurse
○ employer
○ Health and Safety Executive – see *What next?*
○ environmental health officers – see *What next?*

As a member of the public you might like to contact people and groups such as the Citizens Advice Bureau, Friends of the Earth, your MP, British Society for Social Responsibility in Science's work hazards group. See *What next?* for addresses.

Rights for those injured or sick because of work

Various benefits are available for those who've had injuries caused by accidents at work, or who are suffering from an illness recognised as caused by work. If a worker's death is caused by work, widows and dependents can claim.

In all cases you should claim as soon as you know or suspect your problem was work-caused. Accidents at work should always be reported to your supervisor or nurse or employer immediately, in case of claims and disputes later.

Leaflets explaining how claims can be made can be obtained from your local social security office or from the addresses given in *What next?*

Stress and emotions

This chapter looks at what you can do to look after your mental health.

How do you respond, as an adult, to stress and life crises? *Have you learnt*:

○ good responses – so that you can recognise, accept and handle the strong emotions which we all feel at times?

○ that strong emotions can be more bearable if you comfort yourself with food, alcohol, tranquillisers or cigarettes? These can keep your tensions from becoming so painful that you have to admit them and tackle them directly. As short term measures these can work well. But they can become habits which eventually damage your health (see Chapter 4, *Breaking old patterns*), and in the long run they don't help you to tackle your problems.

○ to do something else with your feelings so that they don't come out into the open? For example you may have learnt to keep up a happy front – when you need to be grieving over a loss. Or to turn your anger inwards and get depressed, because it's wrong or dangerous to show anger. Or to feel anxious when you get sexually aroused – because 'nice girls' like you don't want to do that kind of thing. Or to feel you have to go on being endlessly brave when what you need is a good cry because 'brave boys' like you keep a stiff upper lip.

If we don't know what emotions we are feeling – or go on trying to keep them down with pills or by smoking or drinking – it's not surprising that they sometimes swamp us and we become anxious or depressed.

How can this chapter help you?

Stress can affect our physical health as well as our feelings. Yet we often cannot avoid excess stress. The topic on *Stress* helps you recognise the signs that mean you need to take active steps to combat stress. The next topic, *Managing stress*, suggests how you can do this.

Anxiety builds up when we are under stress nearly all the time or our fears, instead of being linked with a special problem, spread thinly across the whole of our lives. The topic on *Anxiety* helps you to work out what makes you particularly anxious and plan what you can do.

We all have passing moods of depression. We feel 'blue', 'low' or 'down'. These moods can go on for a long time or become so severe that they disrupt our lives and we might need treatment for depression. The topic on *Depression* helps you look at what may be behind your feelings and suggests how you can help yourself to handle it.

Depression is also a natural response to a loss. It might be a major loss like bereavement or divorce, or something apparently minor like losing your purse or breaking a special ornament. *Mourning and grief* explains this natural response to a loss and why it is important to go through it and experience it fully.

Although there are many things a person can do to help himself there may come a time of emotional crisis when he doesn't know what to do. *Coping with a crisis* helps you to help someone else who is at such a breaking point.

There is no clear dividing line between being mentally healthy and mentally ill. The topic on *Mental health* looks at this, helps you check on your own mental health and gives some guidelines on when treatment is necessary or worthwhile.

Stress

You feel your heart race and your stomach turns over. Your face flushes and you sweat. Your body is tense. What has happened?

What is stress?

Perhaps you are newly in love and the object of your desire has walked into the room? Perhaps you met a car coming the other way while overtaking on a bend? Both these events can make your body react like this. Both are examples of a stressful situation. Stress is the general response of the body to any demand (pleasant or unpleasant) made on it. So stress is with us all the time.

It happens when our bodies have to respond to many demands at once. We lead complicated lives today. We travel further and faster and meet lots of people.

We drive cars and operate machinery. We have to understand all sorts of rules and regulations and fill in complex forms to get a job or pay income tax, claim supplementary benefit if we are out of work, or just buy a TV licence. Even pleasant events like promotion, getting a rise, marriage or moving to a new home make demands on us.

If these demands get too much we begin to feel stress, our natural bodily response, as a bad thing. But just as some people are more resistant to colds and flu, so some can stand more demands before they get the feeling of being under too much stress.

Of course, some people actually enjoy this feeling – they thrive on it. But for most of us it's a bad feeling. The names we give it show this. We say we feel nervy, on edge, tense, weighed down, strained, anxious, worried, snowed under, up tight, screwed up.

How would you describe this feeling? When you feel like this, do you:
- ☐ bite your nails?
- ☐ light up a cigarette?
- ☐ have a drink?
- ☐ snap at someone?
- ☐ eat something?
- ☐ cry?

Fleeing a wild bear or waiting a long time for a bus – both cause the same stress reaction in your body.

□ withdraw into yourself?
□ take a tranquilliser?
□ wring your hands?
□ pull your hair?
□ chew a pencil?
□ shout?
□ hit someone?
□ hunch your shoulders?

These common reactions to stress help relieve the tense feelings. But only for a short while. They don't solve the problem. So what is happening in our bodies that makes us feel like this? And what can we do about it?

How your body responds

Your body reacts to any demand by preparing for action. If it is something frightening or exciting then the reaction is much greater than for something ordinary. If you are suddenly frightened you can feel the body's emergency action getting you ready to face the 'danger' (fight) or escape from it (flight). Your body needs more oxygen, so you start to breathe faster. You are going to use more energy, so stored food is released into the blood as sugar and fat droplets. This extra oxygen and sugar and fat needs to be carried quickly to the parts of your body where it is most needed.

So your heart beats faster to pump the blood more quickly around the body. The blood vessels in your skin and stomach contract so that more blood can go to your brain, making you more alert, and to your muscles, so that you are ready for physical action. Your blood gets ready to clot in case you should get wounded. Your skin starts to sweat to cool you down.

All of these changes are controlled by a chemical, a hormone, released from a part of your brain.

What can cause stress?

Your body is now ready to jump out of the way of the bus or start to heal itself if you are knocked down. Nowadays, however, there are many times in our everyday lives when we are threatened or excited by happenings which we cannot run away from or fight. Caught in a traffic jam on the way to work, upset by a row with your partner, worried about being late, and with a day's work in a noisy machine shop ahead of you, your body goes into its emergency reaction again and again.

But you can't take any physical action to get rid of the tension. It's all bottled up inside you and your body's defence turns in upon itself. If this happens only occasionally, your body can deal with the hormones and sugar and fat released into the blood, as well as the other body changes, without coming to harm. If there are many such demands on the body it may get damaged.

What stress may cause

It has been suggested that many disorders are partly caused by stress, for example, heart attacks, angina, high blood pressure, peptic ulcers, migraine, asthma, poor sleep, accidents, and depression.

When we are anxious or frightened we may feel sick or get diarrhoea. If we are angry or frustrated we can end up with a headache, indigestion or tense, aching muscles. These are fairly common complaints which most people suffer at some time. But how can stress play a part in illness such as heart attack, ulcers or depression?

In the case of heart attacks it is thought that the fat released into the blood stream, when the body responds to demands, gets trapped in the walls of the heart's own blood vessels. This gradually narrows these tubes. Then one day, during a sudden increased demand on the heart, the narrowed tubes nearly cut off the blood supply of part of the muscles of the heart. This part cannot get enough oxygen and may die, causing a heart attack.

Peptic ulcers may sometimes be caused by too much acid being produced in the stomach at a time of anxiety or worry. Depression may occur when the demands made on a person are continuous. Certain people are always under a lot of stress and never seem to get their heads above water. They are gradually worn down until they feel they can no longer cope at all. They give up trying and then depression sets in.

Too little stress is bad for you

Perhaps your life is so dull that nothing ever seems to happen. This lack of stimulation and lack of demand on the body causes too *little* stress. You seem to lack energy and often feel tired. Although you may have plenty of time when you feel tired like this it's difficult to sum up the energy to go out, visit a friend or invite someone round. It is important to plan how to take up some stimulating activity. (See p 161.)

How much stress in your life?

Some people deal with emergencies without getting panicked and their attitude to life is relaxed and easygoing. But there are others who cannot cope, everything gets on top of them. What about you? Do you feel:

○ 'I can't usually cope, most things get me down'? The demands in your life are too great or you don't know how best to deal with them.

○ 'I normally cope with everything and then strive to do more'? You can cope all right but you are too hard driving and competitive. You never give yourself a chance to relax.

○ 'I usually take life in my stride'? You have got it right! Whether there is too little or too much stress in your life you are able to adjust your pace.

In order to plan how to cope better with stress you need to find out how much stress is in your life now and the main areas in which your problems lie.

Make yourself a chart like the one on the right. We have filled in one problem in each of the four life areas for Jane as an example. You may well have more problems than that so leave yourself plenty of room on your own private chart. There is a lot to think about.

Start with column A, life areas. Work through each of the four areas of your life in column A thinking about what caused your problem. For each problem write down how you felt (column B) and what you did (column C). Try to write comments in all the boxes in the three columns. We hope your comment is 'no problem' for some of them! Now go to column D and consider how you could cope with each of your problems. There are four ways you might deal with stressful situations. Fill in column D with the letter or letters of the way(s) you choose. Could you:

a tackle the problem causing the stress and so remove it?

b avoid the problem and therefore avoid the stress?

c change your attitude to the problem so that it no longer worries you and causes stress?

d learn to control or reduce the stress caused by the problem?

Have another think about column C. What do you normally do in response to a stressful situation? For example, do you light up a cigarette or have a drink? Can you recall a time when, although you did what you usually do at a time of stress,

Some of Jane's comments have been filled in as an example.

A – Life areas	B – How you felt	C – What you did	D – New approach
Where stressful situation/ problems are found	*For example: nervy, on edge, weighed down, anxious, tense, worried, couldn't take any more etc*	*For example: bit nails, lit a cigarette, had a drink, got irritable, ate something, chewed pencil, took pills, snapped at someone etc*	

1 Work and study

Threat of over-time stopping	*Nervy, on edge, tense*	*Lit a cigarette/ got irritable*	*a, c*

2 Family/marriage/sex and intimacy

Child misbehaving at school	*Worried, couldn't take any more*	*Got irritable/ snapped at someone*	*a, d*

3 Social and interpersonal

When meeting someone new	*Anxious, tense*	*Lit a cigarette/ had a drink*	*a, c, d*

4 Leisure and exercise

Can't concentrate on my hobby	*Weighed down*	*Ate something/ chewed pencil*	*c, d*

you didn't in fact have any feelings of stress? You may have learned to smoke or drink at times when you are *expecting* to be under stress. Or it may have become so natural a reaction that you no longer feel the tension and worry. Your body has learned to react to the problem by making you feel you want to light up a cigarette, eat or drink something and not by feeling tense or anxious. This can explain how someone who does lots of things that an onlooker would see as responses to stress can say, 'But I don't feel anxious or under stress'. Regardless of appearances, the changes which happen in stress are still going on inside the body and possibly harming it.

What about Jane?

Work and study
Jane is worried about having less money if her husband's overtime stops. She could tackle this by going out to work herself if she can get a job. She cannot avoid the problem but she could change her attitude towards it so that she is not worried about the money but pleased she will see more of Jim. Or she can learn one of the ways of relaxing and managing stress we describe in the next topic.

Family/marriage/sex and intimacy
Her son is in trouble at school. Jane could tackle this by talking to him and his teachers about the problems. To avoid it she would have to keep him away from school. She can't really change her attitude and think it's a good thing he's in trouble or stop caring about him. But if it's a long term problem she will need to learn to relax to take her mind off it.

Social and interpersonal
Jane is nervous when she meets new people. She could try to tackle it by asking her doctor for some advice to help her make a new start and break the vicious circle. She can't spend the rest of her life avoiding people. She could learn better communication skills so that she gets on with people more easily. She could also learn how to relax and stay calm when she has to meet people.

Leisure and exercise
Because of her other worries Jane finds she cannot concentrate on her knitting and keeps dropping stitches. But worrying about her knitting as well as worrying about everything else won't help. She could look on her difficulty in concentrating on detailed work as the signal for a change and take a walk or go and chat to her neighbour. If this doesn't work then a period of relaxation may help her concentration return.

Managing stress

There are many activities that are enjoyable to do, make you
feel good – and help you cope with stress.

What can help you?

○ If you are alert and fit you can cope
with many demands and problems
without feeling under stress. A well-
balanced diet, some exercise and enough
sleep all help. See Chapter 3, *Looking
after yourself* and 'Sleep problems', p 113
in Chapter 4.
○ Talking about what's causing the
stress can help to relieve it. Having an
unwinding session when you get home at
nights, when someone will listen to
what's been getting you down during the
day, is a good safety-valve that helps stop
the pressures building up. Try talking to
family and friends first. Chapter 2, *Person
to person*, may help you do this. If this does
not help use the chart on p 171 in this
chapter to decide who is best to go to for
help.
○ Stresses caused by work are further
discussed in Chapter 5, *Work and health.*

Rhythmic Exercise

This involves regular repeated
movements of the body. You can do it

alone or with others as part of a sport, or as
an exercise routine best done to music or
by vigorous dancing.

Dancing, on your own or with others,
can be a particularly good 'tonic'. It seems
to improve your body image – you think
of yourself as lively and attractive. This
makes you move in a more alert way,
ready for action.

It helps beat stress in several ways. It
improves your general body fitness so
that you are less likely to suffer ill effects
from stress. And, as we explained in the
previous topic, when our bodies become
ready for action, sugar and fat are
released into the blood. Exercise will help
use these up.

Regular rhythmic exercise has been
shown to lower blood pressure.

By absorbing the body and mind totally
such exercises can help you forget your
troubles. Exercise can also provide an
enjoyable release for bottled up feelings.

As you get better at your exercise you
feel a sense of achievement at improving
your skills. This increases your self-
esteem and so helps to lift depression.

Many doctors believe that there is
another reason why rhythmic exercise

can improve your mental state. A
powerful chemical, a hormone, is
released into the blood during exercise
and acts as a general stimulant. It makes
you more alert, less tired and helps you
concentrate. Exercise may have the same
effect· on the brain as taking an anti-
depressant pill!

Chapter 3 will help you decide what
form of exercise or sport you want to do.
For daily exercise sessions done to music
you may want to get a special tape or
record (see *What next?*) or just use your
own favourite music. You can do your
exercises when you like. (In Chapter 4,
Breaking old patterns, we recommend this
for some people who have trouble getting
off to sleep.)

Relaxation

Relaxing your whole body slows the body
down and also calms the mind. It's easy to
do and is a good antidote to stress. Almost
everyone could benefit from doing
relaxation exercises each day.

Before you can learn to relax you must
first recognise muscle tension. We often

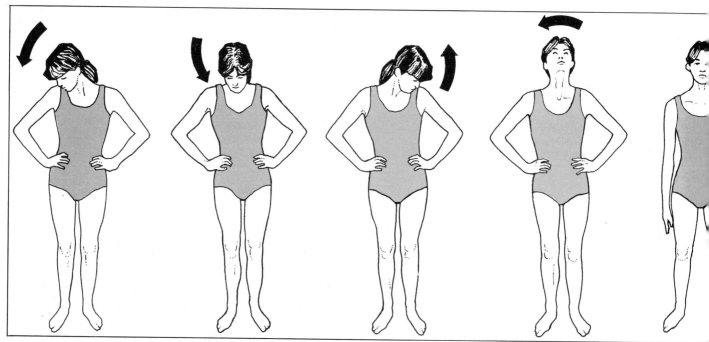

hold our muscles tense without realising it. Try looking in a mirror and doing this simple exercise.

Put your fingers at the side of your forehead by the temples, quite high by the hairline. Grit your teeth two or three times and feel the hard ridge of muscle. Let your jaw sag and feel the difference. Tension headaches and injury to teeth can be caused if you keep up this form of tension for long periods.

You may catch yourself several times during the day with the beginnings of these feelings in your facial muscles.

Once you are aware of the difference between a tense and relaxed muscle you can let go and relax whenever you feel the need to.

Learn in a warm, quiet room where you won't be disturbed. Lie on a bed or sit comfortably in a chair. Start by taking two or three deep breaths, no more. Breathe in slowly and deeply – check that your tummy as well as your chest rises – hold the breath for a few seconds, then breathe out slowly. This helps to calm and relax your breathing. Now breathe normally and quietly.

To relax the rest of your body begin by letting go of your toes and feet, let their muscles relax fully. Let go of and relax each of the main sets of muscles, working up through your calves, thighs, bottom, belly, chest, then your fingers, hands and arms and finally to your shoulders, neck and face muscles. You should then be fully relaxed all over. Stay relaxed for at least ten minutes. It may help you if you try saying a word or phrase to yourself in time with your breathing. You could say

the word 'relax' or 'peace' each time you breathe out. At the end stretch and get up slowly. You should find you feel better.

Quick relaxation

A daily deep relaxation session is a good long term way to help combat stress. Being able to relax quickly helps you cope effectively, at the time, with a particularly stressful experience, such as a visit to the dentist or the tensions created by a quarrel with your partner.

If you are upset you take quick gasping breaths from the top of your chest. So try to remedy this and start by taking two or three breaths as we describe above. This will help you calm down. But it will be better if you can go quickly into full deep relaxation for a few minutes either before or just after a stressful experience.

First you need to learn how to do whole body relaxation (above). Once you have mastered this you will be able to go into full relaxation quickly wherever you are. It may be easier if you have learnt to link your special word with the feeling of being relaxed.

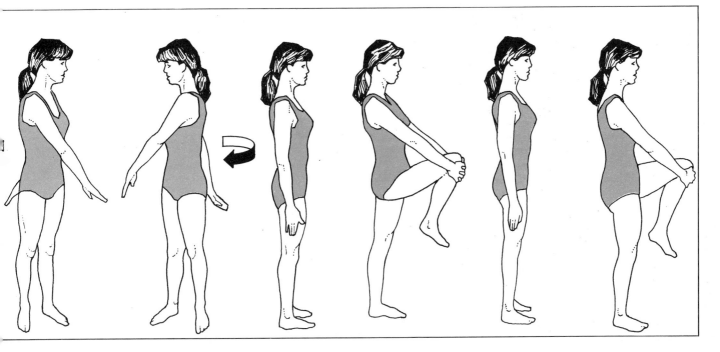

Massage

It's easy to learn how to do massage. You don't need to know a lot of anatomy and there's nothing mysterious about it. But if you don't know much about massage you may think it is not for you. You may think, particularly if you're a man, 'That's not the kind of thing that people like me do!' Some people ask, 'Don't I have to take all my clothes off?' or 'Won't it be sexually exciting?' Well, the answer can be 'yes' to both if that's what you want. But it doesn't have to be. Massage is a sensual (not directly sexual) activity which makes your body feel good. After a massage you feel calm instead of aroused.

More and more people are discovering that massage is a particularly good way of getting rid of the bodily tensions, stiff, tight muscles, that build up in a stressful situation. *What next?* suggests some books which will help you learn how to do massage. Unfortunately there are few classes where you can learn massage. If you can afford it you might treat yourself to a massage in a beauty salon or health clinic to pick up a few tips from them.

You don't have to miss out on a massage if you're on your own. You can massage your own face, scalp and shoulders. However, if you are on your own, yoga is probably a better way to get rid of your muscle tension.

We don't have space here to describe with pictures how to do whole body massage. But here's how to do a shoulder massage. Anyone can learn how to do it. Almost everyone loves having it done to them! It's good after a tiring day when your shoulder muscles are tense.

Get your partner to sit down on an ordinary chair. Stand behind and place your hands on his or her shoulders, close to the neck. Your fingers should be to the front over the top of the shoulders. Hold on with your fingers so that the massage you do with your thumbs won't push her forward. But don't dig your fingernails in! Using the whole side of your thumb reach down and firmly roll the flesh upwards. Work outwards across the shoulders.

Avoid pinching up the tender flesh along the top line of the shoulder towards the neck You don't want to hurt so let your partner tell you what feels best.

Yoga

Yoga is both a physical and mental method for reducing stress. As practised in the West it concentrates on physical exercises and relaxation. But the mental side of the yoga method is not completely ignored.

Yoga sessions begin with a relaxation exercise done in a special position. This is followed by a series of slow stretching exercises in which the final position is held for a while. These stretching exercises help to increase the mobility and suppleness of the body.

All the body muscles are exercised and it is claimed that the slow controlled way this is done also 'massages' and improves the blood supply to the internal organs. The session ends with another period of relaxation.

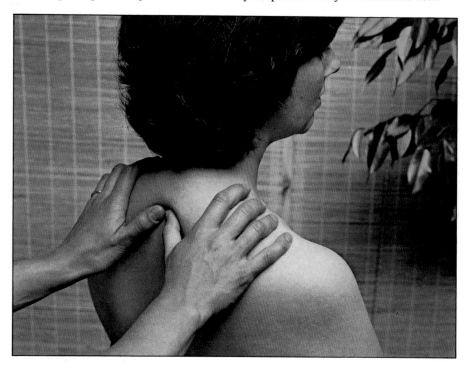

Meditation

Meditation helps the mind to relax and yet at the same time you become more aware of your senses, of what you see, hear, touch, taste and smell.

The idea is to focus the mind:

○ **on a word or phrase (a mantra)** (Many people use the word 'peace' or a very short prayer. Others choose any word that sounds calming to them.)

○ **on an object such as a flower, a lighted candle or an everyday object** (You may like to hold it in your hand so you are aware of its weight and texture.)

○ **on a visual symbol which has a special meaning for you (a mandala)** (Most religions have special symbols. You could draw or paint your own symbol to represent something that's important for you. Or use a memento of a particularly happy time in your life.)

If distracting thoughts arise you just shift your mind back to what you are meditating on. This is contemplation and it involves being calmly and fully aware of something rather than having busy thoughts about it. It's difficult to explain but most people easily get the hang of it – and find it helps them to relax physically as well as mentally. Some people find that saying a word or phrase to themselves in time with their quiet breathing is particularly calming.

Once relaxation is linked with a word or an object or symbol, just calling it to mind when you are in stressful situations will be a signal to your body and mind to relax.

Of course there is nothing new about meditation. It's part of religious practices in almost all the major world religions.

You can teach yourself meditation at home. Find a quiet place where you will not be suddenly disturbed. Stay still – unless you're meditating while you walk. Use your senses as well as your mind. Try to set aside about 15 minutes a day for meditation. But once you've learnt how to do it, you can use it just for two or three minutes at any time throughout the day to offset the build up of stress. Sometimes a person may be given a personal 'secret' mantra by their religious teacher. In other religions simple prayers are repeated, often while looking at a crucifix.

The exercises are done calmly, in silence, with concentration and with carefully controlled breathing. This takes the mind off every day worries and the effect is similar to meditating. The session should leave you feeling mentally refreshed and with an increased feeling of well being.

Done regularly yoga may bring down high blood pressure. It certainly has beneficial effects if you are suffering from too much stress.

You can read more about yoga – and try to teach yourself – in the books listed in *What next?*. But it is better to go to yoga classes to be sure you are doing the exercises properly and the atmosphere at the classes should help you to relax too. There are probably yoga classes in your area. Ask at your library – or write to the address in *What next?*

What's best for you?

Knowing how to relax quickly is useful for everyone. But which activity will best help *you* to combat stress? Perhaps one immediately appeals to you? Good – start with that. But looking at the way you experience stress may help you to decide. Here are some suggestions about where you might start. Whatever method you choose, you will need to try it out for a while to see if it works for you. Give it a fair try because they all take some time to learn to do well.

1 Do you often feel frantic – your mind gets into a whirl – you can't think straight? Are you swamped by worrying thoughts?

We suggest you try meditating. This will give you the benefit of being able to switch quickly into a five-minute meditation session whenever you want to calm your mind.

2 Do you bottle up your anger but sometimes feel you'll explode?

We suggest you try vigorous rhythmic exercise because bottled anger often leads to tensed muscles and aches and pains which are relieved by moving around rather than rest.

3 Do you feel tense and aching and uninterested in sex?

Try massage, if you have someone who will do it with you, as this leaves your body soothed and relaxed so that you can let yourself respond during lovemaking. If you can't do massage, or find you hold yourself tense during it, perhaps some vigorous exercise to dance music will work better for you.

4 Does tension give you headaches?

Try relaxation. Tense muscles in the neck, face and scalp can start headaches.

5 Do you feel you desperately need to stretch your muscles but can't face doing ordinary exercises?

Try yoga – the exercises are done calmly and quietly. Or, if you want to be livened up as well, try vigorous dancing.

Keeping it up

Whatever you choose you should be planning to make your activity a permanent part of your life. Perhaps you would like to try several so that you can compare them and decide which suits you best? For each of the following questions on right, score as follows:
0 – Not at all
1 – Not very much
2 – Quite a bit
3 – Very much
By comparing your total score you should find which suits you best.

Activity you tried	1st	2nd	3rd	4th
1 Did I enjoy doing it?				
2 Did I feel 'better' after doing it?				
3 Would I want to do it for many years?				
4 Does it fit in easily with the rest of my life?				
Total score				

Recreation

Some people say, 'My life is so boring, shut at home all day (or in the same job), nothing exciting ever happens'. They actually need more stress to stimulate them in the form of a new interesting activity. Taking up a group activity or learning together with others at evening classes will provide stimulating company as well as an interesting activity.

Other people say, 'My life's so busy I need some time to myself'. They need an absorbing hobby to do on their own or just time to sit around and unwind.

Recreation should be a time when you take your mind off your work and problems. It could give you a chance to:
○ learn new skills.
○ visit new places.
○ meet new people.
○ think about new ideas.

Try to let yourself become completely involved both physically and mentally in what you do. By having new interests you should find your energy restored.

Unfortunately some people bring the same approach to their recreation as to their work. They drive themselves too hard. They want to win. They want to be perfect. They make their recreation as stressful as their work! It's important to find something to do that you enjoy and which absorbs your interest but which isn't too difficult or competitive.

The best form of recreation for all of us, some of the time, is 'doing nothing'. You don't have to fill every minute of the day with something to do. It's not wicked to do 'nothing'.

Keeping a balance

You may need to reconsider the balance of activities in your life. Take some time off to think about what you want your life to be like. The questions below should help you decide which areas of life you need to give more attention to. We have given you two columns to tick. First of all read each sentence as 'I ought to' and tick that column if it's true for you. Then read the sentence again as 'I would like to'. Tick that column if it's true for you. There may sometimes be a difference between what you feel you ought to do and what you would really like to do. Maybe you haven't worked out a way of doing it that you would enjoy or succeed with. In that case, look at the column below on 'What to do'.

Balance of activities in your life

Should I	I ought to …	I would like to …	What to do?
1 look after my physical needs by: eating more wisely taking enough exercise			1 'Eat more wisely' – Chapter 3 and Chapter 4 should help you do this, 'Take enough exercise' – Chapter 3 should help you choose a suitable enjoyable way to exercise
2 take up activities to help myself combat stress			2 This topic and particularly the quiz opposite, 'What's best for you?' should help
3 escape from my everyday life and do more things on my own			3 This topic and Personal space in Chapter 2 will help you explore your need for time and space just for yourself and suggest solutions
4 get out and meet more people or make new friends			4 Person to person, Chapter 2, should help if you are nervous about getting on with people. Shared interests make it easier to get on together
5 develop new interests such as: hobbies study sports			5 Find out more about possible hobbies, study and sport from your library, evening class or leisure centre. Or contact the Sports Council or the Open University (for addresses, see What next?)
6 get a job or change jobs			6, 7, 8 Your work is discussed in Work and health, Chapter 5
7 cut down on the amount of work I do			
8 reorganise my work so that it's less stressful			
9 spend more time with my family and friends			9, 10 What counts as fun for you? The quiz on p 117 in Chapter 4 helps you think about the pleasures in your life. Try doing this quiz to help you decide what are the things you really enjoy doing and could do more often. You may need to make a special plan – see pages 116–121 – to make sure you do more of them
10 have more fun in life			

Anxiety – fear spread thin

If a thin layer of fear clouds our lives it means we are anxious.

Anxiety should warn us that all is not well in our lives. Taking a tranquilliser will stop us feeling anxious. But then we may not bother to do anything about what's behind our anxiety.

It may be that we have a practical problem that needs tackling instead of worrying over. Or the problem is to do with how we feel or behave or get on with others. Or it may be that worrying is something we have learned to do. It's become a habit which we need to break.

Anxiety shows itself through our being worried, nervous, jumpy, on edge or irritable. It can also affect us physically. Some people seem to feel it in their 'guts' – they feel sick, have a stomach ache, and perhaps diarrhoea as well. Other people 'take it to heart' – literally; their heart races, or thumps oddly, and they may have a pain over their heart. Others break out in a rash. Sometimes it comes as quite a surprise when the doctor explains that these various aches and pains may be due to anxiety.

Anxiety breeds anxiety

Once we feel anxious, whatever the original cause, a vicious circle builds up. When we are anxious we become more aware of minor aches and pains and then these make us more anxious. Also, when we are anxious we feel upset and confused and find it difficult to listen properly. This makes us highly likely to misunderstand what other people say and so become anxious about that as well.

What makes you anxious?

You can't always avoid being anxious. But if you are aware of the main ways in which your anxiety builds up, you can plan how to make those situations less anxiety-provoking. You will also be able to work out the best way to manage your anxiety once it is aroused.

As you go through this quiz tick any of the boxes where the situation described, *or something similar to it*, is true for you.

1 Have you recently had a change in your way of life* such as:
☐ moving house away from your friends?
☐ divorce or separation?
☐ a child starting school *or* a teenager leaving home?
☐ a broken off friendship?
*(See page 170 for why even change for the better can upset us.)

2 Do you worry, rather than doing what you can to make it less likely, about:
☐ being mugged, beaten up or raped?
☐ being in a car accident?
☐ having a heart attack?
☐ developing cancer?

3 Do you often feel:
☐ desperate when your baby keeps on and on crying?
☐ afraid of 'letting yourself go' when making love?
☐ that 'one of these days I'll wring his bloody neck'?
☐ that if you ever started crying you'd never be able to stop?

4 Do you often feel guilty or worry about:
☐ having told lies?
☐ masturbating?
☐ not taking care over your work?
☐ being found out about something?

5 Do you make your anxiety worse by saying to yourself:
☐ 'Oh my God! – I'm starting to panic'?
☐ 'Oh dear! – I feel sick and trembly'?
☐ 'I can't get my breath'?
☐ 'If this goes on I shall scream or faint'?

6 Do you spend quite a lot of time imagining what are for you highly unlikely catastrophies such as:
☐ your house burns down and you are all burnt alive in it?
☐ a nuclear war starts?
☐ your normal, happy child becomes a drug addict?
☐ your partner suddenly runs off with someone else?

7 Do you keep thinking things like:
☐ 'They must think I'm stupid'?

☐ 'I know I'm being silly'?
☐ 'If they only knew what I was really like they wouldn't have anything to do with me'?
☐ 'I'm sure they think I batter my children / nag my partner / don't keep my house clean'?

8 When you feel anxious:
☐ do you feel as though you have 'caught your breath'?
☐ do you say, 'that really took my breath away'?
☐ does your throat feel tight or your chest ache?
☐ do you feel sick or need to keep going to the toilet?

9 Do you say things like:
☐ 'If he gets a motor-bike I'll never stop worrying'?
☐ 'I shan't get a moment's peace until she gets back'?
☐ 'If he loses his job I'll be worried to death'?
☐ 'I just can't stop worrying'?

10 Do certain situations always worry you, for example:
☐ 'Even when I was little I was always frightened of moths / spiders / worms'?
☐ 'I've always been scared of the dark'?
☐ 'I'm scared of horses – I offered one a sugar lump once and it bit me'?
☐ 'I just can't travel on buses'?

11 Do you feel anxious:
☐ speaking in public?
☐ demanding your rights?
☐ refusing a request?
☐ asking someone to go out with you?
☐ if a fuse blows?
☐ if you get a flat tyre?
☐ if a water pipe bursts?
☐ if you're cooking an important meal?

12 Are you unable to talk about your worries to:
☐ your partner?
☐ your parents?
☐ your friends?
☐ your doctor, priest or marriage counsellor?

1 Threat of break-up of a relationship

2 Threat of injury, harm or illness

3 Threat of losing control

4 Guilty conscience

12 No-one to turn to with your worries

5 Talking yourself into it

ANXIETY

11 Lack of coping skills

6 Imagining catastrophes

10 You've learnt to worry

9 Worrying about worrying

8 Catching your breath

7 Imagining what other people will think of you

Look back at the pattern of your ticks. Each numbered question is to do with one of the factors which cause anxiety to build up. These twelve factors are shown in the diagram on this page. If you have one or more ticks for any of the numbered questions colour in the relevant square on the diagram so that you can now see your particular pattern of anxiety.

Of course, being worried about several of these factors needn't mean that you are about to crack up. Everyone gets anxious but there are simple skills that anyone can learn to help them cope. In the next section on *Tackling anxiety* we shall look at the best ways to help yourself deal with these different factors.

Tackling anxiety

There are many ways in which you can learn to control anxiety.

What should you do?

The numbers in brackets refer to the factors as shown in the diagram on the previous page.

Take action over the real problem (2)

Taking tranquillisers or learning to relax are not the right thing to do if you are faced with a real life practical problem. If you are homeless, sick, unemployed, or worried that the lump in your breast is cancer you need every bit of help that is available to you. Your doctor, your health visitor, the social services department, the Citizens Advice Bureau, the Job Centre are all sources of help.

Break the anxiety cycle (all factors)

If you are swamped with anxiety you may need to take tranquillisers for a short while. See your doctor about this. They can break the cycle of anxiety causing more anxiety. You will also have a breathing space in which to consider calmly how best to tackle your anxiety. Tranquillisers – the most common ones are Valium and Librium – work well for a short time. They should not be used as long term props. (*Pills for problems?* p 110 will help you think about what you might do if you are already on tranquillisers.)

Learn to control panic (all, particularly 8)

Learning how to relax and making time to do it each day can help you to cope better with anxiety. In particular, you can learn to manage panic attacks by teaching yourself to relax quickly at the first sign of rising panic. Relaxation techniques are described in *Managing stress* in this chapter.

Are you 'catching your breath'? Even if you didn't tick any items in question 8, you may be doing it without realising it. Try this: quickly snatch half a breath, as though you have been frightened, and hold it. You will feel your chest and shoulder muscles tighten and your throat start to hurt. If you put your hand just below where your ribs meet at the front you will feel that your diaphragm tightens up. You may feel a slight pain in your stomach.

When we are anxious we may take similar short breaths and hold them without realising it. If you don't take in enough air your blood will get short of oxygen and this will make you start to feel panicky. When you feel tense try taking a slow, deep breath. Then put your hand on your tummy and feel your hand lift as you breathe in. Then blow your breath out completely as though you were trying to blow up a balloon. Do this two or three times. (No more as it may make you feel dizzy.) Sometimes after doing this exercise you may find you have released another emotion which the anxiety has been masking. You may discover you feel angry or excited.

Talk to yourself (5, 6, 7 and 9)

The next time you get anxious write down, afterwards, exactly what you felt and, most important, what you said to yourself. Most people, when they are anxious, have a conversation going on inside their heads about how they feel. 'This is awful – I'm going to scream – panic – run away – I feel sick – my hands are sweating – oh dear – I can't stand it!' and so on. This makes anxiety many, many times worse.

You can replace this conversation with one that can help you. It doesn't help if you say, 'I'm not really anxious' or 'I won't let myself get panicky'. You need to go along with the panic and talk yourself through it. For example, if you feel panicky when you are in a lift try saying something like, 'Yes – now I'm getting into the lift I'm starting to panic. I'll do my quick relaxation – tense all my muscles, hold my breath, and count one, two, three. And relax. Now I'll keep up my smooth breathing and not catch my breath. And I'll look around the lift at the other people. I'll lean against the wall and relax my knees. I'd say this was a grade 3 panic – but not as bad as last time'.

These kinds of self-instructions can talk you through the panic. You could ask your GP if a psychologist or therapist at your local hospital can assist you with these techniques if you need extra help.

Desensitise yourself (10)

An extreme irrational fear of certain objects or situations is called a phobia. Some common phobias are fear of dogs, spiders, moths, lifts, bridges, heights, escalators, flying, being in the open or being in an enclosed space. They can make your life miserable.

You may need to get skilled help for your phobia. Your doctor should know who can help. One form of help is a process known as desensitisation. This involves asking you to make lists of situations in which you feel (a) slightly anxious (b) moderately anxious (c) panic stricken. Next you will be taught how to relax properly. Then you will be asked, once really relaxed, to imagine yourself in the first situation on your first list. (The one in which you would expect to feel slightly anxious.)

After a while you will be able to picture the situation without feeling anxious. Then you go on to do the same with your next rather more anxiety-provoking situation. After you can picture the worst situation and still stay relaxed you start practising on real life situations. This usually works well. You can try it for yourself – but learn to relax first. And take it slowly.

There are other ways of dealing with phobias which in effect involve you in tackling your fears face on. But you need exact instructions on how to do it. (See *What next?*)

Learn new skills (11)

If you get anxious because you can't mend a fuse, change a washer or a wheel, turn the stopcock off or speak in public, you have practical problems beyond the scope of this book! How about an evening class or do-it-yourself books to help you learn these skills? You should find Chapter 2 helpful if your lack of personal communication skills result in your feeling anxious.

Look at the underlying problems (1, 3, 4, 7 and 12)

Some relationships (1), such as with your children, inevitably change over the years. Others change abruptly if you move or quarrel. You may not be able to restore the old patterns. But you can get help to come to terms with the new one.

A guilty conscience (4) arises from what you learnt about right and wrong as a child. It may be that what you believe now conflicts with what you were taught as a child. Although you 'know' you are doing what you now believe to be the

right thing your childhood conscience may still make you anxious.

If you get too concerned over what other people think of you (7) it's a fair bet that you secretly feel the same way about yourself. Try saying 'I' instead of 'they' must think I'm silly or wicked or whatever. You may find you are expressing what you think about yourself. 'Owning your feelings' like this is a major step forward towards helping yourself.

You probably need someone to help you. The most important thing they can do for you is to listen while you talk over

your worries. Your partner or close friend may do very well. At the end of the next topic, p 171, there is a chart which shows who can help you. A mixture of anxiety and depression can be particularly worrying so please don't hesitate to seek help.

Most of us can learn skills to help us cope with anxiety. However, at times of extra stress we may find ourselves getting anxious over every little thing. The suggestions in *Managing stress* on pages 156–161 also help you to reduce this general anxiety.

Depression

To stay mentally healthy you need to understand and learn how to cope with disappointment and depression.

Usually we feel depressed only for a while; the mood passes or something nice happens and we feel better. It is only when the low feelings last for a long time or get worse that they really disrupt our lives and cause problems. Then we may need help.

Unfortunately this help all too often takes the form of anti-depressant pills. There are times when anti-depressants can play an important part in managing depression. But even if we do need these pills we shouldn't just sit around waiting for the pills to work! We need to think about how our life-styles may be creating our problems and how we can help ourselves to lift the depression and avoid it in the future. This topic is about how we can help ourselves. People with very serious depressive illnesses, for which they may need hospital treatment, are unlikely to be interested in our suggestions in this topic. They may not realise how ill they are and it can be important that someone who knows them makes sure they get the help they need. (See *Coping with a crisis* in this chapter.)

What are the signs?

Most people think they know what depressed people look like. But you can't tell who is depressed just from looking. However, depression can show up in many different ways such as changes in mood or as various physical symptoms. Their faces are drawn. Their shoulders are hunched and their actions often lack vigour. This may make it difficult for a doctor to diagnose depression. It may also come as a surprise to ourselves to be told we are suffering from depression.

There seem to be two patterns of symptoms of depression:

Depression affects your moods

You may feel:

○ low, blue or sad – 'Life's so flat'

○ despair – 'There's no hope'

○ helpless – 'There's nothing I can do'

○ guilty – 'I blame myself'

○ ashamed – 'I never thought I'd behave like this'

○ empty – 'I don't have any strong feelings nowadays'

○ isolated – 'No-one cares'

○ worthless – 'I've made such a mess of my life that I might as well be dead'

○ unloved and unwanted – 'I have no-one to live for'

○ irritable – 'I fly off the handle over the smallest thing'

○ no interest in sex – 'I've gone completely cold'

You may have:

○ indigestion and wind

○ constipation or diarrhoea

○ increased or decreased appetite (weight gain or weight loss)

○ palpitations (heart races or thumps) and chest pains

○ sleep problems (insomnia or can't wake up)

○ painful joints

○ aching muscles

○ fatigue (tired all the time)

○ headaches

○ agitation (restless and fidgety) – or be terribly slow with speech and movements

○ dry and itchy skin

Depression affects your body

All of these *may* be due to physical illness. In that case there will be other signs or tests which can be done which will enable your doctor to diagnose the real illness. But if you have several of these at the same time (with or without the mood changes) they are likely to be because of depression.

Can you recall a time when you had moods like these? You would probably say 'Yes' because, of course, everyone has normal bouts of depression. However, you may not have been aware that depression shows itself so much in physical illness. But if you have several of these at the same time (with or without the mood changes) they are likely to be because of depression.

Would a doctor diagnose you as depressed?

It is likely that you would be considered to be depressed if:

1 You feel unhappy in any of the ways listed under 'You may feel' (above).

2 You have at least five of these:
○ poor appetite and weight loss.
○ sleep difficulties (insomnia or spend a lot of the day asleep)
○ loss of energy.
○ agitation (jumpiness).
○ decreased ability to think or concentrate.
○ loss of your usual interest in work or hobbies or sex.
○ feelings of self-reproach or guilt.
○ repeated thoughts of suicide.

3 You have felt like this for a month and don't have a serious physical illness.

If your answers show that you would be considered to be depressed then you should see your doctor. Indeed if you are worried about any particular symptom, you should do so. Feeling worried, in itself, is a good enough reason to see a doctor!

Depression may often be part of a physical illness, such as diabetes or glandular fever. Many virus infections including colds, flu and infectious hepatitis are followed by depression.

It may also be a side effect of taking too many tranquillisers or taking some kinds of contraceptive pill. But consult your doctor before you stop taking them!

What's behind depression?

A recent loss? Depression is part of normal mourning when we lose someone we love, by separation or death. We may feel the same way if something of sentimental value is stolen or lost.

This normal mourning and grief is described in the next topic in this chapter. It is important that we are able to express grief so that we learn to accept it.

Unfinished mourning? The depression stage of mourning can sometimes linger on for a long time. Look at the list of 'losses' on p 172 in the next topic. Then, if such a loss happened to you, check whether you:

☐ didn't realise at the time you would have a natural reaction of grief?

☐ never got over the first numb feeling of loss? This might be because somewhere at the back of your mind, you are too afraid of what will happen if you let your feelings out.

☐ tried to pull yourself together too rapidly after a loss and weren't able to let your feelings out?

☐ felt your loss wasn't something you could talk about openly?

☐ couldn't talk about it to anyone?

If you have 'unfinished mourning' that you didn't complete at the time it can leave you with a long-term, low-key depression. You will be likely to get depressed if you hear of anyone else's loss. It also leaves you vulnerable so that later a minor loss can trigger off a major bout of depression. You may need to get help for these delayed reactions because you are, as it were, going back and experiencing the grief you didn't work through at the time of the original loss.

Poor self-esteem? *Self-esteem* in Chapter 2 and *Choosing a partner* in Chapter 7 are relevant to this. **We need to feel loved by, and of value to, others.** As children we got this message via hugs, kisses and cuddles. As adults we often have to settle for having our value affirmed by what other people say to us. We may be given presents or be promoted. But apart from our intimate personal relationships we won't get many hugs or kisses.

Unexpressed anger? Suppressing or denying anger can use up a lot of energy. We talk of 'swallowing our anger'. Depression has sometimes been defined as anger turned in on itself.

The anger doesn't turn in on us if we can assert ourselves when we feel it is right to do so. (See *Asserting yourself* in Chapter 2.) We should be able to tell people how angry we feel. We don't have to swallow the anger in case it bursts out as physical violence.

It's sometimes quite easy to pick up on your anger instead of letting it tip you into depression. Try this:

1 When you get up in the morning look at yourself in the mirror. If someone else was looking at you would they think you were depressed? Or might they think you were angry? If you can 'catch' yourself at this early stage you may be able to stop yourself going into your usual depression. What does your face look like? How are you holding your body?

2 Now hunch up your shoulders and hang your head. Close your eyes and think about how you feel.

3 If you start to feel angry, try saying, 'Get off my bloody back' or, 'Stop pushing me around' or 'I'd like to wring your neck'. Use whatever angry words come into your mind. If it helps you get in touch with your anger, say it several times, louder and louder. What do you start thinking about?

If this exercise works for you you should have a clearer idea of whether your depression is masking anger and what you're angry about.

A life-crisis point? There are certain points in everyone's life where their whole life-style changes. The change may be for the better. But however exciting and enjoyable the new life is we still have to get over 'losing' our old life-style. Many of us experience depression at these times. This can be puzzling if we are at the same time happy with our new life.

Did you feel depressed at any of these crisis points in your life?
○ Adolescence – leaving childhood?
○ Leaving home – to go to work?
○ Changing jobs?
○ Being unemployed?
○ Getting married?
○ Getting divorced?
○ Moving house?
○ Having your first child?
(You're no longer a 'carefree' adult.)
○ Giving up work to look after a baby?
○ Your children leaving home?

Perhaps you can think of other special crisis points in your life which made you depressed?

It's normal to go through a phase of depression at these times. But if you don't know this, or your doctor doesn't ask, you can be labelled as having depression 'out of the blue'. These are often the times when other people say to you, 'why do you need to be depressed – you've got a lovely new baby/house/job/wife etc.'

Depression has its uses

Depression makes you suffer: but it may also do the following.

Cover up for a more painful feeling that can't be faced Substituting one feeling for another is learnt early in life within the family circle. The message that is picked up from the way parents behave is, 'It's not OK to be angry: but you can be depressed'. If this might be true for you, get in touch with your anger, so that you recognise, accept and express it safely. This may make you less likely to get depressed in the future.

It can be used to manipulate other people 'Being depressed' can be a label which entitles you to special treatment! So you can say, 'You hurt my feelings', which means you'd better stop treating me like that or I'll get even more depressed. Or 'I'm depressed, so you must forgive me', which means that however angry you are you can't go on being angry with me without feeling a heel.

These kind of words may not actually be spoken but the message gets across.

It may be thought to act like a kind of magic Some depressed people seem to be acting as if they believed that 'suffering ought to be rewarded'. So if he or she suffers enough something good will happen, e.g. her husband will stop drinking, or his wife will give up her lover. Or 'Everybody has their cross to bear', so that if they put up with their depression it can count as 'their cross' and nothing worse will happen. Or 'I've suffered so much that I'm entitled to buy myself a mink coat, overeat, kill myself.'

If you are depressed now – or can remember being depressed – you may find some of these comments strike home to you. It can be painful to realise that you may be making use of your depression.

What makes depression worse?

The more you think about being depressed the more depressed you get. There are four common habits which help to maintain depression.
1 *Thinking about the past* Depressed people tend to rake over past bad times. They keep things that remind them of bad times and visit places where they've been unhappy.
2 *Thinking about the future* Which they see as one long depression. Even if they do have a good day, depressed people are likely to discount it by thinking, 'Ah, but it won't last'.
3 *Putting yourself down* By making unfavourable comparisons such as, 'I'm not as pretty as her', 'I'm not clever', 'If only I were such a good mother'.
4 *Taking on the cares of the world* Depressed people can despair over any item of bad news they hear. Newspapers and television constantly trigger them off with mentions of accidents, fires, homelessness, and wars.

Breaking these four depressing habits is an important part of tackling depression.

What can be done?

Modern drugs can help, but many anti-depressants have unpleasant side-effects. They can also make you feel that all you need to do is keep taking the pills and that you don't need to learn how to help yourself. Learning how to cope with depression can make you 'stronger' so that you can handle any future bout of depression better.

Day-by-day

The following tips can help many people, but of course they are not the answers to all depressions. You may not feel like trying them but we think you should give them a trial because many people have found that setting themselves small goals to be achieved each day makes them gradually feel more confident and less depressed. If you really are too depressed to make the effort to try any of these ideas, then you need expert help.

○ **Get up – get washed – get dressed** Staying in bed or slopping about in a dressing gown really does make you more depressed.

○ **Set yourself tiny goals,** ones that you are sure to reach. Go out to the shops; write a letter; do some gardening; ring up a friend. All these will give you a sense of achievement. On a bad day you may need a new goal every half hour or so.

○ **Watch out for depressing habits** Read the section on the previous page on 'What makes depression worse?'

○ **Try to stop thinking about bad times** You may need to put away reminders of sad times; stop reading distressing news stories; give up visiting places that you used to go to with someone you have lost. You should be able to detect the pleasantly painful memories that you stir up. It's a bit like a bruise that you have to keep pressing to see if it still hurts! It's easier to stop at this early stage.

These may sound trivial suggestions but some depressed people do seem to collect up depression from all over the place. Each additional sick feeling, as despair washes over them, reinforces their depression.

○ **Don't run yourself down to yourself** Conversations in your head, in which you constantly criticise yourself or compare yourself badly with others, can undermine your self-confidence. You can gradually make yourself stop having these thoughts. If you catch yourself thinking like this, answer yourself back. Say 'stop putting me down', 'shut up', 'whose friend are you?'

○ **Teach yourself new habits** What can you do to make your life more pleasant? In Chapter 4 (p117) there is a quiz on 'What do you enjoy doing?' Try doing that quiz now. If you are depressed you may have to think back to happier times to recall items to add to your list. Use this list and each day choose four or five 'pleasures' and do them. It's so easy when you're depressed to feel you don't deserve any pleasures. So keep a daily count to make sure you do them!

○ **Check your diet** People who get jumpy and irritable when they are depressed tend to eat snacks, cakes, biscuits and sweets most of the day. The opposite type of depression, when you feel slowed down and sleepy, causes a loss of interest in food. You need to try to eat regular meals and have a well-balanced diet. (See Chapter 3.)

○ **Take regular exercise** There is some evidence that taking exercise changes certain chemicals which build up in the brain cells when a person is depressed. Exercise can also help jumpy people to calm down. However, depressed people who feel slowed down also find that regular exercise restores their muscle tone so that they feel more alert. See Chapter 3 on exercise. *Managing stress* in

the samaritans: someone to talk to.

this chapter suggests you try relaxation, yoga or meditation. These can all help with depression.

○ **Sort out sleep problems** These too can be helped by exercise and relaxation. But you probably need to learn new sleep habits (see p 112–3 in Chapter 4).

Change your life-style?

Being socially isolated makes you much more likely to get depressed.

○ A mother of young children at home all day is often seriously isolated. She may have moved away from her own family, her husband will be at work. If they moved to a new home when they started their family she may find it difficult to make new friends. A recent study of young mothers found they were much less likely to get depressed, and more likely to get on better with their children, if they had a job outside the home. Having a job improved their self-esteem and provided a network of friends.

If you can't take a job you may be able to join a mother and toddler club or take turns with a friend in looking after the children. Using a baby-sitter so that you can get away from the children sometimes also helps!

○ Widows and widowers are likely to become depressed. Not only as a natural part of grieving but because they may withdraw from their friends and become isolated.

○ Wives may become isolated when husbands work long hours, bring home work for the evening and spend weekends engrossed in their hobbies. Or if they have to work overtime or go straight to the pub after work.

○ Taking a job or changing jobs can help. It doesn't necessarily have to be paid work – voluntary work is often socially useful and makes one feel wanted and valued by others. New friends are made and one's self-esteem is improved as well.

○ Taking care of your friendships is important too. Many people are terribly busy bringing up children, running a home and going out to work. By their late fifties they may be far from busy, only to find they have neglected their friends and are now quite lonely.

Do you need help?

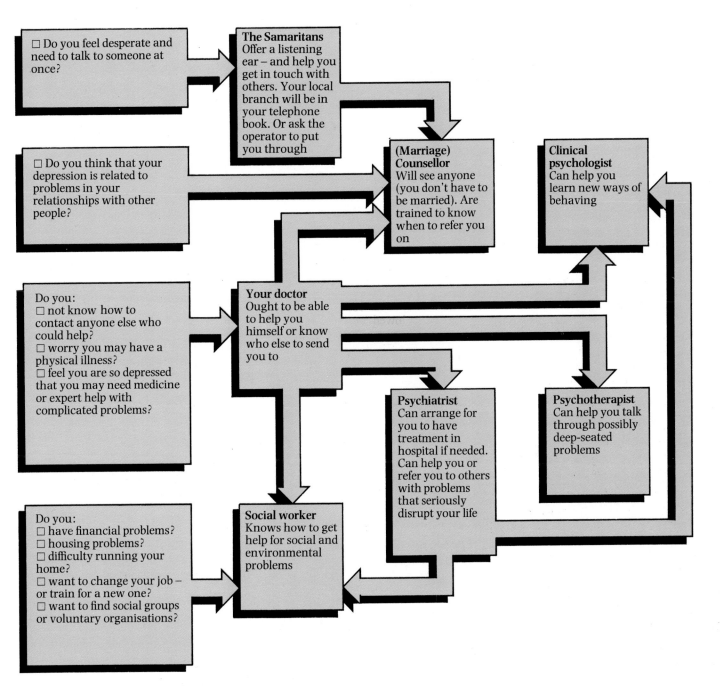

Mourning and grief

Many of us feel uneasy when we have to mention death.
What effect does this have on the bereaved?

It used to be sex that no-one would talk about and everyone pretended didn't happen. Death was written, sung and talked about quite naturally.

Funerals are not what they used to be. The pomp and ceremony common in Victorian times has mostly been abandoned. Few people in our society wear black or observe a formal period of mourning. In many ways this is good because it prevents a morbid dwelling on death. But there were some good things about this attitude to death that we might do well to retain. Death is a tragic event. To take in the idea that someone has gone forever is a hard and painful process. The ceremony of a funeral draws attention to the importance of what has happened. A recognised period of mourning allows bereaved people time to experience their grief in full without having to try to hide it from other people.

The danger nowadays is of going too far the other way. People may be expected to behave as though nothing has happened. They are not expected to grieve. Withdrawal from everyday life and strange behaviour may be seen as signs of mental illness and not as a natural reaction to bereavement. Modern day avoidance and denial of death can be just as bad as the pretence and dishonesty which the Victorians showed. What we need is a balance between the two. But why do we need to grieve and mourn? And what is a natural reaction to bereavement?

Loss and grief

Many different types of loss can be the cause of grief and mourning. Separation from, or death of, a loved one is the most obvious and painful sort of loss. But all of the following can cause us to experience grief and the need to mourn:
○ losing a treasured object.
○ losing or changing jobs.
○ getting married – which involves giving up your unmarried lifestyle.
○ getting separated or divorced.
○ children growing up and leaving the home.
○ losing or changing our home.
○ having an operation.
○ losing a limb or other part of the body.
○ losing or changing our homeland – such as becoming a refugee or emigrating.
○ an abortion or miscarriage.
○ a still-birth.
○ losing our youth – getting old.
○ losing or changing our ideals.

Think about this list. Are any of these events familiar to you? Do you agree that all of them might cause the sad feelings of loss? Or do you feel that some of them are not really a cause for grief?

However, they all have something in common. They all require us to get used to a new set of circumstances. We have to give up an old familiar state or way of life and learn to cope with a new one. This is the basis of all grief. Mourning is the way we achieve this change.

Unfinished mourning on page 167 looks at how not realising we are mourning the loss of something is often behind an apparently inexplicable patch of depression.

The stages of mourning

Understanding how we react to minor losses may help us to understand how we, and others, will react at times of great loss. Think back to a time when you suffered the loss of, for example, your handbag, your wallet, a favourite pet, a job you hoped to get or a boyfriend you really liked. If you have recently lost someone dear to you, doing this activity may be painful but may help you see how natural your feelings are.

Here is a list of statements of how other people have felt at times like these. Put a tick by any you recognise.

When my boyfriend left me:

First stage – *At first*	Tick if you felt like this
I was shocked, I couldn't believe it	
I kept thinking I heard him coming up the path and jumped up whenever the telephone rang	
I felt numb, blank, empty	
I knew it was true, but I couldn't believe he would do this to me	
I felt awful and kept thinking he would make it up again	

Second stage – *Later*	
I began to realise it was really true and I wouldn't get him back again	
I was sure it was all my fault that he had left me	
I felt awful, sad, miserable, depressed, blue, really awful	
I felt so frustrated and helpless that I couldn't keep things as they had been	
Sometimes I felt very angry or very sad	

I cried a lot and couldn't eat or sleep	
I didn't want to go out or do anything or see my friends	
I didn't enjoy my work and got fed up	
I lost interest in life and didn't care what the future held	

Third stage – *Finally*	
After a few weeks the bad feelings began to go	
One day I just began to feel better	
I began to feel I could carry on	
I stopped worrying and started going out again	
Life began to have meaning again	
My new job took my mind off him	
I have another boyfriend now, it's not the same, but I like him	
Last week I went a whole day without thinking about my first boyfriend	
When you get over it you don't forget but you learn how to accept and live with what has happened	

Normal, uncomplicated mourning passes through three stages. The greater the loss, the more intense the grief.

1 *The first phase* is one of shock and disbelief. You attempt to deny what has happened to protect yourself from the shock of the truth. This can last from just a few hours to a few days. If this goes on too long you cannot move into the second stage of mourning which, however painful, eventually helps you recover. You may need help from someone who is used to helping bereaved people. (See *What next?*)

2 *Next* you come to realise that the loss is real. You may feel swept over by a sea of painful feelings. These are distressing but if you try to suppress them they are sure to reveal themselves in some other way, perhaps later as an illness. You have to accept that you will be permanently parted from or never again see the lost person or place or object. Life will never be quite the same again. Old feelings and memories are recalled and it is very common to feel guilty about things you always meant to do but never did.

You may behave in very odd ways and your friends and relatives may think you are 'going mad'. But you are not. Such behaviour is often part of the natural reaction to a loss. You must go through this stage if you are finally to come to terms with your loss. It may last for weeks, months or even years. It all depends on the importance of your loss and the help you have in grieving. Many people remain depressed for a year or more after their bereavement. They need to seek help. Talking over the past with a skilled helper will help them finish this stage of their mourning.

3 *Finally* there is a long stage of recovery, by the end of which the mourning is completed and you recover from the pain of the loss. During this time you get used to living without the lost person or object although, of course, you won't forget your loss. If you understand the importance of mourning – and have the support of someone who helps you express your feelings – you may start this stage within two or three months.

Look back at the statements you ticked. If you have some ticks in all three stages then it is likely that, whatever your loss, you have successfully completed your mourning. If you haven't any ticks in stage two you may have suppressed your feelings too much and not finished grieving. If this is so you may find all your feelings come pouring out when you hear of someone else's sorrow. or you may need to deal with past losses before you can grieve properly in the future. If you have few or no ticks in stage three, then you may need help to make some positive steps towards building a new life.

How to help the bereaved

It is not difficult to give help. It is often our own feelings of embarrassment and awkwardness that get in the way. These feelings can make us insensitive to the needs of the bereaved. Understanding how to give help lessens our awkwardness. What do you think helps the bereaved? (See quiz on right.)

Do you and your friend or partner both agree? Would you like the way your friend would treat you if you were bereaved? What does your friend feel about how you would treat her? Check below for what has been found to help bereaved people.

A helping hand

Support from an understanding helper can prevent grief leading to a serious breakdown or suicide attempt. All grief can be made more bearable by the loving understanding help of family or friends. When more people understand and accept the need for open, natural mourning, society will change so that this healthy process is encouraged. At present those who hide or deny their grief may be praised. Men, even more than women, are expected to keep a stiff upper lip. But we now know that this is bad.

At first, support should take the form of practical help, especially with the funeral details and continued running of the household. The person who is most valued at this time is the one who 'sticks around', quietly performing day-to-day tasks, but who is there to receive any outpourings of despair and anger.

Bereaved people feel they have enough to bear with their own grief. They do not have room for others' grief and hearing about it does not make them feel better. Also, too much sympathy may make them feel more sad. Tablets from the doctor should only be used as a last resort. They can blot out feelings which it is important to have.

Accepting the person's loss, letting them talk, giving practical help and support are the best help to give.

If a friend were bereaved, I would:	You	Friend or partner
accept their behaviour no matter how odd		
ignore their loss, pretend it never happened		
tell them about all my own woes		
let them cry and talk as much as they want		
tell them they are luckier than some		
give plenty of sympathy		
leave them well alone		
help them with practical problems		
tell them about everyone else's misfortunes		
take some burden of everyday chores away		
tell them they'll get over it eventually		
provide food and encourage sleep		
talk about the weather		
try to make them laugh		
stick around for when I'm needed		
tell them it could have been worse		
leave them out of my social circle		
tell them not to worry or think about it		
encourage them to go to the doctor for tablets		

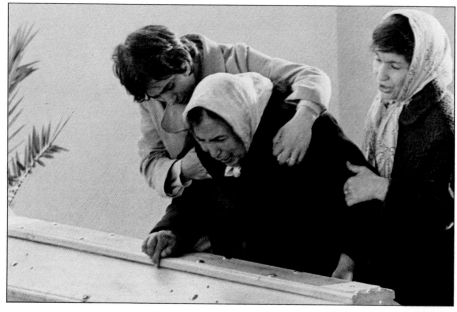

People vary over how long it takes them to come to terms with their grief. If you are helping someone who is bereaved, use your own tact and discretion. If you understand the stages of mourning and know you can talk easily about feelings, then a good guide could be to ask yourself, 'Would I like to be treated that way?'

A bereaved person may not want to turn to a minister of religion and may hesitate to approach a doctor because he is busy or may only offer tablets. But counselling of the bereaved is today included in the training of many doctors and nurses, as well as the clergy.

If you are alone and have no one to help you or would like some support from those who really understand your problem the organisations listed in *What next?* will help you. Unfortunately there are only, at present, a few organisations which can offer help to someone who has suffered a major loss. They tend to give help mainly in the first and second phase of loss. Support may also be needed during the longer third phase when adjustment takes place and a new life is being built.

Hidden losses

Certain types of loss such as a stillbirth, the death of a very young baby or an abortion can be especially hard to grieve over. Talking and remembering help the mourning process. But in these kinds of loss there is apparently no-one to miss, no-one to talk about, no-one to remember. Only an expectation of what might have been. Those around the bereaved parents may take the attitude that what they have never had they never miss. But the parents may have thought about the baby for nine whole months and in their minds they will almost certainly have imagined him growing to adulthood. Even with an abortion of an unwanted baby there can be feelings of loss for 'what might have been' and often a sense of guilt. There may be the extra burden of keeping it a secret. In all these cases the bereaved person can best be helped by someone allowing them to talk openly about their loss.

Coping with a crisis

Stress can drive people to breaking point.
They need help – and this topic helps you to give it.

You can deal with some crises by giving support and attention. Others you may feel are beyond your skill. It can be important to recognise when you can't cope and need to find somebody who can. If someone is very panicky you need to help him calm down. If he is talking of killing himself you need to take this seriously. But these emergencies are rare. You are more likely to be trying to help someone who is quietly desperate and who needs help to talk about his problems.

Calm down

If a person is very panicky you will need to help him calm down. Touch him in some way – hold his hand or put your arm round him. Reassure him that you will stay and that he will soon be able to control his panic. Get him to do something such as sit down, lie down or come for a walk. If you know how to relax quickly try teaching him how to do it. Don't get him to take a lot of deep breaths or he will get dizzy and feel more panicky. He might like you to massage his back and shoulders. When he calms down he will probably want to talk a lot. But if he is exhausted he may fall asleep.

'I'm going to kill myself'

Take this seriously.

It is not true that if a person talks about it he won't do it The majority of people who make suicide attempts *do* tell somebody before hand.

It is not true that if you mention it you may put the idea into his mind If the idea isn't there you will get told that he has no intention of doing that. If it is there he will feel able to be more open about thoughts which he may have felt ashamed to admit.

It is not true that people who make suicidal gestures never do kill themselves Some of them do kill themselves. Even if they may have half-hoped they would be found, if they are unlucky they still end up dead.

Do they need hospital treatment?

Here is a set of guide-lines that some doctors use.

○ Someone with suicidal thoughts needs to be given a strong message of 'Live!' or 'You don't have to kill yourself. Don't!' The last thing he needs is to be given permission to do it by comments such as, 'It's your life' – or 'Well, that's one of the options'.

○ Will he make a 'contract' (a bargain or promise) with himself not to commit suicide? (Not with you, because in certain moods he may be tempted to get his own back on you.) What exactly will he promise himself? Not to do it ever? For at least a year? A month? A day? Help him to spell it out. 'However much I may feel I want to kill myself I won't do it, but instead I will... (go to a hospital if necessary? Don't leave it as 'phone someone', because there may be no answer – and he will then be tempted to say 'Well, I did try but they weren't there when I needed them so ...')

○ If he won't make a 'contract' with himself or a definite plan to get help then he almost certainly does need to go to a hospital.

You can help

Find a quiet place to talk Try to find somewhere that's safe from interruptions. Tell the other person how much time you've got to spend with him. Tell him that you'd like to try and help if you can. Then ...

Listen This is the most important thing to do. Let the other person talk as much as needs to. Try to understand how he's feeling. Try to work out what's making him feel that way. Try to accept what he tells you. Don't rush in with advice. Don't tell him what he ought to feel. Only when you've got some idea of what's happening *in his terms* can you start to think about what to do, so *listen*.

Stay calm If you can't stay calm find someone else who can. If you are upset or agitated you won't be able to listen and probably won't help much.

Follow your feelings If you can start off calm – uncluttered by your own strong feelings – you should find that as you listen you do begin to build up strong feelings. Get in touch with what you feel. It's the best guide to how someone else is feeling. If you're feeling frightened, it's likely the other person is too. If you feel confused, they may do too. In a way you have 'caught' their feelings and can now reflect them back. Tell them what you feel. Check if it's an accurate picture of what's happening to them. For example, 'As you tell me this I'm feeling more and more depressed / angry / despairing. Is that how you feel about it?' Or 'You keep telling me about how good your partner is to you but as you go on, I'm beginning to feel angry. Maybe you feel angry about it too?'

Respect the other person Don't pretend you can do what you can't. If you can't handle the situation find someone who can.

Mental illness

Do we really understand the nature of mental illness?

What does the term 'mental illness' mean? 'Illness' usually implies a physical disorder, something wrong with the body. We expect an illness to be caused by something which produces definite symptoms for which doctors often have a remedy. But 'mental' refers to how our minds work – how we think and feel. The old idea of looking for a single cause and trying to find a medicine to cure it is not a useful way of trying to understand and help the 'mentally ill'.

'Mental illness' is an unsatisfactory label: psychological disorder would be a better term. Many people call the common mental illnesses 'nerves' or 'a nervous breakdown'. This topic will try to give you a clearer picture of what lies behind this vague, unsatisfactory term.

Physical illness can affect the mind A high fever can make you delirious so that you become agitated, see things that aren't there and don't make sense when you speak. Mild depression often comes on after a virus infection, particularly 'flu. It may also be a side-effect of certain medicines you need to take, for example, for some heart disorders.

'Mental illness' starts in your mind – in how you think and feel – but may produce some physical symptoms (See *Depression* p 166.) That doesn't mean the physical symptoms are only 'in your mind'. The pain you feel is real pain but it is caused by upset mental processes calling attention to the problem by physical signals.

With a physical illness it's usually easy to carry out tests to find out what is wrong and to decide which medicines to use to bring about a cure. It's often quite easy to say definitely whether or not you've got the particular illness – and to know when it's cured.

This is not true for 'mental illness'. There is no distinct line between being ill or healthy and medicines are not the best treatment for most kinds of 'mental illness'. And if it's difficult to decide if someone is definitely ill it's just as useless to talk about cures.

If terms linked with 'illness' have to be used then perhaps it is better to call these psychological disorders 'dis-ease' because the mind is certainly 'ill at ease'.

Unable to cope

The one, common typical sign of 'mental illness' is that the person becomes less and less able to cope with everyday life. If they do cope, and don't break down under the strain, they do so by leading a very restricted life. For example, a person with a great fear of going out – agoraphobia – may be able to organise her life so that she doesn't have to go out. Or a person suffering from depression may fend off the actual feelings of depression for many years by working harder and harder, and longer and longer hours.

In our society such a person may be praised for being a hard worker. Restricting his life to continuous hard work takes his mind off the threatening depression. But in the end he may well become exhausted and break down.

THESE PEOPLE KEEP COMING AFTER ME!

What would you do?

Imagine you are walking along a street when you see an old lady shuffling towards you. You can't quite hear what she is mumbling but as you meet she looks desperate, clutches hold of you and says, 'My heart – I can't get my breath!'

How would you feel about her? What would you do?

Now, suppose that she had said, 'They're after me again – they're sending out X-rays from my TV!'

How would you feel about her? Would you feel ashamed, embarrassed, disgusted or want to get away?

What would you do? In the second case the old lady may have a long-term 'mental illness'. She needs help – as much as someone with heart trouble. But her behaviour is bizarre and she doesn't make sense to you when she talks. You may find you can't communicate with her and so you feel anxious or embarrassed. But she may not realise her behaviour is in the least bit bizarre, in which case there is nothing much that you, as a stranger, can do to help.

Out of touch with reality

One of the most distressing things about people who are ill like this old lady is that what they do and say doesn't make sense. They often can't answer questions and their minds are full of upsetting thoughts that they can't control.

In the old days such 'mental illness' would be labelled as insanity or madness. This type of illness is now called a *psychosis* or psychotic disorder. Although this type of illness is relatively rare it is the type that responds best to medical treatment. It can now be relieved and often prevented from recurring with the help of drugs and physical methods of treatment.

However, there is still no satisfactory explanation of why these illnesses develop. Many theories emphasise the importance of their link with social stress and difficult family relationships. More recent theories suggest that they may be linked to upsets of the chemistry of the body. However, although we know that various factors are involved, it is not the same as being able to say that these 'linked factors' definitely cause the illness.

Desperately distressed

In the more common type of psychological upset the person may not behave in such an odd way but he may be far more distressed. His behaviour may not make other people anxious, but may cause irritation or anger. Suppose a person is having an acute panic attack at the foot of an escalator in a rush-hour tube. He may be quite unable to get on the staircase as it moves endlessly away. Most people would think the person causing the bottleneck should pull up his socks and get on with what has to be done! They are unlikely to have much sympathy for him. It would need a skilled observer to understand that here is a man whose severe underlying anxiety has suddenly shown up as a phobic reaction to escalators. This man may have been able to

179

cope with escalators before but sometimes have hesitated slightly. But when his underlying anxiety swamped him he couldn't cope at all.

This kind of psychological upset could be called *neurotic* – but the term has been so misused even by doctors that it has fallen into disrepute. Many people think that a neurotic illness is somehow a 'pretend one' – or something that you could overcome by pulling yourself together. This is completely false. Whatever it's called it *is* extremely distressing. It develops when anxiety, depression or the problems of adapting to change and stress make a person feel unable to cope any longer. This breakdown in coping may be short-lived or go on for some time. Severe depression or anxiety may bring life to a stand-still. The symptoms, both physical and mental, are a way of telling us to take a complete break whilst whatever is wrong is sorted out.

Common complaints

Many of the topics in this chapter have looked at how we can improve our coping skills so that stress, anxiety and depression do not make us break down. However, there may be times for many of us when we cannot cope. Sometimes we get signals that we can't cope much longer. This is likely to happen if we haven't been fully aware of our anxiety or depression. In this case it may show up as increased worry about something that we wouldn't normally worry very much about. For the man on the escalator, his normal slight hesitation turned into a blind panic.

These (see right) are complaints that people who are 'mentally ill' have. Before you rush off to the doctor you should know that each of them is a common complaint anyway. Most people will probably tick off a few of them as applying to themselves. But if you have many of these complaints, or any of them seriously disrupt your life, then your psychological well-being is certainly at a low ebb. (Some of them can occur for other reasons as well, eg lack of energy during flu or palpitations after too much coffee.)

You are not going 'mad' because you feel like this. It may be that your feelings should be a signal to you to think about what is the real cause of stress, anxiety and depression in your life.

You can see now that people with psychological upsets get the same sort of symptoms that we all do at times, but they get more of them, or get them to a worse degree. **There is no sharp dividing line between mental health and 'mental illness'.** Such illnesses are very common. More than one in ten of us will get treatment from a psychiatric hospital at some time or another. But many more of us will go to our own family doctor. No-one knows exactly how common this is, but it has been suggested that 'mental illness' is a part of the problem in as many as one in four of the cases a family doctor sees each day.

What kind of help?

Drugs? Unfortunately, although people turn to doctors for help, the help available is quite often inadequate. It's quite easy to be given something to mask the symptoms but it can be difficult to find someone who can help you learn how to cope better. Unfortunately anti-depressants, tranquillisers or sedatives are prescribed for most people who can no longer cope. For some people they could provide a short 'breathing space' so that the vicious circle of 'worrying breeding more worry' is broken and the person's usually effective coping skills can start to work again. More usually the drugs mask the symptoms. The patient may then become dependent on the drugs.

Indeed a side-effect of these drugs is that they make it more difficult for someone to learn the desperately needed better coping skills which would make him better equipped to deal with stress reactions.

'Talking' cures? Counselling and psychotherapy can help people who have reached breaking point to work out how to cope better. This kind of help can take a long time and needs highly trained people to do it. It's not widely available on the National Health but worth seeking out. Fortunately more and more family doctors are being taught basic counselling skills and know where to send their patients to find help. There are also voluntary organisations such as MIND (see *What next?*) that can help you.

The topics in this chapter should help you understand the importance of taking care of your mental health and provide some 'tips' to help you improve your coping skills.

What about you?

The following things can all indicate that you are finding it hard to cope.

✔ for Yes ✘ for No

1 Do you find it difficult to concentrate? ☐

2 Are you absent-minded? ☐

3 Do you find it difficult to get off to sleep? ☐

4 Do you feel sad or low in your spirits? ☐

5 Do you suffer from palpitations (pounding of the heart)? ☐

6 Do you often feel perplexed? ☐

7 Do you cry a lot? ☐

8 Do you suffer from headaches? ☐

9 Is your appetite poor? ☐

10 Do you have an unpleasant feeling something nasty will happen to you soon (though you don't know what)? ☐

11 Have you less energy than usual? ☐

12 Are you excessively afraid of heights, lifts or animals? ☐

13 Do you have any other very special fears that stop you doing things (eg, going on buses)? ☐

14 Do you find that everything is an effort? ☐

15 Have you lost interest in most things? ☐

Prevention is easier than cure

Perhaps the best thing to do, to prevent yourself reaching a point where you cannot cope, is to discuss your worries at an early stage with a good neighbour or friend.

Don't keep your worries to yourself! It's true that 'a trouble shared is a trouble halved'. Talking about your troubles with the right person helps you to look at your problems in a fresh light and see ways that you hadn't seen before.

You need to decide:

○ who in your life could you talk to about intimate problems? If you really don't have anyone seek help from an experienced counsellor.

○ what are the early signs of stress in your life that should warn you to talk your worries over with someone else?

You can often teach yourself to detect when things are getting on top of you by noticing if you are worrying more about your 'pet worries' than usual. For example, turning off the gas, forgetting your keys, going in lifts or having your lucky mascot or charm with you.

Your sex life

Finding a partner, making love, planning a family are all important for most people.

Many people also think it is important to learn how to make their sexual relationships work better. In sexual matters it's up to you – and your partner – to decide what is best for you.

Learning to love?

Do you need to learn to love? Well, 'what comes naturally' is only the basic urge and ability to have intercourse. All the rest of what is involved in lovemaking and getting on with your partner has to be learned.

We need to learn:
○ how to be good at making love so we can enjoy it and have fun.
○ how to control conception so we don't have to worry about an unwanted pregnancy and can plan the children we do want.
○ how to get on with our partner and so build up a deepening long term relationship in which sex as an expression of love becomes of great importance. It's so reassuring, so good for our self-esteem, to know that the person we love wants to make love with us.

How satisfied are you?

In a survey of people who admitted they were not sexually satisfied the following six statements were the ones which were most often applicable to them. Read through this list and tick those statements with which you agree.
☐ I worry a lot about sex
☐ I don't think I'm as good at it as my friends are
☐ My partner doesn't really satisfy all my physical needs
☐ I would like my sex partner to be more expert and willing to try new things
☐ I can't talk about sex with my partner
☐ I find it difficult to tell my partner what I like or dislike when we are making love

When a large group of other people who did *not* think sex a particular problem were shown these statements most of them agreed with two or three of them. In other words, there is nothing unusual about feeling somewhat unsatisfied with your sex life.

Improving your sex life

It's so easy to make people worry about their sex life. Jokey greetings like, 'Are you getting enough?' reflect a worry that many of us have. We suspect that most other people have a fuller, more exciting sex life than we do.

But some books on improving your sex life can make you feel worse. The danger is that you may come to judge yourself by how often you make love, how long you spend doing it and how many variations you know. Keeping a score and sexual gymnastics are not what real lovemaking is about. Indeed, concentrating on these may stop you looking at what you could do better. Worst of all, the pictures in many books often imply that sex is only for young, slim, fit, beautiful people. That's rubbish.

This chapter can help you make the choices which will be good for you by providing facts, helping you develop skills, and increasing your understanding of how you feel about sexual activities. But what you finally choose to do is up to you. Some people will find this chapter too simple. Others may not want to look at their sex life in such detail. The next topic, *What about you?*, will help you decide which of the other topics in this chapter might be important to read.

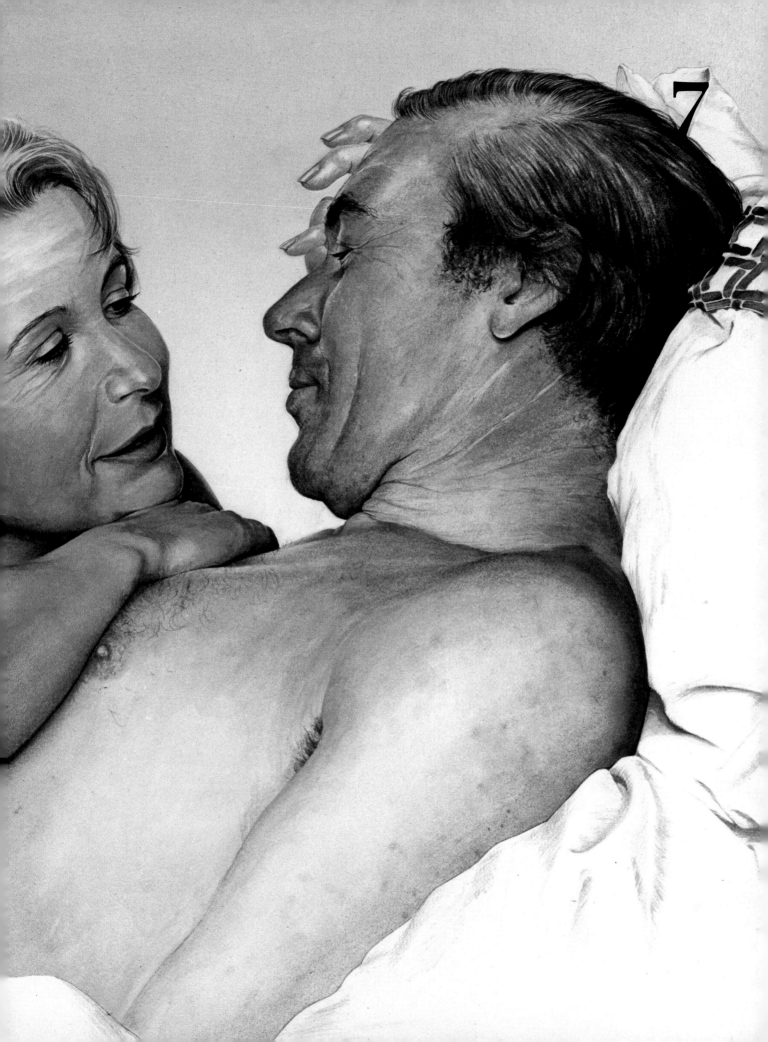

What about you?

Three things are important in sexual relationships –
fun, love and children.

What's important for you?

We think we should spell out what we think is important in sexual relationships. You may not agree with us. Sex can be fun, exciting and give a great deal of pleasure. It enables you to have children if you want to. It can often be *the* best way to express your love. Making love can cheer you up or comfort you. It can be a sign that you and your partner are committed to each other.

These three things don't always have to go together. Their importance can change as you go through life. Which is most important to you at this time in your life? In the chart below we look at birth control first because worries about this can outweigh any other concerns.

As you work through this chart you will be sign-posted to the topics which should be important to you. Have a look too at *But what about me?* These are answers to some of the questions raised by people who helped us test this book.

What's important?	So what?	Topics to read
Sex enables you to have children if you want	You need to look at this first because for many people it is all too easy to get pregnant. Would you agree that every child should be a wanted one?	You need to choose and use the method of birth control which is best for you. See pages 192–3 Understanding how conception can happen will help you understand how the various methods of birth control work to prevent it. Then you can avoid 'mistakes' when using birth control. See pages 190–1
Sex can be the best way to express your love for your partner. Sexual problems can affect your whole relationship. But problems in your relationship can upset your lovemaking too	It can be difficult – but well worth the effort – to work out what each of you is looking for in your relationship	What do you need from your partner? Can you give what he or she needs from you? See pages 194–7 Are there strains on your relationship? See pages 198–9
Sex can be highly enjoyable	Your attitudes to sex may affect how much you enjoy your sex life. It's worth learning the skills of lovemaking so that you can enjoy it more	How did you develop your attitudes and do you want to change any of them? See pages 186–9 Do you want to learn the skills of being a better lover? See pages 204–7 Do you have any problems with lovemaking for which you need help? See pages 208–9

What did you decide?

Come back to this part of the chart when you have finished reading this chapter. It's easy to want to change but more difficult to make the plans and carry them out.

You should find it helpful to review your life, take stock, and *decide* what you want to do as a result of working through this chapter. These steps may seem very simple. But they can make the difference between meaning to do something and actually doing it. Keep your own written copy of what you plan to do – it can be your contract with yourself. Like a new year's resolution. Only you must try to keep it!

I am going to –

1 Be more careful about using birth control ☐

2 Discuss with my partner how we should use birth control ☐

3 Change the method of birth control I use ☐

4 Find out more about some of the methods ☐

---

1 Make plans to overcome the difficulties we have in talking about what we want from each other ☐

2 Get advice or help for other strains on our relationship ☐

---

1 Discuss with my partner our attitudes about what's OK in lovemaking ☐

2 Plan time to do the exercise in *Good lovers* in this chapter ☐

3 Read some more about love making ☐

4 Find someone to talk to about my sexual problem ☐

The next step

1 Get hold of a book about birth control? (see *What next?*) ☐

2 Get some leaflets from the FPA or local family planning clinic? (see *What next?*) ☐

3 Go to see my doctor? ☐

4 Go to my local family planning clinic? ☐

---

1 Reading a book together can help you to start talking. Get a copy of '*Treat yourself to sex*' (see *What next?*)

2 You may need information or practical advice (see *What next?*). If you have all the facts you need but your feelings still cause problems you need to find someone who can counsel you

---

1 When are you going to do this? Make a note of what you particularly want to talk about

2 When? Where? Have you got a body lotion or oil you would like to use?

3 See *What next?* for what to read and how to get hold of it ☐

4 Ask your doctor who can help. Or ask your local marriage guidance council for help. There is also a Directory of Psycho-Sexual Clinics (see *What next?*)

But what about me?

'*I'm heterosexual, satisfied with my partner and reckon I'm pretty good at love making. Is this chapter of any use to me?*'

Your pride will probably ensure that you take a look at *Good lovers*. Talking with your partner about what you think about sex and, particularly, the activity on page 189 may give you new ideas.

'*I'm homosexual – and want to be. All the sex books I've read are for heterosexuals. Is this chapter of any use to me?*'

Men and women, pages 186–189, and *Choosing a partner*, pages 194–197 should be just as helpful to you as to anyone else. Read the bit that applies to you in *How our bodies respond*. The activities in *Good lovers*, pages 204–207, will help you to improve your lovemaking. Homosexuals may have very much the same problems in love making as heterosexuals so, if you need to, read *Getting help*, pages 208–9. Psycho-sexual counsellors usually work with homosexual as well as heterosexual couples. See *What next?* if you want to find a counsellor.

'*I'm not really interested in sex.*'

No-one has the right to say you ought to be. Many people choose, for good reasons, to be celibate and lead perfectly happy lives. And many married couples are happy without an active sex life. Stick to the way of life you have chosen if you are happy with it. You will probably want to read this chapter if you help people who need to talk about their sexual relationships.

'*All this depresses me. I haven't got a sexual partner. I'm unlikely to get one. I was just beginning to accept this and now I read all this about how important sex is.*'

Yes, sex is important, and it is sad if you can't have the kind of sex life you would like. Pretending it's not important or criticising those who spend a lot of time on it won't really help you feel better about what you haven't got. It's quite reasonable to feel sad about the good things in life that we may miss out on although it's better to feel positive and enjoy the things we do have. For, of course, although sex is important, it's not everything in life.

Men and women

The way you were brought up and the society you live in both help to shape your views about sexuality.

But just what are your views? Do you know what your opinions are? More importantly, are you happy with the effect they have on what you do? Do you realise that attitudes are learned and that you can change them if you want to?

Where did you learn your attitudes?

The place where you first learn attitudes to sexuality is at home, with your family. Your parents probably never sat down and gave you a lesson in what you should think about sexuality. You picked it up from what they did. Even the things they didn't do may have told you a lot. For example, you may never have seen them kiss or cuddle or never heard them say, 'I love you' to each other. Perhaps they always steered the talk away from sexual subjects. Or did they keep the bedroom and bathroom doors locked so that you never saw them naked?

You learnt a great deal, even if no-one spelled it out to you, when you were very young. This is one of the reasons why sexual attitudes are often so hard to change. They seem like second nature. You hardly know you've got them.

Unless your parents were unusual you'll have found that most of the attitudes you learnt at home were confirmed at school. Other children thought the same or similar things. If you thought differently you probably changed your mind or kept quiet in order not to be left out of the group. As you grew older, television, films and books most likely added to the information you had.

What did you learn?

Your whole personality is coloured by what it means to you to be a woman – or a man. You soon learnt how to be a little girl or a little boy; and what kind of woman – or man – you should grow up to be. You learnt what kind of behaviour is 'right' for your sex. You learnt what to expect from the opposite sex. These sexual 'stereotypes' – the fixed patterns of what a woman and a man should be like –

are being challenged more and more today.

Many women and men feel these stereotypes are restricting. But the old views and opinions die hard. Here are two examples of the views of today's teenagers.

○ Sixteen-year-old girls still think mainly in terms of marriage, home and children when asked about their futures.

○ Sixteen-year-old boys still think mainly in terms of the job they will do when asked about their futures.

Are your opinions changing? How well do you agree with the following five statements? Have you always held these opinions?

1 Men shouldn't show their feelings.

2 Men can be as good as women at looking after the children.
3 Leadership comes naturally to men, but not to women.
4 Household chores should be shared equally between husband and wife.
5 A woman's first responsibility is towards her children.

What does your partner think?

Sexual activities: what's right, what's wrong?

Old attitudes about sexual behaviour are also being questioned nowadays, particularly by women. Some people are changing their minds about what they consider to be OK. But other people sometimes feel pushed into adopting views they don't quite approve of or feel unsure of, just because others they know are changing. This can cut both ways. Sometimes people feel pushed into adopting more permissive views than they would like. Sometimes people feel they would like to express more permissive views but are afraid of what those around them might think.

This quiz will help you and your partner or friend to sort out your opinions.

	My view	Partner's view	Friend's view
1 It's OK if people kiss and embrace in public			
2 It's OK to have homosexual relationships if that's what you want			
3 It's OK to masturbate if you want to			
4 Sex before marriage is OK for men			
5 Sex before marriage is OK for women			
6 It's OK for a woman to ask for what she wants in lovemaking			
7 It's OK for a woman to invite a man to sleep with her			
8 It's OK for a woman to take the lead in lovemaking			
9 It's OK for a woman to be unfaithful			
10 It's OK for a man to be unfaithful			

Score one point for every tick you have in column one. Clearly the more ticks you have the more easy-going you are in your views. But more important, whatever your views, is whether you are happy with them. Look back at your answers in column one and mark with an asterisk (*) any opinion which, in certain circumstances, you would hesitate to admit you hold. One or two asterisks may indicate that there are some people in your life from whom you sensibly withhold your opinions. More than that and it could indicate that there is a conflict between the views you hold and the circles you move in. Do you want to do something about it?

How far do you and your partner or friend agree with each other? Were you surprised by any of your answers or any of your partner's answers? If you were, does it mean that one of you wants the other to change? Or are you happy to disagree in your attitudes?

Why change your attitudes?

Of course it's one thing to change your views. Changing what you *do* can be another story. So, why change your views at all? Will it help?

1 You may not want to change what you do

For instance, you may decide that there is nothing wrong with homosexual relationships. But this need not mean you want to have homosexual relationships yourself. You can be happy to tolerate other people's sexual practices without wishing to join in with them. **So changing your views may just mean becoming more sensitive to what other people think and do.**

2 Changed circumstances may need changed attitudes

You may find that the way you are living is different from the way you grew up. Perhaps your old attitudes are being called into question. You may feel unsure now as to why you hold a particular view or opinion.

Let's look at what happened in the Rogers' family. June and Jim Rogers were surprised by the way their teenage daughter thought and behaved. Julie, their 18-year-old, had left home. When she came home to stay for a week-end with her boyfriend they expected to sleep together. June felt shocked and insulted. Her first response was simply to tell them that on no account would they sleep

187

together in her house. She didn't believe in it. Her own parents wouldn't have allowed her to do such a thing. What had been good enough for her should be good enough for her daughter. When she'd calmed down a bit she realised that her views and feelings were more complicated than she'd thought. These were the kinds of things that she discovered were really bothering her.

○ She realised that she didn't actually think it was wrong if young people slept together. The view that it was wrong was one that she'd picked up from her parents and had never really questioned before.

○ But she was upset that her daughter hadn't asked her beforehand if she and her boyfriend could share a room.

○ She was worried that her daughter might get pregnant.

○ Also, as her husband Jim pointed out, she was perhaps a little bit jealous of her daughter's sexual freedom which she herself hadn't been allowed when she was younger.

Sorting it out

So, when you find you have strong views about sexual matters it is always worth asking yourself the following questions.

Do I hold a particular view because:
○ I believe it to be morally right?
○ I just happen to have always thought it?
○ someone told me it was true years ago and I've never really thought about it since?

What feelings are attached to this view? When people oppose your point of view do you feel angry? Indignant? Upset? Afraid? Or worried?

Examining her views and the strong feelings attached to them helped June Rogers sort out what she really thought and felt. In her case the strong feelings weren't really about the moral issue at all. They had more to do with feeling upset and threatened by her daughter's attitudes and expectations.

So questioning your own attitudes may enable you to understand those close to you better. It can help to close the gap between the way you live (or want to live) and the things you think.

3 Changed attitudes can lead to changed circumstances

If you want to change the way you live and behave, changing your attitudes may be a first step towards changing your behaviour. Starting to question your attitudes, views and beliefs can help you to see how they restrict or help you. You can start to choose what you think instead of just thinking it.

Let's look at what happened to Marie. Marie got married when she was 17. Her family were very strict and conventional. She was brought up to believe that sex before marriage was wrong. She was a virgin when she married and knew little about sex. She thought the only point of sex was to produce children. She thought it was wrong to think about or talk about sex. She found her husband's advances distasteful at best and unpleasant or unbearable at worst. Her attitudes fitted her family's expectations of what a good wife and mother should be but they didn't make her very happy.

Eight years later, when she was 25, her husband left her. He complained that she was frigid. They hadn't slept together for a year.

Beginning to question things

The shock of her marriage breaking up led Marie to question some of her views. Was it really true that:
○ women shouldn't expect sexual satisfaction?
○ women didn't enjoy sex?
○ women weren't meant to look after themselves?
○ it was wrong to talk about sex?
○ sex was only for making babies?

For Marie, questioning and then beginning to change her attitudes in turn led to her changing the way she lived. Questioning her view that women didn't enjoy sex led her to want to talk to other women about it. After much hesitation she managed to talk to a close woman friend. Gradually she came to see that her views on sex were tied up with the way she had been brought up and had contributed a lot to the unhappiness of her marriage.

Just changing her views wasn't enough, of course. Knowing that it was not wrong for women to enjoy sex didn't in itself help her enjoy it any more. In the end Marie decided to get expert help and she went to see a counsellor who was able eventually to help her overcome her sexual problems.

So questioning and changing your attitudes can lead you to change what you do, even in an area like sex, where people have such strong views.

Attitudes and feelings

Both Marie and June found that questioning their attitudes about sex brought up a lot of strong feelings. Most people feel strongly one way or another about sex. It can be useful to ask yourself why your feelings are so strong. Is it because your view is very important to you? Or are there other reasons too, as June discovered? Deep down most people have some fears and worries about sex. These may be fears about sexual performance, feelings of guilt about enjoying yourself, feelings of jealousy or inadequacy compared with others. When views on sex are discussed these feelings can come out as anger or indignation towards people who oppose your particular view.

What about you?

Now that you've read so far it may be a good time for you to think about how your own attitudes have changed. Write your answers on a sheet of paper.

Q. 1 Can you think of any examples of how your attitudes, as an adult, are different from those your parents taught you when you were a child?

Q. 2 What views have you changed in the last few years? What led you to make these changes?

Here are the replies of some of the people who helped us when we were writing this book.

My parents said – but I don't now agree
'Sex outside marriage was wrong.'
'Sexual happiness is unimportant in marriage.'

'Homosexuality is wrong – I'm not homosexual but I don't now agree with their point of view.'

'Sex was regarded as non-existent, never to be talked about.'

I've changed my opinion

'I've seen the results of my relatives handling situations badly and learnt from that.'

'I'm now in favour of abortion on demand as a result of knowing friends with problems.'

'My partner helped me to be more demonstrative than I used to be.'

'Some of the magazines I've seen at work have broadened my ideas about sex. But sometimes I feel abnormal because I don't do some of these things (oral sex).'

Attitudes and actions

Is there a conflict between what you would like to do and what actually happens when you make love?

Try doing this when you have some time alone together with your partner.

Either write down what you would like to say to complete the following sentences. (Use a separate piece of paper.) Get your partner to do the same. And then together read what you've both written.

Or talk to each other about how you would like to complete the sentences.

We suggest that, at least to begin with, you only give two examples for each statement.

When we make love I would like to ...
do more **(1)**

(2)

stop doing **(1)**

(2)

try doing something different like
(1)

(2)

What happened when you compared your ideas? We hope that you had some ideas that you are happy to try out. But – did you disagree strongly over any suggestions? If so, try looking at them again. Read again the sections on 'Sorting it out' and 'Attitudes and feelings' on the opposite page. Each of you needs to try to be honest in working through the questions in 'Sorting it out'.

You may find you end up having to choose between these two views: 'partners should never put pressure on each other to do something they don't want to do' *and* 'try it out – you may like it when you try it'. *Good lovers* and *Getting help* are two topics in this chapter that should help you if you still disagree about what you like to do when you make love.

189

Lovemaking and birth control

Most couples want to have some children.

But most couples think that two or three are enough.

However, these same couples look forward to many years of making love. Therefore they need birth control.

Birth control

Getting pregnant can be avoided. There are now several reliable methods of birth control that can be used. (On page 192 we help you to decide which method suits you best.)

It is important to understand how the various methods work. Why? Let's look at how often the various methods fail. When the failure rate of the methods is calculated by scientists, they look at the weaknesses of the contraceptives themselves. They assume that the couple using them will not make any mistakes. But people do make mistakes. When contraceptives are used by couples who don't understand *how* they work the failure rate turns out to be much higher. The figures given below were worked out in 1976. We have shown the failure rate as: the number of women who get pregnant out of every 1000 women using the method for one year. They had intercourse about two or three times a week. None of the couples wanted another baby.

One group (**A**) was just told to get on with using their chosen method of birth control. The other group (**B**) was given extra advice on how to use their method as carefully as possible.

1000 women using the method for a year	Number of pregnancies	
	Group A– 'ordinary users'	Group B– 'very careful users'
The Pill	70	3
The Mini Pill	70	12
IUD (Loop etc)	50	20
Sheath and spermicide	50	9
Cap and spermicide	170	30

This table shows you that using an extremely 'reliable' method, such as the Pill, without much care can result in more pregnancies than using a 'less reliable' method very carefully. In fact,

the sheath and the cap are very good methods of contraception, if they are used properly. To use a method very carefully you need a lot of information as well as a 'careful' nature. For example, many women on the Pill do not know that

sickness and diarrhoea or taking certain types of antibiotics can make the Pill fail to work. Many people do not realise that, if they use the cap, they should insert more spermicidal cream before each time they make love in one night.

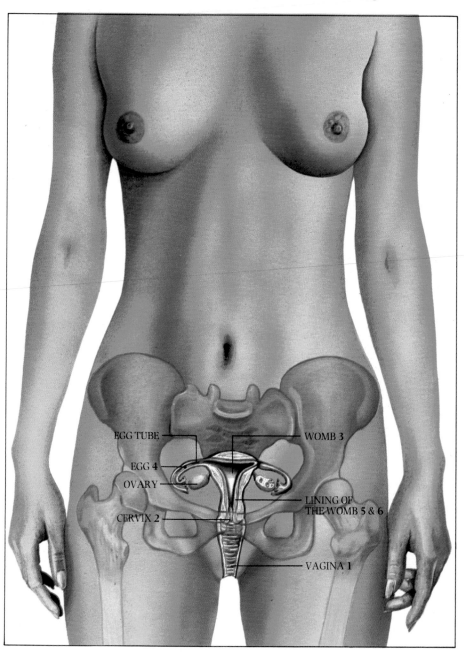

EGG TUBE

WOMB 3

EGG 4

OVARY

LINING OF THE WOMB 5 & 6

CERVIX 2

VAGINA 1

How conception occurs

You need to understand exactly how you can get pregnant if you want to make the best use of the various methods of birth control. In the description below each step towards conception is numbered. As you read, check with the numbers on the diagram to see where that stage happens. (The asterisks (*) mark each point along the way at which a method of birth control could work. This is explained in the section on 'How does birth control work?')

1 At the end of sexual intercourse the man's seed (semen) spurts out into the woman's vagina.*

2 The semen contains many millions of sperm. These sperm swim through the opening (the cervix) into the womb.*

3 They travel up the womb and out along the egg tubes (Fallopian tubes).* The eggs that are produced in the woman's ovaries travel down these tubes.

4 If the sperm meet an egg * near the end of the tube, one of them may penetrate the egg. If so, the egg is then said to be fertilised. This is the moment of conception. The fertilised egg then travels on down the tube and into the womb.

5 Once in the womb it will burrow into the lining of the womb.*

6 Then it will develop into a baby.*

A woman usually only produces one egg at a time, about once a month. This happens about 14 days before the next period is due.

If the egg is not fertilised it lives only for about two days, after which it dies and passes out of the vagina, along with the lining of the womb which is also shed about once a month. This is menstruation – a 'period'.

You need to know more!

Your method of birth control is a very personal decision. See our chart on the right for details of how all the different methods work. Overleaf we help you decide what might be right for you.

The most effective methods, the Pill and the IUD, have disadvantages for some women. So if it would not be a disaster to have a baby – or you would be prepared to have an abortion if you did – you might feel happier using one of the other methods.

We don't have space here to explain exactly how you use these methods. *What next?* tells you what to read to learn more and whom you can approach for help. Sheaths and spermicides can be bought from chemists and some other shops. For other methods you need professional advice.

How birth control works

1 The sperm can be stopped from getting into the vagina

A The man can withdraw his penis before he ejaculates. This is so unreliable that it isn't worth considering

B The man can stretch over his erect penis a rubber sheath (condom, french letter). This catches the semen. Spermicide (see D) should be used as well. Putting on a sheath may interrupt lovemaking but it can help prevent infection being passed from one partner to another

C The man can be sterilised (vasectomy). This cannot be reversed, so you must be certain you won't want more children. In this case the sperm tubes are cut and tied. The man ejaculates just the same way as before but there are no sperm in the fluid

2 The sperm can be stopped from getting through the opening of the womb

D A cream or foam which kills sperm – a spermicide – can be placed at the top of the vagina. Use with a sheath (see B) or a cap (see E). These may also help reduce the risk of infection for the woman

E A rubber cap can be placed over the neck of the womb (use with spermicide (see D)). Used carefully – as the table shows – this can be a good reliable method of contraception. It may also reduce the risk of cervical cancer

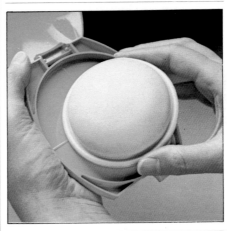

3 The egg tubes can be cut or tied so that the sperm cannot get through

F Sterilisation. A fairly simple operation allows the tubes to be cut and tied or heat-sealed or clipped shut. This cannot be reversed – so you must be certain you don't want more children

4 The egg may not be in the tube

G You can work out the time of the month when ovulation (the ovary releasing an egg into the tube) occurs and avoid intercourse at this fertile time (natural method). This method is often unreliable because it is difficult to know when ovulation occurs. The egg lives for about two days; sperm can survive three (sometimes more) days inside the woman's body. So it may be necessary to avoid intercourse for many days

H Ovulation can be stopped by taking the Pill so that no ripe eggs are released. (Taking the Pill also makes stages two and five more difficult because the hormones in the Pill keep the opening of the womb blocked with sticky mucus and prevent a thick lining building up in the womb.) Which type of Pill to take needs careful discussion with a doctor. Many women are not prepared to accept the possible side-effects of the Pill. The risks for you must be discussed with your local doctor

5 The fertilised egg can be prevented from settling in the womb

I A loop or coil can be placed inside the womb. This is an IUD – intra-uterine device. It is suspected that the presence of the IUD hurries the egg along the tube so it is less likely to get fertilised (stage 4). It may also stop the fertilised egg from being implanted in the lining of the womb. (See also H) Certain types of loop can only be used if you have had a child. Modern types of the loop can be used even if you haven't had a baby

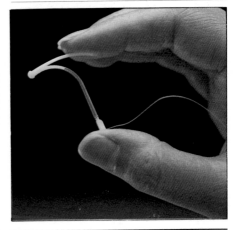

6 The developing foetus can be removed from the womb

J This is abortion. It isn't a method of birth control, ie, a way of preventing conception. But it does stop unwanted births. The lining of the womb, together with the foetus, can be removed by gentle suction (vacuum extraction) or by scraping out the womb. With an older foetus a brief labour is brought on, dislodging the foetus before it is able to survive

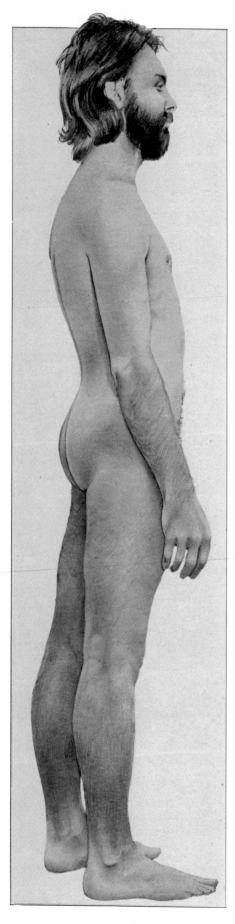

Which method suits you?

Follow the questions in the chart to work out which method should best suit you. But bear these things in mind.

○ **You have to decide why it would be a 'disaster' for you to have a baby** Because of money or housing problems? Giving up a career? You have enough children already? You feel, or your doctor advises you, that you are too old to have a child? There are sound medical reasons why you shouldn't have a child? You don't want to risk passing on an inheritable disease?

○ **If you reach 'think again'** on the chart you may have to choose second best. Perhaps use a method you don't like using but which works well.

○ **If you keep reaching 'think again'** ask yourself these questions:

a do I want to find an excuse for not having intercourse?

b perhaps I secretly want a baby?

○ **Some of the methods may not be acceptable to you** on moral grounds eg. sterilisation or abortion, or artificial methods in general or the IUD in particular, if it does prevent the fertilised egg from embedding in the womb and therefore works as an early form or abortion.

Using it – but not liking it

All methods of birth control have some disadvantages. Most people put up with them because they consider it is even more important not to get pregnant. But the disadvantages can affect how you feel about love-making. Here are some comments.

'Having to stop to put on the sheath makes me go limp – and I can't get it on.' *Man, 29*

'The foam from spermicides drips out for ages. That's why I won't make love in the mornings any more.' *Woman, 23*

'When I know it's not "safe" to make love I get very keen. I think it's really the idea of forbidden fruit.' *Man, 31*

'I feel fat and cow-like on the Pill and honestly I don't fancy having sex much nowadays.' *Woman, 25*

'If I go to all the trouble to put my cap in and then he doesn't want to make love, I get really mad.' *Woman, 36*

'I felt sick on the Pill. Got cramps with the loop. Foam makes me itch. My doctor says I'm just being difficult.' *Woman, 33*

Have you ever risked starting a baby by making love …

☐ when you didn't have a contraceptive with you?

☐ when you felt that romance or passion

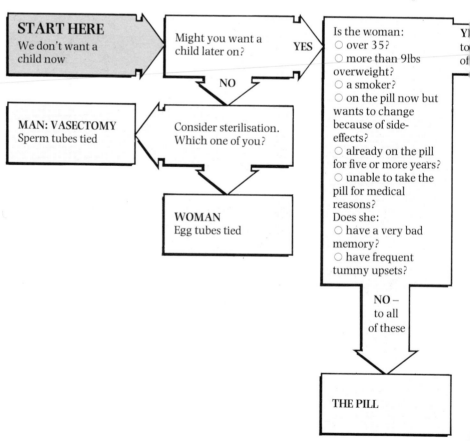

would be spoiled by using birth control?

☐ without contraceptives because if you said 'no' your partner might leave you or be angry?

☐ without contraceptives and believing in 'magic'? ('I'm sure I won't get pregnant' or 'Just once won't make you pregnant.')

☐ when you weren't prepared, because you wouldn't admit to yourself in advance that you might make love?

☐ when you didn't care because you had had too much to drink?

☐ without using your birth control method properly, because you secretly dislike using it? ('Why should I risk harming my body? – damn the Pill!')

☐ without contraceptives because in the back of your mind you know you want a baby

☐ to prove you are fertile?

☐ to hold on to your partner?

☐ to have someone to love and look after you?

☐ because you think it's about time you had one?

Almost everyone would agree that if you make love but you don't want a baby then you ought to use birth control.

But in Britain there are about 12,000 abortions a year *and* one in three babies born were conceived by 'accident' (though that doesn't mean they were unwanted by the time they were born).

That all adds up to a lot of 'accidental' pregnancies. Few of these were due to an unavoidable failure of birth control. Some people did need more information or advice. Perhaps they didn't know where to go? Or were nervous about asking? Or made mistakes because they weren't given enough information?

But very many of these 'accidents' seem to be linked with situations where common sense is overruled by other considerations. The reasons for risking pregnancy may have a lot to do with it.

Trying to get pregnant

Making love when you want to get pregnant can be the best time of all. But some couples have great difficulty in starting a baby. For them lovemaking can lose its passion and turn into rather grim attempts to conceive. But they may know that the woman is more likely to start a baby if they make love when she has just released an egg (ovulated). This usually happens two weeks before her period is due.

To find out more you can consult your doctor or a book (see *What next?*).

If you have been trying to conceive for nine months without success (or for six months if one of you is over 30) most doctors would advise you to seek specialist help.

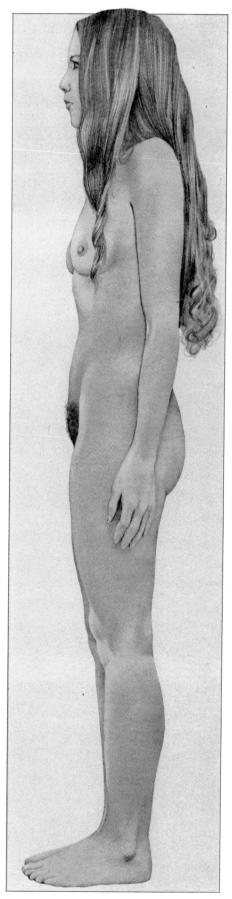

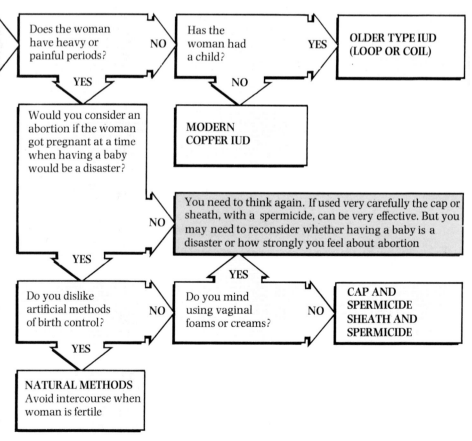

Does the woman have heavy or painful periods? — NO → Has the woman had a child? — YES → **OLDER TYPE IUD (LOOP OR COIL)**

YES ↓

Has the woman had a child? — NO → **MODERN COPPER IUD**

Would you consider an abortion if the woman got pregnant at a time when having a baby would be a disaster? — NO → You need to think again. If used very carefully the cap or sheath, with a spermicide, can be very effective. But you may need to reconsider whether having a baby is a disaster or how strongly you feel about abortion

YES ↓

Do you dislike artificial methods of birth control? — NO → Do you mind using vaginal foams or creams? — NO → **CAP AND SPERMICIDE SHEATH AND SPERMICIDE**

YES ↓

NATURAL METHODS
Avoid intercourse when woman is fertile

Choosing a partner

Why do people choose whom they do?
It all goes back to experiences of early childhood.

All kinds of things go to make up these choices but the most important are probably shared interests, physical attraction and love.

What is love?

Sexual relationships in which there is no love or affection usually don't last. They can be exciting and totally absorbing for a while. But they're rarely permanent.

Most people look for love as well as sex from their partners. But, as the song says, 'What is this thing called love?'

We may think of loving as second nature. It's just something we do. But in fact it's something we *learnt* how to do from the moment we were born. The early bonds which build up between parent and child help the child to learn that the world is a safe place and that people are to be trusted.

The child inside us all

A good early experience of being loved can make it easier to build up adult loving relationships. Bad early experiences can make it hard.

As children we all needed the following things.

Affection This can be shown by gazing into eyes, smiling, talking, kissing and singing. We needed to learn as children how to show affection in actions. We started to learn this from the day we were born. But things can go wrong. Maybe the mother or the child was ill and they were separated. Or the mother may have had too many worries to be able to relax and show affection.

Tender physical closeness This ensures that we learn to be at ease with how our body feels. As adults we shall be able to enjoy physical contacts and lovemaking. Again, things may go wrong. Perhaps the child was seldom picked up and cuddled for fear that it might be spoilt. Or perhaps the parents learnt when they were young not to expect kisses and cuddles and, in turn, don't feel at ease cuddling their children.

Approval We needed to be wanted and accepted regardless of what we looked like or what we did. It wasn't enough if we felt we were only loved for our looks, our cleverness, or for being obedient. We needed to be loved regardless of any 'naughty' things we did.

All this, if it goes well, builds up into the experience of being loved. We have to have experienced affection, the pleasures of physical contact and being wanted in order to be able to show all of this to others. That's to say, we learn how to love from experiencing what it is like to be loved.

But if all did not go well in childhood it may be hard to build up loving adult relationships. Then the child who didn't get enough of its needs met lives on inside you. You tend to look to your partner to satisfy needs in you that have got left over, as it were, from childhood. In some sense or other you are looking for a parent as well as a partner. You make demands that can't be met. You find it hard to satisfy the demands of others.

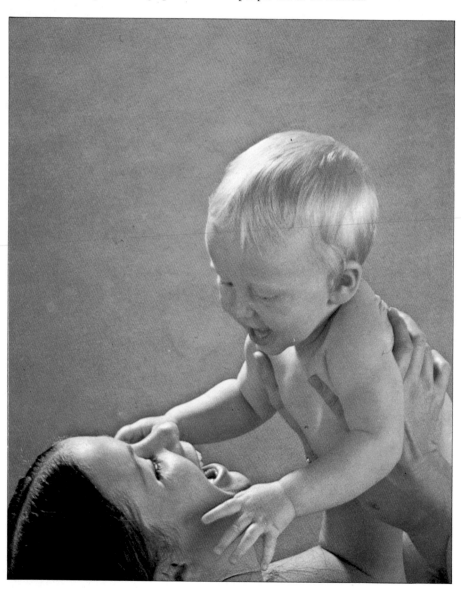

Richard, Simon and Tracey

Let's take a look at three people whose childhood experiences *did* make it very difficult for them to form close adult relationships.

Richard – 'Don't try to come close to us'

Richard was kept at a distance by both his parents. His mother had too many worries of her own to have much time for him. She looked after her elderly sick father as well as doing a part-time job. When she got home at night she was too tired to do anything more than dump Richard down in front of the television with his supper. He never plucked up courage to get close to his mother and share his news with her.

Richard's father, a postman, was at home in the afternoon and would have had plenty of time to play with him. But Richard's father had never been close to his parents and he, in turn, didn't know how to show affection to his son. When Richard grew up he was looking for a girl who could give him everything he had missed out on. He wanted a lot from his partner, but had little to give in return.

Simon – 'You're bad'

Simon was considered by his parents to be one big nuisance.

They hadn't saved enough before he was born for the house they wanted. His father had wanted a little girl. Simon was a big, demanding boy. Simon didn't like waiting for four hours when he wanted to be fed – but he had to learn to like it.

Simon grew up making the usual childish mistakes on the way. Each time his parents made him feel that he was 'bad', 'wicked', and 'stupid'. He grew up without ever having felt accepted as a lovable individual. He had such poor self esteem that he felt he didn't deserve good things to happen to him. He was tempted to hold back from relationships with women because he expected them to go wrong.

Tracey – 'I'll always take care of you'

Tracey was born prematurely. Her parents had many fears for their tiny doll-like daughter in her first years of life. They were unable to have more children, and Tracey was their precious baby. They felt anxious if she set out to explore or experiment on her own.

Tracey didn't have much chance to make decisions for herself or to try to manage on her own. She was quite timid and easily gave up and ran to mummy or daddy for help. She was actually quite fit and robust but she picked up from her parents the idea that she was 'a fragile little doll'.

Tracey grew up to be a pretty young woman who attracted a lot of men. She was looking for someone to take care of her. But she knew that if anything went wrong she would still be 'daddy's precious girl'.

Choosing partners

We have drawn a pen portrait of three extreme types of people. Those who have been deprived of affection like Richard. Those who have poor self esteem like Simon. Those who never achieve independence but remain dependent on others like Tracey. In each of them the 'needy child inside' remains strong.

Supposing the three of them met. What would they think of each other? What kind of partnerships would they make?

To Richard Tracey seemed soft and pretty. He liked the fact that she admired his practical skills and always wanted to be with him. In short she made him feel he was loved.

To Simon Tracey was the perfect woman. Her demands for attention made him feel he had something to give after all. But at the same time he felt he didn't deserve such a perfect woman. He was worried that he couldn't satisfy her.

To Tracey both Richard and Simon seemed the sort of men you could lean on.

So what would happen if Tracey were to marry either Simon or Richard? Take a few minutes to think about it. Then write down:
○ what things you think Richard wants from a relationship.
○ whether you think Tracey could give him those things.
○ what things you think Simon wants from a relationship.
○ whether you think Tracey could give him those things.
○ what things you think Tracey wants from a relationship.
○ whether you think Richard or Simon could give her those things.

On the right is what we think some of their concerns would be.

What about you?

We have just looked at three extreme cases. Simon, Tracey and Richard would probably need help to understand what it is they really want from a partner. And to realise what they are able, or unable, to

Richard wants:	Tracey wants:	Simon wants:
○ someone to love him	○ someone to love her	○ someone to love him
○ a woman to make up for the mother he feels he never had	○ someone to take care of her, make decisions for her, do things for her, comfort her when things go wrong	○ someone constantly to reassure him that she loves him
○ frequent sexual satisfaction – since deprivation makes him feel so insecure	○ plenty of kisses and cuddles	

He finds it difficult to:	She finds it difficult to:	He finds it difficult to:
○ show affection	○ offer support and be the strong one	○ believe he deserves to be loved
○ accept the arrival of a baby	○ play an active part in sexual activities	○ get enough reassurance from one woman
○ see why two women to love him wouldn't be better than one	○ persevere when things go wrong	○ demand sexual satisfaction from his perfect woman
	○ be apart from her man for any length of time	

give to each other in a relationship.

They all want a lot – but find it difficult to give. Simon not only wants a lot but finds it difficult to believe he is loved when he is. Richard can't show the affection which would make his sexual demands more acceptable. Tracey wants support for herself but can't give it to others.

But what about you? We all make demands on our partners. We all find some of the demands on us difficult to meet.

What do you and your partner want from each other? Which things are most important to you? The next quiz should help you look at these things. It's for you and your partner to fill in together, on separate sheets of paper, if you prefer, or cover your answers if you use the book. Tick ✔ for 'yes' or put ✘ for 'no' against each statement on page 197.

Your answers to this quiz will show you two things:

1 whether or not you agree about what is important.
2 whether you understand what your partner thinks.

So now fill in the quiz on page 197. When you have done that, come back to this page, where we start to look at some possible patterns of answers.

You both agree – and know you do

Which questions have you answered like this?

 or

You may feel that the more of these you have the stronger your relationship will be. That may be true – up to a point. It could certainly make for a quiet life with few disagreements. But it might seem boring and lack excitement!

You disagree – but you know you do

Which questions have you answered like this?

| ✔ | ✘ | ✘ | ✔ | or | ✘ | ✔ | ✔ | ✘ |

My answers

Column 1	Column 2
It is important to me that:	*I think it is important to my partner that:*

**It is important to me/
I think it is important
to my partner that:**

1 we should be sexually faithful to each other

2 we can rely on each other at all times

3 in our relationship it's OK to be rude / impossible / grumpy if that's what we feel like

4 we are together every possible moment of the day

5 we should stand by each other in all circumstances

6 marriage is a contract for life

7 it's possible to say exactly what we feel

8 we never have arguments

9 it's all right to get angry

10 we always agree with each other in public

11 we often tell each other we love each other

12 we often kiss and cuddle

13 we make love frequently

14 we need never feel lonely

My partner's answers

Column 3	Column 4
It is important to me that:	*I think it is important to my partner that:*

Many couples enjoy being able to hold separate opinions. Neither feels threatened that the other disagrees. Nor do they feel they must change the other's opinions.

But sometimes this disagreement can lead to one partner's actions being seen by the other as putting a great strain on the relationship (see the next topic). At least knowing each other's opinions should make it possible for an open discussion of your disagreements.

You don't know each other's feelings

You may have discovered from your answers that you and your partner have some wrong impressions of each other.

Which questions have you marked as below in columns 2 and 3?

A [| ✓ | ✗]   B [| ✗ | ✓]

or for columns 1 and 4

C [✓ | | ✗]   D [✗ | | ✓]

(It doesn't matter what you put in the columns we've left blank.) Perhaps you should make a special list. Make one list of 'What I didn't know about my partner' (A and B above) and another of 'What my partner doesn't know about me' (C and D above). You are going to need to talk about these things. Because now you know you guessed wrong about how your partner felt.

It is these areas which, in the past, may have put extra strain on your relationship. If you don't talk them over, now that you do know about them, they can be a threat for the future.

What can you do?

Some misunderstandings are easy to get over. It can be a relief to discover what the other person really thinks. Others are more difficult. They may point to conflicts in your relationship that aren't easily solved. They may be difficult or painful to talk about. The next topic, *Strains on relationships*, looks further at these kinds of problems.

Strains on relationships

Your partner may be the person you love most but he or she probably bears the brunt of any strains on your life.

Most couples expect a lot from each other. Your partner is probably the one person you feel really free to express yourself with. Maybe you let rip from time to time. Maybe you take out your frustrations and disappointments on him or her.

What kinds of things produce strains on relationships? Mark with a tick those which you think might be a strain on your relationship.

☐ **Money** Shortage of money or difficulties in managing money.

☐ **Work** Is it tiring or demanding? Does it involve moving house frequently? Even success at work can cause strain, for you may need to adjust to a new way of life or one of you may feel jealous of the other's success.

☐ **Unemployment** This is often bad for your self-esteem as well as causing money worries.

☐ **Illness and disability** The outcome may be worrying. It's also a strain to have to accept being looked after – as well as having to do the 'looking after'.

☐ **Bad housing** Overcrowding or poor living conditions can mean a lack of basic comfort and privacy for everyone.

☐ **Drink and gambling** If one partner drinks or gambles heavily he or she is likely to spend a lot of time away from home. There may be money problems too.

☐ **Sex problems** If your sex life is unhappy, the rest of your relationship suffers.

☐ **One partner away a lot** Maybe because of work or 'play' and when there's only one of you left to cope, life can get to be too much.

☐ **Religion** You may have agreed to differ about this but as the years go by religious beliefs may seem more important.

☐ **You've grown apart** People change. You start to want different things.

☐ **A new baby** This changes the relationship between husband and wife. The mother becomes bound up with the baby. The father may feel left out.

☐ **Children leave** There's a gap in the family. How do you fill it?

☐ **A relative moves in** Life will have to change a bit. But who's going to do the changing? You? Your partner? The relative?

☐ **Can't talk to each other** Difficulty in talking about things can make all other problems seem worse.

Talking your problems through

The solutions to most problems begin with talking. Sometimes just talking can help you to feel better or to see an answer. Sometimes it's a first step towards taking other actions. At any rate, whatever the problem, it's important to tell your partner what you're feeling and thinking. It's just as important to listen to him or her. Try and understand what he or she is thinking and feeling. Put yourself in the other person's shoes.

When you don't talk about things you build up all sorts of fantasies about what the other person is thinking and feeling. So if difficulty in talking about things is one of your problems – that's what you need to tackle first.

How do you begin?

'Every time I open my mouth he accuses me of nagging. He gets abusive or rushes out to the pub.'

'He's so tired when he gets home from work all he wants to do is put his feet up in front of the telly. I don't remember when we last had a serious talk.'

'All she does is scream at me or burst into tears if I try to talk about things. It worries me if she does it in front of the children, so I've given up trying.'

These kinds of statements are probably a far cry from the hopes with which you began your relationship.

If you are trying to bring up a difficult subject:

○ **choose your time and place** Try to make sure you won't be interrupted. Choose a time when you're not tired and not in a hurry.

○ **take one thing at a time** Be satisfied if you manage to talk about one thing that's troubling you. Start with something small. Leave the major problems till talking becomes easier.

○ **try not to throw the blame** It's all too easy to get into a slanging match. Try to say what it is you'd like the other person to do rather than criticising the way they are. Chapter 2, *Person to person*, tells you more about ways of doing this.

Once you start talking

It may help if you take each of the subjects you ticked (above on the left) and then go through these steps.

○ **Ask yourself** What do I think about this? How does it make me feel?

○ **Share with your partner** Tell your thoughts and feelings and listen to his thoughts and feelings about it too. Some problems *can* be solved just by talking to each other. Both sides need to understand the difficulties the other person has. Understanding can help you to see ways of making things easier.

○ **Look at all the possibilities** The first ideas you have about what to do about a problem may not be the best. But it can be tempting to act on the first idea so that you can stop talking about a painful subject. Keep asking yourself, 'what else might we do?'

○ **Do you need to ask others for:**
facts – to help you decide for yourself?
advice – on what's best for you?
support – someone who can listen and help you talk over your feelings and ideas about what could be done. It may be that you know what the sensible thing to do is but your feelings still get in the way of putting it into practice. Or you may realise you can't avoid a long term strain on your relationship and need someone to talk to who can help you bear the strain.

What next?, at the end of the book, suggests who can help.

How do our bodies respond?

If your sex life is unhappy, the rest of your relationship is bound to suffer. Do we need to learn how to make love?

Imagine this. You know that people drive cars but you have never seen anyone doing it. You know in a rough sort of way how cars work – they have an engine, four wheels, can go backwards and forwards, and need to be steered.

At a certain age you are told that it's now OK for you to get into a car and drive off. But you still don't know *how* to drive. You do have a Highway Code which tells you what you must not do. You very much want to drive – so you start off. How skilful a driver will you be? What do you think are the chances of an accident?

Try reading this again but now substitute the idea of lovemaking instead of cars. 'You know that people make love but …' We think that lovemaking and car-driving are both highly skilled.

Old questions

Much of the research into how our bodies respond during lovemaking was carried out in America by two sex therapists called William Masters and Virginia Johnson. Once they understood exactly what happened during ordinary lovemaking they were able to work out ways to help with sexual problems. (See section on *Getting help*.)

Understanding how their bodies respond has helped many people enjoy lovemaking more. So they needed the answers to questions such as these.

1 When is a woman ready for intercourse?

2 Can a woman's vagina be too small?

3 Can a man's penis be too small – or too big?

4 How important is a woman's clitoris? And where is it? Should it be as tiny as it is? Why is it sometimes so difficult to find during lovemaking?

5 What is an orgasm?

6 Which is the best way for a woman to reach an orgasm?

7 Should a man and woman try to have their orgasms at the same time?

8 How long should intercourse last?

9 Is too much intercourse harmful?

10 Is masturbation harmful?

Of course you don't have to know the answers to all of these questions before you can enjoy making love. But our guess is that the answers to some of these questions would interest you. A description of how our bodies respond provides some of the clues. We'll come to the actual answers in the section called 'New answers' on page 203.

How our bodies respond

Excitement

Getting 'turned on' and excited about making love can take two seconds or all day! Thoughts and feelings often play a more important part than physical contact in helping someone to become turned on. Indeed physical contact before you are in the mood for lovemaking can put you off.

What turns you on?

You might like to try the following activity some time when you have a quiet five or ten minutes on your own. Think about the partner you have now – or a partner you did have. And try to recall all the different things which turn you on and make you want to make love.

What are the triggers for you? Are they to do with:
☐ what your partner looks like?
☐ something they are wearing?
☐ the way they move?
☐ something they say – or their tone of voice?
☐ the way they smile?
☐ imagining touching them?

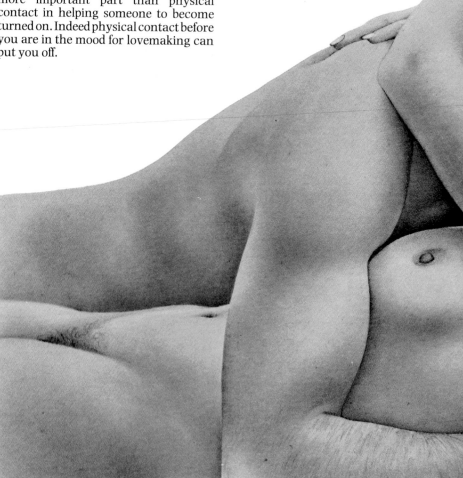

□ imagining your partner touching you?
□ how they smell?
□ being in a certain place?
□ listening to certain music?
□ just thinking how wonderful they are?

This activity should help you realise how important your thoughts are when you make love. Sexual problems are much more likely to be caused by your feelings getting in the way, than by there being something wrong with your body.

As you might suppose, the physical presence of your partner tends to turn you on even more than if you are imagining them. Of course, if your partner has been around for many years, or you are feeling tired and quarrelsome, their mere presence may not do much for you. But when you suddenly remember a 'trigger' from your more carefree times it is easy to get aroused again. You may find it helpful sometimes to do the activity we suggest above when you'd like to feel like making love.

Ready for intercourse

Our bodies should be completely ready by the time intercourse begins. If you rush the early part of lovemaking the woman is unlikely to have an orgasm. But it's an important enjoyable stage in its own right. Not just a lead up to an orgasm. This is when skilled lovers can express their love in a variety of ways.

Pacing yourself – assuming you both want an orgasm – can be tricky at this stage. Too much stimulation can make a man come sooner than you would both like. On the other hand a woman usually needs to be on the brink of an orgasm before intercourse begins. This different pacing explains why it is difficult for both partners to reach an orgasm at the same time. Sometimes men and women do climax together. But making this the goal can take your mind off enjoying yourself.

Why does the woman need to be on the brink of an orgasm? Well, the movement of the penis in and out of the vagina is often not very stimulating for the woman. The lower third of her vagina becomes swollen when she is fully aroused and grips the penis and feels good because it is quite sensitive. However, the most sensitive part of the woman is her clitoris. This is at the front where the inner lips (labia) meet. (When she's not aroused these labia fold across over the vagina.) It is stimulation of the clitoris which triggers off orgasm. But, because of its position, it only gets a little stimulation during actual intercourse and it is often not enough to bring the woman to orgasm unless she is well aroused.

The woman may need to find out for herself how she enjoys being touched and then show her partner.

Physical changes in the woman

The lining of the vagina becomes wet when a woman starts to get aroused. A moist vagina allows the penis to move easily within it. Most women know when this happens. You can always use a finger to test out.

The top part of the vagina expands and lengthens. There is now plenty of room for the penis. If the woman is used to feeling inside her vagina she will know that when she is not aroused she usually feels quite tight. The tip of her finger may also be able to touch the rubbery neck of the womb at the top of her vagina.

The lips (labia) which usually fold over together become swollen and they spread apart so that the penis can enter the vagina more easily.

As the lips swell they cover the clitoris and it may become difficult to find. However, at this stage, it is usually so sensitive to touch that just general rubbing or stroking over it is enough.

The sensitive lower part of the vagina, near the entrance, becomes swollen. It can now fit closely around the penis. Remember the vagina is now damp and quite long. The tight grip of the lower part of the vagina increases the stimulation for both partners.

The woman is now completely ready for intercourse.

Physical changes in the man

What happens to the man during this love play? His penis has probably been erect since the start of lovemaking. As he reaches the final stages of arousal the ridge around the head of the penis gets bigger. The skin of the scrotum becomes swollen and tightens up so that the testes are pulled up close to the base of the penis. A few drops of fluid often come out of the penis before he ejaculates. (This is why the withdrawal method of contraception is unreliable.)

Reaching a climax

In both partners breathing and heart rate speed up. Many muscles become tense. There are a few seconds of suspense before these tensions are released.

The man's semen is pumped out in a series of spurts. How much pleasure the man feels seems to vary from one orgasm to another. But all orgasms result in the release of sexual tension.

In the woman the first sensations of orgasm are usually felt in the lower part of the vagina. This may contract from three to 15 times. The contractions gradually get weaker. Sometimes the womb is felt to contract as well. Other times the response may seem to involve the whole body.

Women seem to vary a great deal when they explain the pleasurable sensations of orgasm. The feelings of any one woman also seem to vary from one orgasm to another. (This probably explains why reading about how other women respond doesn't seem to help women who have not yet learned to have an orgasm.)

An orgasm is over in less than a minute.

Relaxation

The man's penis goes down to about half its erect size. At this time the head of the penis may be so sensitive that it is painful if it is touched. The penis then slowly returns to its limp state and there will be a stage when no amount of stimulation will enable the man to have intercourse again. This compulsory resting stage varies from a quarter of an hour to two or three hours, or even days. It tends to take longer in an older man.

In the woman the release of tension is followed by the swollen lips and lower parts of her vagina returning to their normal size. The woman *can* have another, or even several more, orgasms right away. She doesn't seem to need the resting stage that a man must have. Some women never feel they want to try for another orgasm right away. Others find it easy or sometimes want to do so. Second orgasms are often not quite so strong. Do whatever feels good for you. Let your feelings decide. Trying too hard to have an orgasm is a sure-fire way of not enjoying yourself, and not having an orgasm either.

Sometimes both partners want to go to sleep straight after sex. More likely the man does but the woman would still like to spend time on gentle caressing and talking. You may need to work out how to adjust to each other over this, if it applies to you.

New answers

Look back at the list of questions on page 200, at the start of this topic. Many of them have been answered by this account of lovemaking.

1 The woman is ready for intercourse when she has been so aroused that her vagina is moist, and the upper part of the vagina has lengthened. Sex will feel even better if she is so excited that the lower part of the vagina is swollen and grips the penis better.

2 A woman's vagina can't be too small because excitement makes it expand. After all, a baby has to come down the vagina when it's born, so the vagina must be stretchy!

3 The penis can't be too big because the vagina stretches. (See 2 above.) The sensitive lower part of the vagina swells and grips the penis. So even a very small penis can stimulate the vagina perfectly well. (A small penis swells more than a large one when it becomes erect. So don't judge a penis by its size when it's limp.) However, after childbirth, sometimes, the vagina may be looser. Exercises to tighten the muscles around the vagina are usually taught with other post-natal exercises.

4 Read the section on how our bodies respond to find out the importance of the clitoris.

5 We've explained what happens to the body in an orgasm. How you would describe the pleasure experienced will be very much up to you. Women who have never had an orgasm often need to learn to have one by masurbating (see *Good lovers*).

One way of learning how to have an orgasm is to use a vibrator against the clitoris (not the vagina). A vibrator usually stimulates a quick, short, intense orgasm. Using a vibrator can be fun – either with your partner or on your own. But in the long run a machine is no substitute for skilled lovemaking.

6 A woman's orgasms are caused by her clitoris being stimulated. Either directly or indirectly, as the penis moves in and out of the vagina.

7 It's not worth trying too hard to reach a climax together. See 'Reaching a climax'.

8 There is no set length of time that intercourse should last. It should be just long enough to suit the couple concerned.

9 There is no such thing as too much intercourse. How much intercourse you want is up to you and your partner.

10 Masturbation is not harmful. It can actually be helpful as it allows you to explore your own body responses.

What next? suggests books to help if you don't know many of the terms that are commonly used for sexual matters or if you need help to understand your body.

Good lovers

Good lovers know how to please their partners.

How? Because good lovers show their partners how to please them.

People vary so much that each couple has to work out their own pattern of lovemaking. They need to show each other how to please. So each partner has to take the responsibility to ask either by words or actions. And each has to feel happy and relaxed about giving and receiving pleasure.

Perhaps 'receiving pleasure' sounds too greedy to you? Well, as in most other activities, there are some 'rules of the game'. There has to be a sharing if both partners are to get satisfaction. But that doesn't mean that both partners have to have an orgasm each time. Also both partners have to be sensitive to the feelings of the other, so that one person doesn't feel obliged to make love when they really don't feel like it, or feel they have to do something they find unpleasant.

It is, perhaps, ideal if each partner feels like this.

○ I can really enjoy my body.

○ Sexual excitement and lovemaking make me feel great.

○ I can show my partner how to please me.

Fine! But what if this isn't true for you? This book can give you facts on how your bodies respond during lovemaking; and on how pregnancy happens and how to avoid it. That's quite easy, but you also have to learn the skills of lovemaking. Telling you what to do step by step isn't the best way to help you. That's where some books go wrong. However, you can be helped to discover for yourself what best suits you.

What pleases you?

The following two activities will help you to explore your body and find out exactly what gives you pleasure. You can then help your partner to learn how best to please you. You will need to find time to be alone in a warm place where you won't be interrupted and at a time when you don't feel too tired. Some of you may find this difficult to arrange but it is well worth trying.

Why do anything?

Many people have already tried out these activities and found they really did help them. Even experienced, skilful couples said they made them think again about their lovemaking.

Here is what one woman wrote to us after she had read a draft of this topic and tried out these activities.

'I found it very difficult to accept the idea that I could try and "find out alone". Having decided to give it a try I found the experience interesting (although obviously not as pleasurable as lovemaking with a partner). An interesting result (one that I had not anticipated) is that I now feel my body belongs to *me* and am less embarrassed about touching or looking at myself. This exercise is not one that I would feel I would need or want to repeat.

'Having taken a (for me) major step in "finding out alone" I discussed the "finding out together" activity with my partner and we decided to give it a try. I think we were both surprised at how unembarrassed we felt and how enjoyable the activity was. The slowed-down pace improved for me what I had always considered a very good love-life.'

However some of the people who were asked to do this activity needed some reassurance first.

○ The women often liked stroking themselves or being stroked but felt anxious about going on to more directly sexual stimulation. On the other hand, the men felt they might feel silly about the gentle stroking. How sad that in our society girls can get the message, 'Be tender but don't be sexy' and boys the opposite one, 'Be sexy but it's cissy to be tender'. Lovemaking involves tenderness *and* sexual excitement. We think it is useful to explore how touching is involved in both.

○ Men were quite likely to say: 'I know very well how to make myself "come" – why do I need to do this?' They probably *are* good at giving themselves quick satisfaction. But this activity helps them to explore a wider range of feelings and to concentrate on slowness and variety in ways of doing it.

○ Some people don't feel that it is OK to touch themselves or masturbate at all. If you feel that way, maybe you need to help yourself get over beliefs picked up as a child that sexual activity is dirty or naughty? Or that you shouldn't touch yourself? If you feel that giving yourself pleasure in this way is morally wrong, you may find it more acceptable if you look on it as a step towards learning how to make better love with your partner.

Finding out alone

You may like to try this while you are soaping yourself in the bath. This may help if you feel shy about getting started. But a warm bed is probably a better place to do it. In this case, so that you are not rubbing dry skin, use a small amount of cream or lotion to smooth on to your body. Use whatever you like as long as it feels right and smells good. Some people particularly like sun creams or oils.

Start stroking yourself all over. Experiment with soft stroking or firmer massage. It's often a good idea, particularly if you are tired or tense, to start by stroking your face, and then your ears and then the back of your neck.

Or, if you've been standing up all day, start with a quite firm massage of your feet and legs. Try touching all the parts of your body that you may not previously have thought were sexually sensitive.

You may find it difficult to concentrate on how your body is responding because you start thinking of other things. In this case try to imagine you are being made love to.

Now concentrate on the more sexually exciting parts of your body. What kind of touching do you like here? Perhaps more vigorous rubbing or a steady rhythm suits you? Try to work out exactly what gives you most pleasure. You may want to go on to have an orgasm. But spend plenty of time first exploring your responses. Remember we have been trying to encourage you to get to know your body on your own, so that you can find out all the things that please you. Knowing how your body responds will make it easier to help your partner learn how to please you.

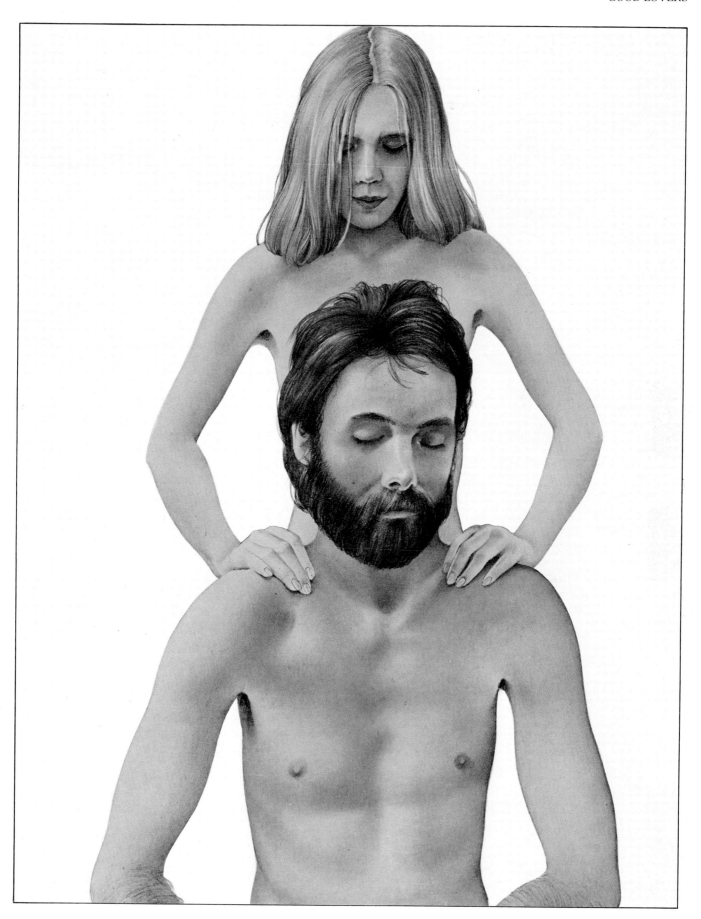

Finding out together

We often find that we fit our lovemaking into the left-over times of our life. We expect to start making love after we've worked all day, cooked the supper, washed up, and watched TV until closing down time. Or after we've had a late night out at the pub or cinema.

This time try making a date to make love. Choose a time when you won't be interrupted. Get the room warm so that you won't be cold when you take your clothes off. Have some background music or a drink or whatever makes the two of you feel relaxed and at ease with each other. Leave the light on so that you can see each other.

Choose which of you shall start this activity. The other person can take the lead later on or next time. There is no hurry, and you should not start off with the idea of having intercourse. Maybe you will, maybe you won't. It's not important this time. You are going to help your partner learn how to please you. You can show your partner what to do by telling or by guiding his/her hands. Use a little cream or oil to heighten the pleasure. Try to tell your partner how you feel while you are teaching him or her how to please you. You may find you like to show them the kind of rhythm you like in the stroking or rubbing. This can be done by stroking or rubbing their back or thigh at the pace you like or by moving their hands for them.

Keep your thoughts on how your body feels when you are teaching your partner like this. Some people find any kind of lovemaking difficult because they get distracted and start watching what they are doing and talking to themselves about it. 'Goodness, we look stupid!' 'He must be getting tired.' 'My hair's getting mussed up.' Doing this makes it difficult to abandon yourself to the pleasures of lovemaking. If you find it difficult to concentrate on enjoying yourself you can try imagining a sexually exciting scene. Do whatever suits you.

Keep on for as long as you like. Don't start thinking you're being selfish. Just remember that your partner's turn for pleasure will come next.

Want to learn more?

These activities in which you concentrate on exploring the sensations of your body rather than having intercourse are called sensate focus exercises by sex therapists. They are the start of most programmes designed to help people with problems. But many people who are already good lovers have enjoyed doing them too. If these activities help you, you might like to read more about them. (See *What next?*)

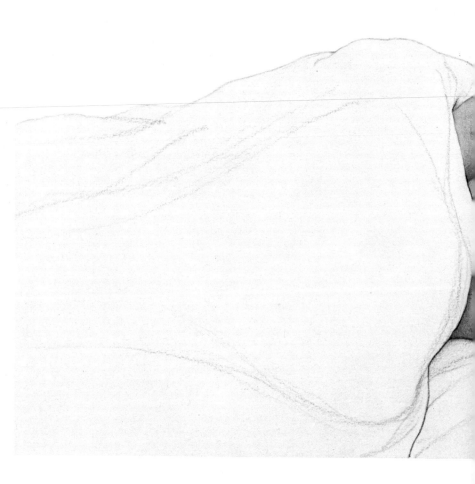

Getting help for sexual problems

Most sexual problems can be helped.

Yet many people with problems don't go for help.

Is it because they don't know that they can be helped? Or where to go to be helped?

Or is it because their feelings get in the way? They may be worried about what the therapists will do. Or they may not like to admit they have a problem.

Or is it because they think they shouldn't have to learn? They think lovemaking should come naturally. Or that it's not OK to talk about their sex life?

Problems – not illnesses

Sex problems are not like an illness, which a doctor could cure with medicine. Problems have to be solved. People with these problems need to understand how they came to get the problem and what they can do about it. Sex therapists try to help their clients to do this.

Modern sex therapy is based on methods called behaviour modification. This means helping people to learn more useful ways of doing things. Sex therapists William Masters and Virginia Johnson were pioneers in this field, in the USA, and their methods are being used more and more by therapists in Britain today. This approach is based on the following ideas.

○ What happens when you are learning the basic skills of lovemaking is vitally important. If you have a sex problem it is highly likely that your body has 'learnt' a poor pattern of responses to sexual excitement. Most likely ignorance or fear had something to do with it. (It is important to remember that you start learning about how your body responds when you are a small child.)

○ Most people have a strong sexual drive which makes them want to enjoy sexual activities.

○ New and better lovemaking skills *can* be learnt.

Of course many people also need to be helped to understand how their own bodies respond. They also need help to sort out their feelings which may make it difficult for them to learn new lovemaking skills.

How can a sex therapist help?

A good therapist will:
○ **reassure you** that many other people have had your problem and have been helped. The trouble is that worrying about a sex problem is the quickest way to make it worse. Embarrassment, shame or guilt also add to the problem but the therapist will help you talk this over, if this is the case with you.
○ **teach you,** if need be, to understand and explore your own and your partner's body. And how your body responds during lovemaking.

○ **plan with you** how you can practise new lovemaking skills which will help you enjoy lovemaking more. As 'homework' to do at home between visits to the therapist, you will be set 'practice sessions'. The therapist will explain why you are being asked to do them and how they will help. (*Good lovers* in this chapter describes two such practice sessions which anyone who wants to increase their pleasure in lovemaking should find helpful.)
○ **encourage you** and help you get over any 'blocks' you discover when you carry out your practice sessions. By seeing you

Men – *I'm worried because:*	The experts' term for this:
I've never been able to get an erection	
I used to be able to get an erection, but I don't get one very often nowadays	erectile insufficiency
I start to get an erection but just go limp again	
I come (ejaculate) before I can get into her vagina	
I come as soon as I enter	premature ejaculation
I feel I can't keep going long enough	
my partner tells me I come too soon	
I can keep going for ages but hardly ever (or never) come	retarded ejaculation
I come when I masturbate but can't manage it with a partner	
I'd like to be more interested in sex	
I'm too tired to make love	low sex drive
nothing seems to turn me on nowadays	
Women – *I'm worried because:*	
I want to make love but never get very excited	general sexual dysfunction
his lovemaking leaves me cold	
I reach a climax when I masturbate but not when we make love	orgasmic dysfunction
I like making love but I've never had an orgasm	
we try for ages but I'm just left feeling tense and angry	
my vagina is too tight	
his penis is too big	vaginismus
I'm really very scared and hold my legs tight together	
he thinks I should be more interested in sex	low sex drive
I ought to want to make love	

regularly over a period of weeks the therapist can guide you step by step in learning new skills.

Sometimes, as a couple start to tackle their sex problem, they find that other areas of their relationship need to be looked at. It may be that anger, which they couldn't express directly to each other, has been dampening their sexual response. Or 'forgotten' guilt about something long since past has blocked them from enjoying sex. A good therapist will know how to help with these problems too.

Who can be helped?

Look at the chart (left). These are the common ways in which most people describe their problems. If you can recognise any of these statements as true for you – then you *can* be helped.

We've given the labels that the experts use for sexual problems. But labels aren't always very helpful! In this case we think you may find it reassuring to know that what worries you is so common that it has a definite label. Knowing the terms may make you feel more at ease about seeing a therapist. However, most therapists prefer to use whatever terms the couple commonly use with each other. It's even more important to feel at ease talking to your partner. Some people like to use the medical terms, others feel more at ease using everyday words. If you have never talked with your partner you could make a start by sharing all the words you know for sexual activities and parts of your bodies. Try writing them on pieces of paper if you can't bring yourself to say them. You may end up laughing – and that can be good therapy.

Self help?

Can couples help themselves? It's worth trying. But we can't give you enough information in a short chapter like this. There is a very good book to help you called *'Treat yourself to sex'* (see *What next?*). The authors believe that: 'Good sex is based on the skills of relating together which can most definitely be learned'. This book will take you, in sequence, through a series of exercises, which, if followed carefully, honestly and, most importantly, in order, will enable you to develop your own good sex.'

This book is careful to warn you about when self-help is likely to do you little good and you should find a therapist.

Finding help

Not all sex therapists are doctors. There is no reason why they should be medically trained since their job is to help you solve your problems, not to cure illness.

To find one try asking:
○ your doctor.
○ your local marriage guidance council.
○ your local hospital – they may have a clinic for psycho-sexual problems.

What next? – at the end of this book – has details of organisations which can help you find a good therapist.

A healthy community

Many of the factors affecting our health may be beyond our control as individuals.

So far in this book we have looked mainly at the ways of promoting health which you can tackle on your own. But some things you can't do much about alone.

For example, when it comes to buying food, you can only choose from what's available and you cannot do much about its cost. You cannot easily reorganise the place where you work or clean up the atmosphere in which you live.

But changes such as these can be brought about by education, government action and the collective action of committed people.

So why have we used most of this book to talk about what you can do for yourself? Usually education, government action and collective action take a long time to have any effect. Changing food production methods may make things better for our children, but it will be too late for most of us.

Many people want to get on with it and do what they can for their own health – now! This is a good idea but we must be careful not to forget the very important long-term efforts needed to make our society a healthier place in which to live.

It has long been known that certain illnesses affect groups of people who live in the same area, or do the same kind of work, or generally have the same way of life. Whether or not a particular person develops the illness may be determined by such factors as their age, sex and physical condition – but the main causes lie in society itself.

The National Health Service often works on the basis that individuals are somehow personally responsible for the illnesses they develop and that it is up to each person to change his ways. But we think that, since the causes lie in the way society is organised, that is also where they must be tackled.

In this chapter we have taken a brief look at some of the longer term things people can do to help improve everyone's health.

The first topic, *Who told you that?*, looks at where you get your information about health and the effect this has on how you think and feel about health.

The next topic, *A healthy environment?*, looks at the way factors like where you live, how much money you have and what you do for a living can affect your health. Some ways of tackling these problems are suggested.

Help from the community is about the health and social services provided in our society today. You are asked to think about how you use them and whether you are satisfied with them.

A good relationship with your family doctor is vital because he is the key to so many of these services. *Talking to your doctor* helps you get the best out of your visits to him.

But some people find that the NHS does not have a helpful solution for their health problems. This has led to a new interest in self-help groups. The topic on self-help aims to help you decide whether they can offer anything for you and if so how to start or join one. *Alternative health care* is also about health help provided outside the NHS. It looks at what alternative health care offers that NHS care seems to lack.

The final topic, *The politics of health*, asks you to imagine what you would do to promote health and prevent disease if you were Minister of Health.

Who told you that?

We all know a lot about health and illness. But where does our information come from? How much of it is fact?

The role of advertising

How do you know when you are unwell? How do you know what to do about it? Most people have learned what they know about health and illness from a variety of sources. They learn from personal experience, from friends and relatives, from the family doctor, from newspaper articles, from radio and television programmes, from government publicity and health education material and from advertising. **Advertising is probably our biggest source of information. But how reliable is this information? And who controls it?**

The effect on you

How much does advertising influence your views about health and illness? Try this activity to find out. Take a magazine and a newspaper and look through them for the advertisements. Don't bother with the small ads, just read the big, obvious ones. First of all work out roughly how many of the advertisements relate to health and well-being or illness. Is it about half or much more than this? If you happen to be watching TV or visiting the cinema you could also note how many of the commercials relate to health or illness.

Then draw up a chart like the one on this page for some of the advertisements you've noted. We have filled our chart in with our own examples.

For each advertisement think about which fears and weaknesses the advertisers are trying to exploit. Do some advertisements work by trying to scare you with images of overweight adults, sick children, tense nervous housewives or bored and dissatisfied husbands? Do others claim to make you and your family healthy, beautiful, successful and loved if you use their products? Even the cigarette and alcohol advertisements, which may encourage you to do things which are *bad* for your health, are promoted with healthy images such as young, beautiful people leading energetic lives in glorious countryside.

Many advertisements try to mystify you with the technical details of their products. They feature men in white coats making scientific-sounding statements and saying that doctors or dentists recommend their brand.

Finally, make a note of how many different brands of pain killers, indigestion tablets, tonics, cough mixtures, toothpastes, breakfast cereals containing roughage, margarines and cooking oils, glucose drinks or vitamins

Advertisements chart

What was being advertised?	Where did you see it?	What fears/worries did it play on or what false hopes did it raise?	Did it associate the product with being healthy?	Did it mystify you with technical details and medical names?
Brand X cigarettes	Cinema	The fear of not being accepted by others, not being a 'he-man' if you don't smoke. It implied that you'll seduce beautiful girls if you do smoke this brand	Yes, it showed youthful people running about by a mountain stream. It suggested that your life will be like this if you smoke this brand	Yes, information on low tar content and menthol
Brand Y breakfast cereal	TV	The fear of not being a good mother and the children not thriving. It implied your family would be made happy if you fed the children this brand	Yes, it showed a happy smiling family all beaming with health while eating the cereal. It suggested your life will be like this only if you eat this brand	Yes, information on added roughage and vitamins needed for health
Brand Z headache and neuralgia pills	Newspaper	The worry that a headache will get worse and you won't be able to cope if you don't take pills. It implied that this brand of pill makes everything better, relieving all stress and tension and calming nerves	Yes, it showed coping capable Mum cooking for a happy, healthy family	Yes, it showed a diagram of 'relief' flowing through nerves in the body

you come across. The more brands of each product there are, the more claims each advertiser must make to encourage you to buy his product, not someone else's.

The World Health Organisation said in 1968, 'Human beings have always been searching for the magic cure to their ills and it is very easy for an advertiser or charlatan to take advantage of human credibility'.

Selling medicines

Even in this country, where there are standards of advertising practice and certain controls, we still find that health is used as a selling point by advertisers. One survey showed that 70 to 80 out of every 100 advertisements related to health in one way or another.

Much of our health information comes from advertisements for drugs and food. We have come to associate getting better or keeping well with taking or using something bought or prescribed. It is not in the manufacturer's interest to remind us that taking nothing could work just as well. Many advertisements are aimed at people who suffer from constipation or mild complaints such as colds and coughs which soon clear up by themselves.

Similarly, clever advertising is aimed at sufferers of chronic ailments who will try anything because doctors have not been able to cure them. This can sometimes induce such strong faith in a drug that a cure is brought about by the power of suggestion alone.

This is known as the 'placebo' effect. (Placebos are pills which are made of sugar instead of active drugs. They are used in research to help test whether a new drug is effective.)

Selling foods

Our fears about our health are exploited not just by advertisers of drugs but also by manufacturers and advertisers of food. The manufacturers of cooking oils and margarines have traded heavily on our worries about the causes of heart disease. There is still uncertainty on this issue, but this is not apparent from a reading of the advertisements which extol the virtues of butter and cream, regardless of the high animal fat content. Advertisements for glucose drinks also play on our fears about being ill and lacking in energy. Such drinks are expensive and unnecessary because ordinary sugar is converted into glucose in our bodies.

Advertising to doctors

Even doctors are not immune from the powers of advertising. In fact, a great deal of advertising is directed solely at them. The British general practitioner receives about one hundredweight of advertising literature and assorted gifts every month.

There is one drug company sales representative for every eight general practitioners. The doctors also see advertisements in free medical papers and other journals and may be invited to see educational films, with lunch and drinks thrown in, and to attend conferences at the expense of particular drug companies.

Your busy doctor very often has little option but to rely on drug companies for his information about new drugs. The drug companies exploit his lack of knowledge in order to sell him their particular (and often more expensive) brand of medicines.

They also exploit his feeling of helplessness when confronted by a patient whose problem he either hasn't the time for or can't solve. Prescriptions for drugs which change your mood now account for one in five of all NHS dispensed prescriptions. Their effect, in dulling anxiety and therefore making bad social or economic conditions bearable, is promoted by advertisements.

Perhaps you might think that the excessive influence of advertising is due to the lack of any other information (from government sources etc) which could counter or compete with the advertisers' claims? It is true that information that comes from one source only is often suspect, but let us take a look at the job government agencies are doing in this country to control advertising.

Who controls advertising?

Advertising is controlled by manufacturing companies' need to make a profit. They hope to keep their position in the market, or improve it, by the use of clever advertising. It would not be done if it did not bring material rewards.

Manufacturers' interests are not necessarily met by providing useful health information. It is difficult for either the government or the health authorities to have much control over advertising except by ensuring that advertisements do not tell lies (the Trades Description Act controls this).

Indeed the government can be seen to be in an awkward position. It gets revenue in taxes from the sales of the products which are advertised, no matter how bad for your health they may be.

The government's main effort to provide alternative information to the public is through the Health Education Council. Compared with the budgets of advertising companies, however, what they can do on theirs is limited.

In the opinion of many people the Health Education Council is no real answer to the power of advertising. It tends to emphasise individual responsibility for health rather than government and collective responsibility. A recent campaign to reduce prescribed drug-taking laid the responsibility firmly on us to stop expecting drugs from doctors. No campaign to cut down on drug company high-pressure advertising or doctors' over-prescribing was publicised.

Fact or opinion?

Your chart should give you a good idea of the role advertising plays in forming your views about health and illness. You will now be aware that many of the 'facts' you believe about health may in truth be no more than ideas and opinions. But how did you come to believe these 'facts'? Is it all due to the power of advertising? Or is some other factor at work?

We are all selective about the information we retain and what we believe. One of the key factors affecting this is our own position in life. For example, if you smoke 50 cigarettes a day and can't give them up you will resist accepting the fact that cigarettes cause lung cancer. Someone who has never smoked and finds cigarettes unpleasant will find this fact easy to believe. (It *is* a fact, scientifically proved. What is still a matter of opinion is how cigarettes cause lung cancer.)

Similarly, if you are well-off, you may find it hard to accept the fact that poor people have much more illness than people who are comfortably off. It may make you feel guilty. However, if you are poor, you know it's true – ill-health is part of your life. The relationship between money and ill-health is a fact. What is still open to opinion is *why* poor people are less healthy.

Some opinions are eventually shown to be facts, others aren't. So you need to think carefully about your 'facts' and try to check whether they are really opinions. Try asking yourself these two questions.

1 Where did I get the information from?

2 What personal interest do I have in believing or not believing certain information?

But what else can I do?

If you think you would like to take further action on health information you could:

○ contact your local community health council – their address is in the telephone book. The council is a group of people from your area, some nominated by the local health authority, others representing local voluntary organisations. Their job is to see that your views about the health service are passed on to the people working in it. Their other jobs include helping you contact the right people to deal with your problem, and helping you if you need to make a complaint.

They should keep a check on the adequacy of local services and press for improvements. You might like to suggest starting up patients' committees in any of your local health centres. This way you may be able to influence your local doctors.

○ contact your own local councillor to enlist his help and interest.

○ write to your MP and tell him of your concern. Ask him to do something about it. Remember the government gets revenue from advertising.

○ join or form a self-help group concerned with health information. Remember that a group of people which has a special point of view is always given more attention than individuals.

○ write to the Patients' Association – address in *What next?* They provide help and information on all aspects of patients' rights to medical care.

A healthy environment?

Every aspect of your life can have an effect on your health and well-being.

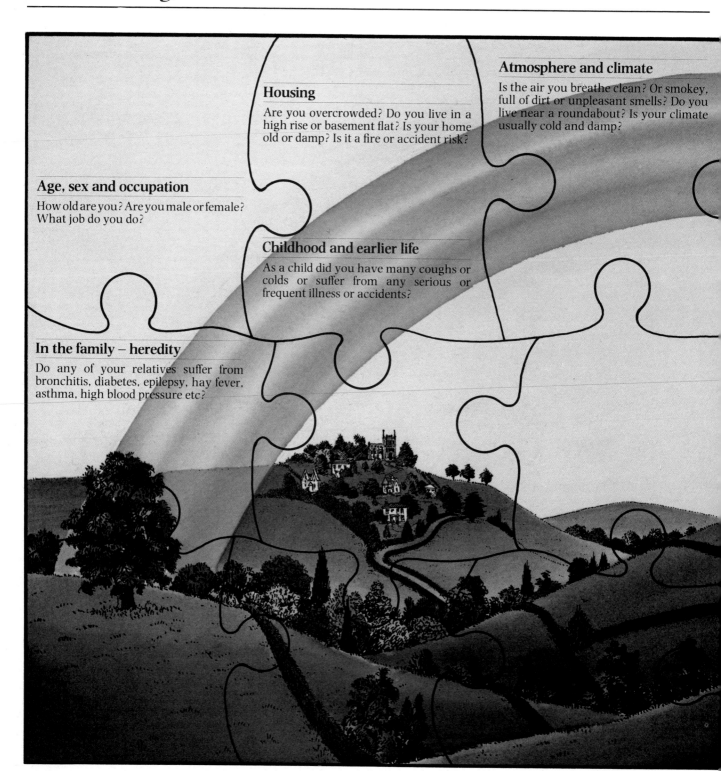

Housing

Are you overcrowded? Do you live in a high rise or basement flat? Is your home old or damp? Is it a fire or accident risk?

Atmosphere and climate

Is the air you breathe clean? Or smokey, full of dirt or unpleasant smells? Do you live near a roundabout? Is your climate usually cold and damp?

Age, sex and occupation

How old are you? Are you male or female? What job do you do?

Childhood and earlier life

As a child did you have many coughs or colds or suffer from any serious or frequent illness or accidents?

In the family – heredity

Do any of your relatives suffer from bronchitis, diabetes, epilepsy, hay fever, asthma, high blood pressure etc?

Many things affect your health

Health isn't just a personal matter. It's affected by the people around us, where we live and what we do for a living. Everything in our lives works together to make up our state of health. It's rather like the way the pieces of a jigsaw go together to make up a picture. You can't tell what the picture is going to be if you see only one piece, and if a piece is missing the picture isn't complete.

So, with our health, unless we consider together all the factors affecting it we don't get a complete picture. For example, the kind of house you live in probably depends on your income but income depends on your work which depends on your age, sex and where you live.

This jigsaw aims to help you start looking at these things. In the spaces provided fill in your details. It will help you see more clearly how all the factors in your life work together to make up your state of health.

Policy

Do you have any say in what goes on in your neighbourhood? Such as where the roads go, whether your children have somewhere to play or whether your local hospital stays open?

Family life

Do you have a family? Does your family life provide a chance to relax? Do you have too many chores? Are there many arguments and fights? Money problems?

Income

How much do you earn? Do you have to work overtime or shifts to make ends meet? Can you afford good food, adequate heating or a holiday?

Your workplace

Is your workplace noisy or dirty? Are there dust particles or chemical fumes in the air. Do you work with vibrating machinery, X-rays or dangerous chemicals? Is the temperature too hot or too cold? Do you find your work boring or stressful?

Social life, leisure and personal habits

Is your social life relaxing? Exciting, stressful, worrying? How much do you rest and exercise, smoke, eat or drink?

What affects your health?

This quiz will help you take a closer look at the factors that affect your health and what you can do about them. First think of an ailment or illness which you get quite often and use this for your example. If you never seem to be unwell then use something you are worried you might suffer from in the future. It doesn't need to be anything serious, perhaps a tummy upset, backache or a headache. But it could be something like bronchitis, heart trouble or stomach ulcers.

Take a pencil and a piece of paper. Read through the quiz and write down your answers to the questions in column 2 using your own case as an example. See if you can work out what may have helped bring on your ailment and what makes it get better or worse. To help you we have looked at George and his arthritis in column 3.

Doing the quiz helped him to see what, if anything, he could change in his life. Later we look at the changes he decided on and how he tried to make them.

If there are gaps in your information you can get the books we suggest in *What next?* or you could ask your doctor or health visitor.

Age, sex and occupation	Questions to ask yourself	George
Certain age groups are at risk from specific illness or accidents, eg, young adult males – motorbike accidents; middle aged men – heart disease; middle aged women – breast or cervical cancer. People in certain occupations are more likely to get certain illnesses, eg, miners – chest diseases; labourers – back injuries; lorry drivers – stomach ulcers; radiographers – leukaemia	Your ailment? Your age? Your sex? Your occupation? Is your ailment more common in men or women? Is it more common, or does it get worse, at certain ages? Do people doing particular jobs suffer from it more?	Osteoarthritis 53 years Male Sheet metal worker My doctor says that arthritis is more common in people who put a heavy strain on their joints, eg, sportsmen and labourers. Arthritis tends to get worse as you get older. My job probably did not cause my arthritis but almost certainly aggravates it
In the family		
Some ailments do run in families, either because children grow up in the same place as their parents and are exposed to the same things, eg, bad housing and air pollution. Or because they pick up their parents' 'bad habits' such as smoking or over-eating. Other things are definitely inherited, eg, sickle-cell anaemia, or a tendency to heart disease or asthma	Did your parents or any other relative suffer from the same ailment? Do you still live in the same place as your family? Have you learned their 'bad' habits?	Some types of arthritis are thought to be partly inherited but the evidence is not very clear yet
Childhood and early life		
What happens to you as a child may cause problems later on. Certain illnesses such as rheumatic heart disease or pneumonia may leave you with a weakness later, eg, in the heart or chest	What happened in your childhood that might affect your ailment? Did you suffer from any serious illnesses or constant coughs and colds?	When I was a boy I smashed my right knee-cap in an accident. Nowadays when my arthritis is bad my right knee swells up more and is more painful than the left one
Atmosphere and climate		
A clean atmosphere promotes good health. Polluted air, whether from smoke or chemicals, can cause all sorts of illnesses, particularly respiratory ones. Damp climates can aggravate rheumatism	Do you live in or near an industrial area? Do local factories belch out dust and dirt, or smoke and fumes? Do any particular weather conditions affect your ailment?	The atmosphere doesn't affect my arthritis. But on particularly cold days my joints, particularly the knees, seem to be stiffer than usual
Housing		
Cold and damp housing can aggravate conditions like bronchitis or rheumatism. Isolation in a tower-block or bedsit can lead to depression. Overcrowding encourages the spread of infectious diseases and makes accidents more likely	Is your home warm and dry? Or does it need improvement? Do you live in a friendly area? Or are you cut off from others? Do you suffer from overcrowding?	I live in a small house which is cold in winter. This makes the arthritis worse. I'm worried that as I get older I will not be able to get up and down the stairs to the bedroom

Your workplace	Questions to ask yourself	George
This is covered more fully in Chapter 5, *Work and health*. Briefly, your workplace may be too hot or too cold or dirty and full of hazards. Noisy and stressful workplaces have higher illness rates	Are you happy at work? What are the physical conditions of your workplace like? Are there any special hazards? Do many people have accidents or get ill? Do you ever find that certain things at work aggravate your ailment?	I work in a noisy machine shop. I used to find that when I did overtime my arthritis got worse. I put this down to the stress of rushing to get things done. So I don't do overtime anymore
Family life		
The size of your family and their state of health can affect your health, eg, spreading infections like flu. Marital problems can place a strain on you, leading to depression and mental illness or can lower your resistance to infections	How many people are there in your family? Are they healthy? Do they suffer from the same ailment as you? How well do you get on with them?	I live with my wife and teenage daughters and our family life is happy. But I did notice that when my younger daughter was being troublesome my arthritis seemed worse. Worrying about her upset me a lot, I think
Social life, leisure and personal habits		
If your social life is happy and relaxing it can be a great antidote to the stresses and strains of work and even family life. But you do need to balance the benefits of fun and friendship against the possible harmful effects of, say, cigarette smoke in pubs and clubs; or perhaps upsetting your partner and family by going off too much without them	How do you spend your leisure time? Is your social life relaxing and beneficial? Do you smoke or drink too much or eat too much? Do you drive wildly or work too hard?	I've always loved fishing and this is how I spent most of my leisure time. However getting cold and wet and sitting in one position for a long time aggravated my arthritis. I do eat too much and drink a lot of beer. This has made me rather overweight and my doctor says this puts strain on my joints and so also aggravates my arthritis
Income		
How much you earn can determine your whole lifestyle. Generally people with more money have better housing and food. Money can mean that you have good holidays, warm clothes and your own transport. Poorer people make less use of NHS care even though they have worse health	How much does your income dictate your lifestyle? What things would you give up or take up if you had more money? Could you do something about your ailment if you had more money? Do you make good use of the NHS?	I really need to work overtime to get enough money for any luxuries. But this makes my arthritis worse – so I have to balance one against the other. If I spent less on beer, my wife could afford better food. But my pints after work are part of the relaxation and important to me
Policy		
Government policies can have a profound effect on your health. Decisions about the kind of health service we have, which illnesses are priorities for spending and who has access to care are all policy decisions	Can you think of how policy decisions may affect your ailment? Is it a low priority illness because it's not life threatening? Is it something more common or exclusive to women so that male researchers are less interested in it?	There is not a lot my doctor can do for my arthritis. I get pain killers and I'm supposed to lose weight. But, because arthritis is not life threatening or dramatic, little money is spent on research into it. Still arthritis causes an enormous amount of pain, invalidism and time off work

What can you do?

You can see from the exercise on p 218 how the parts of your life interlock. They combine to affect your mental and physical health. Some factors are under your control but many are not. Good health is not just a personal issue but one which must involve the whole community.

But can you influence your own health by trying to influence the community in which you live? It is possible. Work through the ten areas and make your own list of things you might like to do. Again we have used George as an example.

What can be done	What George did
Age, sex and occupation	
You can't change your age. But as you get older you can take more care not to get infections, make your home safer to reduce the risk of accidents, have regular check-ups with your doctor, pay attention to your lifestyle to help prevent the diseases of old age. If the health risks of your job are very bad you may wish to try to change them or to change your occupation. See Chapter 5, *Work and health*	As George gets older he is becoming more concerned about his health. He does regular gentle exercise, such as swimming, to keep his joints mobile. He keeps himself warm and tries to avoid infections like flu because he finds that a bad bout of flu can make his joints very painful and stiff. George feels he can't change his occupation because there is high unemployment in his area, but he has stopped doing overtime
In the family	
You can try to minimise the effect of inherited factors by taking extra care as you grow older. You can try to change the 'bad' habits you have picked up from your parents. For example, if there is a history of heart disease in your family you would be wise to watch your diet, avoid smoking and stress and get some exercise. See Chapter 4, *Breaking old patterns*	George picked up the habit of overeating from his family. His wife and mates won't take him seriously when he wants to slim, so he would like to join a self-help slimming group for men

What can be done	What George did
Childhood and earlier life	
You can't change the past but you can take better care of your health now, take special care over your lifestyle as you grow older and try to change things for the better for your own children	George has given up cycling to work because of the risk of being knocked over and possibly breaking another bone. Of course, this doesn't help his weight problem so he needs other, safer exercise
Atmosphere and climate	
If your area doesn't suit your health you need to consider moving if you can, even if it involves requesting rehousing on medical grounds. If this is not possible you can try to get your local atmosphere cleaned up. Your first step should be to approach your environmental health officer at the Town Hall	George's town is now much cleaner than it used to be. George doesn't smoke and doesn't like his friends to smoke in his house. George makes every effort to stay warm in winter. As he is a low wage earner he applied for a heating allowance from supplementary benefits
Housing	
Improving this takes money. If you need a grant your local housing or social services department at the Town Hall may be able to help. If your health is already affected see your GP or health visitor. They can sometimes help with rehousing on medical grounds	George's house only has a coal boiler and fire. He is saving up for central heating. He used to have an outside toilet but got an improvement grant to get an inside one fitted
Your workplace	
Your work probably has more effect on your health than anything else, yet can be most difficult to change. You will probably need to take collective action. See Chapter 5, *Work and health*	George's work is stressful. He can't change his job but is thinking of joining with others in his factory to push for change in the way work is organised, to make it less stressful
Family life, social life leisure and personal habits	
These are areas where many people like to make changes by exercising personal choice. See Chapters 2, 3, 4 and 7	George eventually gave up his fishing because of his arthritis. His family life affects his health because he cannot get any support to lose the extra weight which aggravates his arthritis. A self help group is his best bet
Income	
It's hard for you to influence your income except by changing jobs, promotion or getting a wage rise. However, many people are entitled to grants and supplementary benefits which they never claim. These are designed to improve the standard of living of anyone in need. Ask for a list of your entitlements from your local social security office	George cannot improve his income but he does apply for any grants or benefits he is entitled to, such as roof insulation, a heating allowance and a rent rebate
Policy	
It is not easy for you to have a voice in decision making about health care services. Some channels you can use are your community health council, your local councillor, your MP and any local or national pressure groups	George would like to see more of the resources of the health service go towards research into the causes, possible cures and treatments of arthritis. It is very common and yet there is still little known about some particular types

Conclusion

George decided there were changes he could make in all ten areas of his life. He felt he needed the support of others to put these changes into practice. He decided to try and locate a local or national organisation devoted to arthritis sufferers and, if he couldn't, to start one up himself. You too will need to decide which areas in your life to tackle first and how to go about it. Almost certainly, taking some kind of action with others will be one of the most effective ways you can influence your health.

Help from the community

What can you do to improve the health services in your area?

There are many different services available to help you if you have a health problem. But most of them are concerned with the cure of sickness rather than with preventing illness and promoting health. Most services are run by the government but some are run by voluntary organisations, particularly if there is a gap in NHS provision or insufficient services to meet needs.

The services available

By doing the following activity you will become more aware of the services available to you and how to use them. You will also be able to decide which services you think need improvement.

Make a chart for yourself like the one below. You need to think back to the last time you sought help for a problem. Fill in the five columns for each problem you can remember. (You could use the 'Guide to commonly used health and social services', on pages 224–225 to jog your memory.)

When you have filled in all the problems you can recall go back to the Guide and take a look at the services you have not yet used. Think about your life in the future and imagine which ones you might need to use. Make another chart like the one right for all the services you think you might use. From what you

know of these services (recall what you have heard from friends and relatives or read in your local paper), do you think you would be satisfied?

You might consider trying to get those services which don't seem satisfactory improved before you need them. The following case study will help you see what we mean.

Josie was a young wife with a full time job in the local town. She travelled there each day on the bus from the village where she lived. Going home on Fridays she noticed that the bus was always full of tired mothers with babies. She heard them saying how awful it was to have to go into town to the child health clinic. Why couldn't they have a clinic even once a month in their village hall?

The village had a new estate and an increasing number of children under five. Josie herself was planning to start a family soon. She became friendly with the women and enjoyed amusing the children during the bus journey.

But she didn't like the prospect of that journey with a baby of her own. She decided that, while she had the time and energy, she would suggest that they get together to campaign for their own local clinic. So they formed a group with Josie as secretary. They wrote to the community health council to enlist their support and now they are about to get their own village clinic once a month. If the village population continues to grow they will campaign for a more frequent local clinic.

Services you might need

Which	Why? Examples:	What have you heard?
Ante-natal clinic	1 Expecting a baby	The mothers sometimes have to wait for ages. But the midwives seem very good about answering your questions
Chiropodist	2 Getting older – I can't reach my feet easily!	I know you can get seen to free if you're elderly. Suppose my doctor could tell me how old you have to be
Screening clinic	3 Worried I might get breast cancer	I've read about Well Women Clinics in the paper. I could ask the community health council if there's one locally or, if not, if they could investigate the possibility of getting one

Services you have used

Reason you went Examples	First contact	Were you referred on? If so, where?	How often do you use this service? Every day/week/ month/year?	How satisfied were you? Very satisfied/OK/not satisfied?
1 Check-up on my high blood pressure and heart trouble	Doctor	Yes. Outpatients at general hospital to see specialist about new drug treatment	Go to outpatients every month to have blood tests to see what new drug is doing	OK but sometimes have to wait a long time
2 Child has speech difficulty	Health visitor	Yes. Referred to speech therapist at local child health centre	Child has to go each week for exercises	Not very satisfied. She seems more aware of her stammer
3 Needed a wheelchair for elderly aunt who was visiting us	Doctor	Yes. County St John's Ambulance	Probably once a year	Very satisfied

Will you take action?

In your first chart we asked you to say how satisfied you were with a particular service. There are many reasons why you might be dissatisfied with a service. We have listed some here. Take each of the services with which you are dissatisfied and fill in the empty column in the table (right). Tick off each of the reasons on the list which apply. Then add any other reasons which apply particularly to the services you are considering. The chart shows what one woman thought of her ante-natal clinic.

Next, see if your friends who also use these services agree with you. If they do, put an asterisk (*) beside your tick. If you are the only one to feel dissatisfied you may decide not to take any further action. (You may well feel this way if it is a service you don't use very often.) If several of you feel the same this is a good indication that the service needs changing.

What can you do?

Most people are very reluctant to complain. But if we don't complain no one will know that anything is wrong and so it won't be put right. It is difficult for one person to change things. To do so would take a great deal of time and energy and even money. The best solution may be to join or form a group which aims to put right whatever is wrong. There are many campaigning special interest groups in this country. (See *What Next?*) If there isn't a suitable existing group you may wish to start one yourself. See the section on self-help groups in this chapter.

Your local community health council will help you make your views known to whomever is responsible for these services. The council may decide to review an existing service and recommend how it could be improved. Even if you are, as far as you know, the only one who is really dissatisfied it's still worth telling your community health council. They can tell you where you should go to make a formal complaint. If many individuals complain about the same service the community health council will automatically look into the matter.

One of the problems associated with trying to improve services is that there is only a limited amount of money to share around. For example, money spent on the elderly could mean less money available for the under fives. The last topic in this book asks you to imagine what you would do if you were Minister of Health and how you would share out resources.

Reasons for being dissatisfied

	Antenatal clinic	Your examples		
		1	2	3
1 You have to travel long distances				
2 It's difficult to get to – ○ a long way from the bus or station	✔			
○ you need a taxi if you don't have a car				
3 It's not available/open very often				
4 There's a long waiting list				
5 You have to wait a long time when you get there	✔			
6 There's nowhere comfortable to wait				
7 There's no provision for children if you have to take them with you	✔			
8 It's so disorganised that you have to wait longer than you need to. (Perhaps they book 15 patients in at the same time?)				
9 You can't get a cup of tea				
10 The toilets are terrible	✔			
11 They don't have up-to-date equipment				
12 Some of the staff don't seem to understand what you say				
13 You feel the staff treat you in an impersonal way				
14 You don't get a chance to ask any questions				
15 It costs a lot				
Your other reasons				
16 By the time I've finished I have to travel home in the rush hour	✔			
17 I have to take time off, without pay, to go in the afternoon	✔			

Guide to commonly used health and social services

Health services you can go to without being referred by a doctor

Ask at your local health centre or doctor's surgery. (You may have to pay for some of the more specialised services.)

○ **Family doctor** – can be visited either by appointment or by attending surgery at certain times. Will do home visits in certain circumstances. Free.

○ **Health visitor** – can be visited at the child health centre or in her office. She will visit you automatically if you have young children but you can request a visit at other times or for any family health problems. Can be asked to visit by your district nurse, midwife or GP. Free.

○ **Child health centre** – can be visited with or without appointment to have your baby weighed, talk to a health visitor or clinic doctor, have your child's progress checked (sight, hearing, speech, physical, mental and social progress) and to have your child immunised. Free.

○ **Family planning clinics** – provide contraceptive advice on a walk-in or appointment basis. Free.

○ **Dentist** – appointments can be made to visit a dentist for a check-up and for treatment of teeth or dentures. Usually some payment.

○ **Dental hygienist** – appointments can be made to have your teeth cleaned and polished but only after referral by your dentist.

○ **Opthalmic optician** – appointments can now be made without a doctor's referral for eyesight tests and prescriptions for lenses. Usually some payment.

○ **Chiropodists** – no need for doctor's referral to have your feet looked after. Appointments necessary. Usually some payment – but free for the elderly, if referred by their doctor. Chiropodists may also make home visits to the elderly.

○ **Accident and emergency** (casualty) department of your local hospital – can be visited at any time for urgent treatment only, or when your own GP is not available. Free.

Health services which need some form of referral usually from family or hospital doctor

○ **Hospital outpatients** – usually visited after appointment has been made by family doctor over the telephone or by yourself with doctor's letter. There are many different departments for all different kinds of ailment. Free.

○ **Psychiatric day hospital** – provides care and treatment during the day. Patient returns home at night. Free.

○ **Ante-natal and postnatal clinics** – appointment made by family doctor after confirmation of pregnancy / delivery. May be at doctor's surgery, health centre or hospital outpatients. Free.

○ **Screening clinics** – may be for breast or cervical cancer checks, chest X-rays, high blood pressure etc. Some are walk-in but most are referral only. Free.

○ **District nurse** – may visit after referral from GP or be asked to visit by midwife or health visitor. Carries out any nursing care needed in the home, particularly for the elderly and those home from hospital. Free.

○ **Midwife** – may be seen in ante-natal clinic or in hospital once pregnancy is confirmed. Carries out home visits for home deliveries and mothers and babies discharged home after 48 hours. Free.

○ **Clinic nurse** – works at doctor's surgery or health centre, may be a district nurse, but more usually employed by GP. Provides dressings, treatments, injections that don't require home visit or hospitalisation. Free.

○ **Speech-therapist** – may be seen by appointment in health centre, clinics or hospital. Usually referral made by health visitor to GP or doctor at the child health centre. The doctor then arranges for a speech therapist. Helps mainly children

and patients who have suffered strokes to develop and improve speech. Free.

○ **Physiotherapist** – works mainly in hospitals, health centres and clinics. Helps all kinds of people to recover use of injured or deformed parts of body by special exercises. Also teaches breathing and relaxation exercises. Free.

○ **Hospitals and nursing homes** – you can enter hospital as an in-patient directly from the accident and emergency department or by referral from your family doctor in an emergency. Referral from an outpatients' clinic usually means going on a waiting list. Specialist regional hospitals (such as spinal injuries units) can only be entered by referral from a district or general hospital. Free.

Social services available in the community

○ **Social workers** – you can arrange to see a social worker by phoning or visiting your local Town Hall or social services department. They will also visit you at home. Social workers help people with any personal or welfare problems. They can help you get grants and supplementary benefits.

○ **Meals-on-Wheels** – usually are requested by family doctors, social workers, health visitors or district nurses. Hot meals are delivered to an elderly or disabled person. May be a small charge.

○ **Home helps** – requested in same way as Meals-on-Wheels. Help is given with shopping, cooking, housework, and laundry depending on need. Usually for old or disabled people but sometimes for mothers after the baby is born. May be a small charge.

○ **Day centres for the elderly** – run by the local authority to help older disabled people to get out of the home and meet others. Individuals usually referred by GP or social worker. Free.

○ **Day nurseries** – for children of mothers who have to go out to work. Run by local authority. Special priority may be given to single parents. Usually some payment.

Voluntary organisations

St John's Ambulance and the Red Cross are probably the most well known services. They provide training courses in first-aid and home nursing, supply their services free on public occasions and loan home nursing equipment, from wheelchairs to bed pans and air cushions. Another very well known organisation, Marriage Guidance, does not need a referral from anyone but appointments are usually made. Helps with all kinds of relationship problems, sex, marriage, divorce, homosexuality etc. Usually free.

There are hundreds and hundreds of other voluntary organisations. Your library should keep a list of all the ones in your area. Or you could ask your local Council for Social Service or contact the Patients' Association. See *What next?*

Talking to your doctor

It is often difficult to explain to a doctor what exactly is wrong with you and what you would like done.

A visit to the surgery

What happens when you go to see your doctor? Look at the list (right) of the kind of things that can happen. Have they ever happened to you? Ask your partner or friend if anything like this has happened to them.

Do you usually feel ...

Successful? If you ticked **1, 6, 10,** and **13** then you know what it is like to be able to talk over your problems and get the help you need.

Frustrated and upset? Did you tick **2, 5, 11** or **12**? It can be difficult to get involved in the decisions that are made about your problem. The doctor has trained for many years. He is seldom taught how to explain things simply to his patients. Sometimes (such as in situation **12**) the control which the doctor has is very obvious. It's up to the doctor to decide whether you get a prescription or whether you need to be referred to a specialist. Your feelings and wishes may not seem to be considered. Knowing how to discuss your problem will help you feel less frustrated.

You like to leave it all to the doctor? Some of us are happy to leave the responsibility for our health with the doctor and are quite happy if situation **3** or **11** happens when we visit the surgery. In one way it's true that you don't need to understand what's making you ill or how the treatment works for the doctor to be able to make you better. However, this does make it difficult to do anything to avoid getting the illness again. And it may mean you are more likely to give up the treatment if you don't know how it's supposed to be working.

Perhaps you feel it's easier to leave it all to the doctor because it's so difficult to ask questions? Or you may have always had doctors who insisted on making all the decisions and never discussed the problem with you. You need to remember that it's your body and your health for which, in the end, only you are responsible. It's not really like an old car you can dump at the garage for repairs!

At the surgery ...	Tick statements that apply to you		
	You	Partner	Friend
1 The doctor reassured me that the problem was not serious. I was really relieved			
2 The doctor gave me a prescription but I didn't really understand what the problem was or what made it come on the way it did			
3 The doctor didn't waste any time. He just gave me a prescription and I was out in two minutes			
4 I couldn't seem to get the doctor to listen to what I had to say			
5 I was so embarrassed. I started to cry while I was telling him about the problem			
6 I knew that I'd already tried all the remedies the doctor was suggesting, so I told him. Once he understood, he gave me some new medicine to try and said to come back if it didn't work			
7 I had a lot of questions to ask but when I got into the surgery they all went out of my mind			
8 When I did ask a question the doctor wasn't able to answer it fully			
9 I know I should have told him I'd stopped taking the tablets he had prescribed, and I did want to tell him, but there just wasn't a chance to say it properly. I was in and out before I knew it			
10 The instructions were complicated so I decided to make notes when the doctor was telling me what to do			
11 The doctor told me the results of the test but I couldn't understand			
12 The doctor wouldn't give me a prescription. She just told me to go away and think about what she'd said			
13 I just went to the doctor because I needed someone to talk to about my problem			

It's my body but I'm not in charge? Both you and the doctor have a part to play during the consultation. The way the surgery is run will affect both of you. For example, if it's been a busy surgery there will be pressure on you both to hurry. Number **9** on our list shows what can happen if the doctor is running late.

The doctor may control the situation simply because he is so used to his job. He sees many patients each day. This means he will have developed a routine of his own based on what he thinks is the best way to solve the problems patients bring. In situation **4** the doctor may have quickly made up his mind what the problem was and what was the best solution for it. That's why he didn't seem to be listening to the patient! But, if the patient doesn't realise that, he may lose confidence and not bother to follow the doctor's instructions.

If you are not used to going to a surgery it is easy to become flustered and forget to ask the questions which are really bothering you (situation **7**).

Information from the doctor

Many people want to get information from the doctor about the problem which has brought them to the surgery. They don't always get it. Or, if they do get an answer, it is difficult to understand. You need information about your ailment so that you can cope with it satisfactorily. Being well informed means that you are more likely to understand your treatment and be happy to carry it out.

When a number of doctor-patient interviews were tape-recorded for research purposes it was found that hardly any time was taken up by the patients' asking questions. Does this mean that people do not want information? Would you agree with this? Two out of every three people who were interviewed after they had seen their doctors said they would like to have been given more information.

The most important thing is for you to decide which questions you want answered. It will help if the doctor can answer them simply; ask him to explain if he swamps you with medical terms. You may find he gives you some of the answers without your needing to ask exact questions.

The key questions

When a large number of doctor-patient interviews were analysed it seemed that, even if the patients didn't know exactly what questions to ask, they were hoping to get the answers to certain underlying concerns. These could be expressed in five basic questions:
They wanted to know:

1 which part of their body was actually affected by the ailment.

2 how serious was the ailment. In a way, they wanted to know how much they should worry about it.

3 what would be the likely course of the illness. How long would it last and what would happen to them?

4 what could be done. What treatment was available?

5 what they could do to help themselves avoid it happening again.

Of course the patients often had some idea of what the answers would be, though they didn't always guess right! This is Brian's experience.

Brian had a pain in the middle of his chest. It felt worse when he lay down at night or when he bent over to tie his shoes. When he had the sharp pain he was worried that he might be going to have a heart attack. He didn't know what to take for it. Of course he was quite right to go and see his doctor. (If you are unsure of whether you should see your doctor, see *What next?* for a book which helps you decide.) Although he didn't ask the five questions above he did get the answers as you'll see indicated by the numbers in the text.

After the doctor had asked questions about exactly where he felt the pain, what kind of a pain it was, when it came on and what made it worse or better, he was able to give Brian the information he needed. Brian had 'heartburn' which is an irritation of the bottom part of his food pipe (**1**). There was sometimes a back-flow of the contents of his stomach into the food pipe. The acid food mixture irritated the lining of his food pipe and gave him a sharp, burning pain which he felt in the middle of his chest.

Bending over or lying flat made the back flow more likely to happen. It wasn't serious (**2**). The pain would soon pass off (**3**) if he took an antacid medicine which would make the contents of his stomach less acid so that they wouldn't irritate his food pipe so much if they flowed back (**4**). He could also do several things to avoid getting it (**5**) such as not lying down after meals, and avoiding eating or drinking for two hours before he went to bed. He could also use extra pillows, or prop up the head of the bed, and not wear a tight belt during the day.

These main answers were given even though the interview was short. However, Brian's worry about his heart wasn't discussed. Your doctor should ask you something like, 'Were you worried you might have something more serious?' If he doesn't and you do have secret worries, it's important to bring them into the open. Worry itself is bad for you and you may well be worrying for nothing.

Think about the last time you went to your doctor. Did you get the answers to our five key questions? The questions may help you to be sure on future visits that you don't forget one of your important areas of concern.

Getting the answers

You may not get all the answers at the first interview. This may be because some tests to confirm the diagnosis are needed, there is not time to tell you all the details or you may feel too ill to ask, or to remember, the details if you were told.

There may not be a straightforward answer because doctors themselves may disagree as to the cause or the best treatment. Your doctor has to make a judgement about what would be best in your case.

But you still have a right to ask about all this. In fact your life-style and the kind of treatment you would find easiest to comply with should be taken into consideration.

You may want to know the risks of certain kinds of treatment – for example the side effects of drugs, or what might happen if you didn't keep up the treatment. An open discussion of the pros and cons helps you have a say in what's best for you, and also helps you understand (and therefore not worry unduly about) certain unexpected effects of the drugs.

Your plan

Before you go to the surgery Make a list (in your mind or on a piece of paper) of the symptoms that are causing your concern.

You might also note how long you have had the symptoms and whether you ever had them before and, if so, what happened. And what kind of treatment did you have?

When you get there – ask your questions
If you have a written list tell your doctor you made it because you don't always remember to ask your questions when you see him. Write down his instructions if they are at all complicated. Tell him if you can't take medicines at the times he suggests and if you've been prescribed that medicine before and it didn't suit you or you stopped taking it for any other reason.

Changing your doctor

If after trying the suggestions in this topic you still find that you cannot get on with your doctor, then you should consider changing to another doctor. A survey in England showed that one in six people who change their doctor do so because they are dissatisfied with him. (Many more of the people in the survey said they would like to change but didn't know how to or felt embarrassed about doing it.)

If your doctor is part of a group practice then this should not be difficult. Simply ask to see one of the other doctors. If you want to change to a new doctor in another practice you will need to register. Go and see your old doctor and say you want to leave and get him to sign your medical card. If you don't want to see him send your medical card to your local Family Practitioner Committee and say you would like to change. You don't have to go into details unless you want to. They will mark your card so that you can take it to your new doctor.

Finding a new doctor

Your own local Family Practitioner Committee produces a list of local doctors which should be available at your post-office.

Ask your friends and neighbours how they get on with their doctors. But only take the advice of those who want the same kind of relationship with their doctor as you do.

If you have difficulty getting a new doctor the Family Practitioner Committee will help. (See *What next?*)

229

Self-help health

Self-help health means helping yourself to health
by joining forces with other people.

Self-help groups – what are they?

Have you ever heard of any of the following? Be Not Anxious, The Phobic Society, La Leche League, Lincolnshire Group for Depressives, Merton Action Group for Epilepsy, Physically Handicapped – Able Bodied, Spinal Injuries Association, Mastectomy Association, Weight Watchers, Alcoholics Anonymous? They are just some of the many groups who would call themselves self-help groups. You can find out about these and all sorts of other different groups from books listed in *What next?*

The modern self-help movement started around the turn of the century. Its aim has been to help people to help themselves without assistance from professionals. Both the size and number of self-help groups have grown rapidly in the last ten years. They are concerned with many different issues, not just health, and you will find them in all parts of the country.

Self-help health isn't just self-treatment such as going to bed with a couple of aspirins when you feel a cold coming on. It can involve a wide variety of health related activities. Most of the self-help comes about through people being helped by, or helping, others in the same position as themselves. Perhaps it would be better to call these groups mutual-aid groups.

The idea of self-help has become very attractive to those who, for various reasons, can expect little help from the statutory health services. This includes a wide cross-section of people from agoraphobics (those who are afraid of wide open spaces) to sufferers from chronic cystitis (urinary infection). Because there are so many different types of self-help groups it is difficult to generalise about them. But most groups have three main functions, described below, though some may concentrate more on one of these than another.

How they carry out these three functions will depend on the cause which brought them together. Most self-help groups are democratic with few or no membership restrictions. The main reason for joining a self-help group seems to be that the applicant is 'in the same boat', and shares the same experience as the others, whether it is alcoholic addiction or physical handicap.

What self-help groups do

Sharing of information Some groups come together to share information on a mainly practical level. They may talk about dietary advice, physical aids, rights, official agencies. They feel that practical knowledge about common problems and how to manage them can help patients and their relatives to cope with the day-to-day tasks of living with their problem. Most people find that the social life and support they get from these groups make them both valuable and enjoyable.

Pressure group activity Some groups wish to go further than just sharing information and giving support. They hope to change and improve the circumstances which cause their problems. These activities range from small local campaigns to fight against the closure of a local hospital to big national campaigns run by national charities. Age Concern fights for better care for the elderly and Shelter campaigns for more and better housing for all homeless and destitute people.

Services and fund-raising Groups with the main aim of providing services and raising funds are formed by people who see a gap in the NHS provision which the authorities don't have the money to fill. The groups provide services on a voluntary basis but such activities need funds to survive, so the service function goes hand-in-hand with fund-raising.

Criticisms of some self-help groups

They let the state off the hook Do self-help groups undermine campaigns for more and better services from the NHS by providing services themselves? Some people would argue that a voluntary group should not raise money for services that the NHS has a duty to provide. This danger is even more apparent at a time when public expenditure cuts are already affecting services. It's easier for a local authority to give a small subsidy to a voluntary group to carry out work on a small scale than to provide better services themselves. Even when these services are much needed on a larger scale. Many self-help groups are aware of this problem and try to combine their provision of services with pressure group activity. A good example of this is MIND (National Association for Mental health). It tries to influence government decision making, as well as providing home or hostel services itself. It is a national organisation funded mainly by trusts, legacies and donations but also receives a government grant in recognition of the value of its work.

Self-help groups treat the symptoms but ignore the cause Some groups see self-help as a major solution to our health problems. They don't seem to acknowledge that ill health is caused by many factors which are not under the individual's control, such as pollution, hazards at work and a low income. (See topic in this chapter, called *A healthy environment?*) So they don't offer a cure or solution to our health problems but rather a way of making the symptoms more bearable. This usually happens by chance rather than by design. For example, if a group spends all its time, energy and money helping members, it may never have the time to look outside and tackle what is causing the problem.

Examples of this sort of self-help group are some slimming groups, stop-smoking groups, and alcoholics support groups. They gather people together for mutual aid and try to cure their ills by individual action. Though their work is undoubtedly valuable at the individual level it does fail to remove the wider causes of these ills. But this is by no means true of all self-help groups. We gave some examples in the section on pressure group activity.

Do you need a self-help group?

Have you ever thought about joining or starting a self-help group? Three people (right) all had different problems which they found were helped by being involved with a self-help group. Reading their case studies may help you to see how a self-help group might help you.

Perhaps you can think of other situations in which the best approach to a common problem would be to join or form a self-help group. As you can see from our examples, there is rarely just one reason for joining a self-help group. Use the following list to help you decide whether you would like to join a group. If you have a health problem, or are concerned about someone who does, some of these reasons may apply to you. Circle the ones that do.

Why start or join a self-help group?

1 Desire to help others in the same position by sharing your experience.

2 A need for practical information and support from others in the same position.

3 No suitable or attractive NHS service for people with your problem.

4 Need for money for equipment, appliances or services the NHS is unable or unwilling to provide.

5 Inability to cope with the problem yourself without outside help.

6 Social or physical isolation because of illness or handicap.

7 Need for the public to be educated about the problem so that they can understand and help sufferers.

8 Need to educate doctors about the problems and self-taught treatments that sufferers know of from experience.

9 Desire to put pressure on government organisations, nationally or locally, to change environmental causes of ill-health, stop cuts, improve services and to ensure your rights.

How to join or start a self-help group

How are self-help groups started? Many groups are brought together initially by sympathetic health workers who have made contact with several sufferers through their work. Some are formed after an article about the subject in a local or national newspaper, others by relatives anxious to do something to help.

If you are considering joining or starting a self-help group, check first with the list of national groups in *What Next?* There may be an appropriate national body which has local groups all over the country, offering the kind of help you want. Other useful sources of local information are your social services department, the council for voluntary services in your town, the community health council, doctors and health visitors. If you find nothing suitable, it is probably best to start on a small scale, finding as many interested people nearby as possible. You could put leaflets or notices in the health centre or surgery, the library, launderette, and so on. Publicity in the local press would almost certainly attract fellow sufferers.

Once you have brought together a group of like-minded people you will need ·to decide what you want your group to do. It may not be enough just to meet and talk. Most people want some kind of planned activity to make coming to meetings worthwhile. Your group needs to decide which type of activity is most appropriate. You may decide to:
○ share the information you have each gained about your common problems and give mutual support.
○ pressurise local authorities for better services.
○ fund-raise for appliances and equipment.
○ publicise your problems, thereby educating both the public and the medical profession about your needs.

There are many other activities your group could start and few groups are short of ideas. In your group you have the chance to organise help in the way you think it should be done.

Mr Brownlow is an elderly man, suffering from terminal cancer, but still cheerful and able to get about. He is helped and nursed by his wife, who is fit and well. But they are worried about how she will be able to nurse him if he becomes bed-ridden. He doesn't like the idea of having to go back into hospital.

They also have money worries. His private pension brings his income to just above the supplementary benefit level but he and his wife are finding it difficult to manage financially with his extra needs.

He discovered a national charity concerned with cancer through his local welfare rights group and was able to receive a weekly supplement to his income for his extra needs. He has also found out about going into a hospice for the dying if things get too bad at home.

Alan is 21, physically handicapped and spends most of his life in a wheelchair. He enjoyed being away at a special school when he was a child. But when his school days were over he had to come home to live with his parents. He hasn't managed to get a job since he left the school he used to attend and is feeling very depressed about the future. He also misses the social life he used to enjoy and is feeling very isolated.

Alan heard about a local branch of a club for both physically handicapped and able-bodied people, which, although it couldn't give him a job, has provided him with a new social life.

Mrs Gregg has a small child with hearing difficulties who has been attending an excellent clinic nearby. The authorities intend to close down the clinic, as they are transferring the service to a district hospital in the nearest large town. After toying with the idea of getting private treatment for her child Mrs Gregg decided that the clinic they had was worth fighting for. She and some of the other mothers have grouped together and are campaigning against its closure by writing letters to their community health council, local councillors, MPs, and the press and anyone else they can think of. They have also been attending public area health authority meetings – with placards!

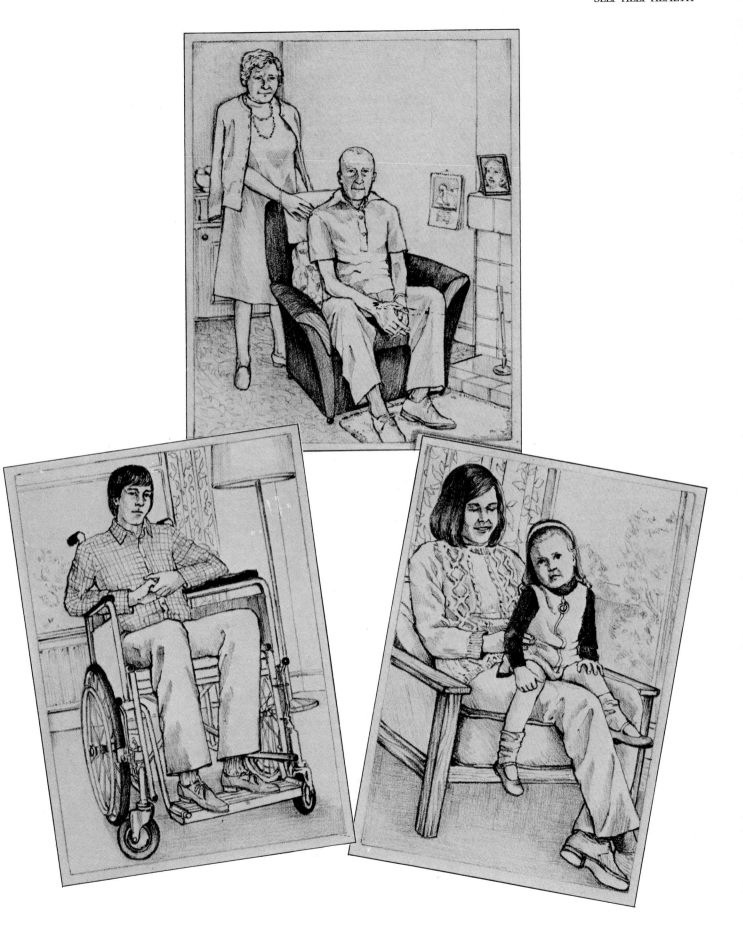

Alternative health care

Why do people go to osteopaths, acupuncturists, herbalists, spiritual healers – or pay their doctor for private treatment?

Is it because they can't get what they need from a doctor within the National Health Service?

National Health (?) Service

Western medicine today is often based on the idea that any one illness has one cause for which there is one cure. Where this is truly the case modern scientific tests to find the cause and powerful drugs to bring about a cure are of great benefit.

Unfortunately many illnesses do not fit this pattern. The important killer diseases of today, heart disease and cancer, don't. Nor do ailments such as backache and headache that take the joy out of life, and result in so much time being taken off work.

The one disease, one cause, one cure approach has also had unfortunate side effects. It leads the doctor to concentrate on the part of the body which is diseased instead of on the whole person.

It also leads to doctors thinking their job only begins when you get ill. They do little to prevent illness, let alone promote health. Hence the wry joke that the National Health Service ought to be re-labelled the National Illness Service.

Outside the NHS

One thing most alternative therapies have in common is a view about health which leads them to look at the whole body, not just its individual parts. Some of them share a belief in the power of unseen spiritual forces influencing our health. Others are less concerned with treatment of the sick body than with promotion of health through diet, exercise, meditation and personal development. The most widely practised therapies in this country are homoeopathy, osteopathy, naturopathy, herbalism, spiritual healing and acupuncture. (See *What next?* to find out more about them.)

Many people feel it is only a matter of time before some alternative therapies are officially recognised by the medical profession. Already within the NHS attention is beginning to be paid to the beneficial effects of exercise and diet on the mind as well as on the body and to the usefulness of relaxation techniques for combatting the strains of modern life. Some doctors will now refer patients with chronic back trouble to an osteopath. And doctors are also now allowed to refer people to faith-healers, if they think fit.

Why do people go?

You may never have considered alternative health care. But many people do. The table shows some of the reasons why. Before you read through this list try to think of a problem you have had, or are likely to have, where you might consider seeking help outside the NHS. Circle any of the reasons which would be important for you.

Why go? Because ...

1 They often deal with disorders which:
a doctors don't understand the cause of.
b doctors don't know how to treat.
c doctors have already tried, without success, to treat.

2 They may offer alternative treatment which:
a doesn't involve powerful drugs, with their possibly unpleasant side-effects.
b is quicker than traditional treatments.
c doesn't involve surgery.

3 They usually provide:
a a sympathetic treatment of the 'whole' person.
b a friendly, helpful and unhurried patient-therapist relationship.
c information, so that the patient can understand the disorder and the treatment.

4 They often stress the importance of:
a the prevention of future illness.
b improving health by reviewing your life-style and making changes where need be.
c the patient taking responsibility for his health.

5 They usually do not have long waiting lists.

The reasons given in sections **1** and **2** are to do with the kinds of therapy which are not medically approved or which are not considered to be part of the work of the NHS. These would include manipulation of the spine by an osteopath for a long-term back problem or investigation of possible food allergies as a cause of various disorders. It would also cover seeking help from spiritual healers or those offering unorthodox physical 'cures' for what the doctors consider to be an incurable illness. Many people would feel that, if their case seems hopeless, then it's worth trying anything on offer – provided they can afford it.

People who are unhappy with the idea of taking powerful drugs (**2a**) often prefer to consult herbalists, who prescribe 'gentler' drugs extracted from plants, or homoeopaths, who prescribe minute doses of drugs.

Osteopathy often offers a quicker method of treatment than the NHS for back troubles (**2b**) – perhaps just a few sessions of body manipulation instead of weeks of bed rest or months of wearing a support corset. Acupuncture, an ancient Chinese healing method which involves the insertion of long needles, also often offers the hope of a quick cure.

Avoiding surgery (**2c**) can be a dangerous reason for choosing an alternative therapy. Except for the very few people who refuse surgery on religious principles it would be better if these people could have their fears of surgery allayed by sympathetic explanation of what is involved and why. Reputable alternative therapists who discover that patients visit them because of this fear often help their patient cope with his fears and encourage him to go back to his doctor.

How important for you were the reasons given in sections **3**, **4** and **5**? The personal involvement which is usually found in most alternative therapies is probably the key to their rising popularity. It is what many people feel is missing in doctor-patient relationships within the NHS. This is often what people are paying for when they consult a doctor privately. They get exactly the same kind of medicine as that available on the NHS but the doctor spends more time with them and gives them more attention. Of course they also avoid having to wait a long time for hospital treatment.

Helping people choose a healthy lifestyle, and avoid illness as far as possible, is an important part of health education. Many people believe it should be given more emphasis within the NHS if it is to change from an 'illness' into a 'health' service.

Change the NHS?

This is an issue that needs action at both the national and local level. Nationally you can lobby your MP and write to the Minister of Health. The more people who do this the better, so why not start a self-help group (at local level) to campaign for better health care.

A Brief Guide to Alternative Therapies

Homoeopathy is based on the idea that symptoms of illness, the aches and pains we suffer, are caused by our bodies trying to throw off disease. Homoeopaths give minute doses of special medicines to stimulate the body to fight disease.

Osteopathy treats back pain and other related disorders by manipulating the muscles and tendons. This effectively removes pain but may not treat the cause of the disorder.

Spiritual healing works through interpersonal relationships without using medicines or machines. Healers lay their hands on the affected part of the patient's body so that their special 'healing power' is transferred.

Herbalism uses the long known healing qualities of herbs to help the body fight off disease. Many modern drugs are based on herb extracts, but herbalism uses the whole plant, as this helps avoid unwanted side-effects.

Acupuncture is based on the ancient Chinese belief that good health occurs when vital energy flows freely around the body. Needles are used to restore this balance of vital energy which illness is thought to disturb. Some Western doctors believe acupuncture may have a rational scientific explanation.

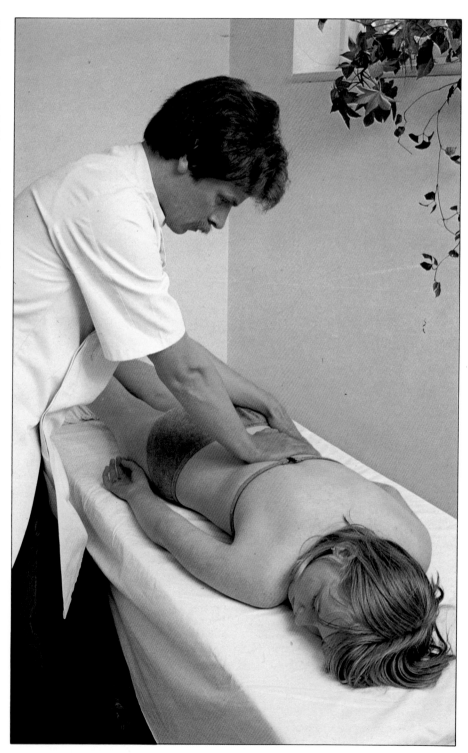

The politics of health

If you have a car accident, a heart attack or bronchitis, is it totally your fault? If not, who should see that things change?

The politics of health is about these sort of questions. In *A healthy environment?* we looked at some of the causes of health and illness in our society. We suggested ways in which you as an individual might change them through your own action or by collective action in a group. Here we take a wider look at the causes of ill-health in our community and the ways in which we might tackle them.

Changes in the pattern of health and illness

Many people do not realise that the major contributions to the better health we enjoy in this century are social and environmental. Investment in better housing, sewage disposal schemes, legislation about purer food, pensions, education and higher income, have led to the improved standard of health we have today. The killer epidemics of tuberculosis, cholera, diptheria and so on are now almost unknown in the UK.

When the NHS was set up in 1948 many people believed that more spending would mean better health. And that in due course there would be less and less need for a health service. Yet today we are spending more money on health.

The reason for this is that, as our patterns of living have changed, the diseases we suffer from have also changed. Heart disease, strokes and cancer have replaced infectious diseases as the main causes of death. Most of today's diseases are due to environmental causes or to what are called 'self-imposed' risks of life. Some of these risks are chosen (eg, climbing mountains). But many risks, such as those arising from doing a very inactive job, are dictated by the kind of society we live in.

Ways in which our society creates illness

By inequality If you are an unskilled worker, you are not only twice as likely to suffer from chronic illness, but your life is likely to be shorter than that of professionals or managers. Your child has less chance of surviving to its first birthday than the child in a professional family. Unfortunately this doesn't mean that you are more likely to get good medical care. In fact, there seems to be an unwritten law that the more you need health care the less likely you are to get it. The reasons for this could be:
○ the social gap between doctor and patient, causing difficulties.
○ the greater difficulties working class people have in getting access to medical services. For example, they are more likely to work unsocial hours, live further from doctors' surgeries, have to rely on public transport and so on.

By the way we live We drive fast cars, causing accidents, we eat sweets which rot our teeth, we drink too much alcohol and smoke cigarettes. We have to make a positive choice not to live like this. And it's difficult because these are the images of the good life pushed at us every day by newspapers, magazines and TV.

By the way work is organised The work we do may severely affect our health, and the by-products of the things we produce may pollute our neighbours' environment.

By the time span we live By living longer more of us encounter the infirmities and chronic diseases of old age.

By changed patterns of living The fact that people move around the country to live and work has destroyed the old patterns of care in the community. Now people are more likely to look for health care in institutions rather than turn to their own friends and relatives.

So the diseases we suffer from today are mainly those caused by the way society is organised. Faced with this, what can a health care system do? Some people say we have a National Disease Service, a salvaging service. The NHS doctor has been compared with a man on a riverbank who sees a drowning man in the river. He dives in and rescues him, but just as he gets one man out, he sees another man drowning and has to dive in again, and then again and again. He never seems to have time to go upstream and see who is pushing them in.

'So there we are, spending more each year on health but not getting rid of illness. Recently governments have been promoting campaigns to persuade people to look after themselves, to eat wisely, and to take more exercise. This approach implies that the individual is wholly responsible for his or her own illness, and that if people pulled up their socks and fastened their seat belts they wouldn't be ill. As we have seen, illness is not always caused by an individual person's 'bad' habits, and the solutions to ill-health are not always in the hands of the patient. A government which really wanted to reduce lung-cancer would change the situation we have now where it spends little on health education yet condones the tobacco industry spending many millions a year on advertising.

If you were Minister of Health …

In *A healthy environment?* we talked about what individuals can do. In this activity we'd like you to consider what you think the government should do about the health of the nation.

Imagine you are Minister of Health in a new government which is eager to reorganise its departments.
○ Would you limit your health service to the job of curing disease, or would you change its responsibility to include things like housing, provision of school milk, health and safety legislation?
○ Would you spend money on services for those who are most in need, like the elderly, the mentally ill and the young? Or on those who live productive working lives and are most useful to the economy?
○ Whose priorities would you consider? The patient's needs and preferences? The doctor's desire to work where it is convenient for him to work? The administrator's need to keep down costs? Or the community's need to keep friends and relatives close by them when sick and not send them to hospital?

Each decision, whether it is about providing meals on wheels for old folk, or intensive care for heart patients involves a range of different opinions.

Piecing the jigsaw together

Take a pen and paper and write down your answers to the questions in the jigsaw, which we first looked at in topic 2. The questions are somewhat different now!

Would you provide more money for the care of the elderly and for research into the ailments of old age? Would you introduce national health checks and advice sessions for those approaching middle age to help prevent future illness? Or do you think that this is each individual's problem? Would you simply treat the sufferers of diseases caused by certain occupations or would you also try to remove from the environment those factors known to cause the diseases? Would you consider altering the production system so that those harmful conditions could not occur again?

With better food, housing, sanitation and ante-natal care, more babies survive now than earlier this century. But more babies die in the first year of life in Britain than in Sweden and some other European countries. Diet, housing, hygiene and health care are still important factors. In Sweden the general standard of living is higher. Both mothers and fathers can take time off work to take children to the child health centre or to nurse them when they are sick. What would you do for the children of the future? Leave everything to their parents or try to change some of our laws? Is this the job of the Health Minister?

Many people still live in houses which are damp, or over-crowded. Many have outside toilets and no baths. Young mothers still live in high rise flats with small children. History shows that better housing has greatly improved health in the past. Is this the concern of a Ministry for Health?

You could start with stricter factory legislation to control harmful emissions. This would cost the factories money in the short term, but would cost your health service more in the long term if you didn't. And what would you do about those car exhaust fumes? There isn't much your health service can do about our wonderful climate. But it could help people protect themselves against it. Many old people die from hypothermia every year. Could you provide them with more money, better housing, subsidised food and fuel, or better social services?

Any factory worker will tell you how his own work conditions could be improved by shorter hours, less noise, cleaner air. But who would pay for this – the employer, the worker, or the health service? Should the health service be directly responsible for health and safety at work? Should all work places have an occupational health service?

Why do tendencies towards particular illnesses run in families? If your health service is going to do some research, what will its priorities be? More and better ways of treating the illnesses which run in families? Or research into the wider causes of illness and the medical and social solutions?

Would your health service see it as part of its role to educate young people about personal relationships and living with other people? Would it look for ways of showing them how to be responsible and caring – not only for their own family, but also for the community of which they are a part? If so, should the health service have some say about what is taught in schools?

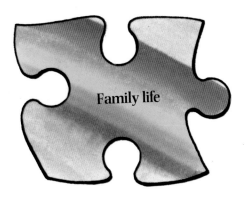

Should our social lives ever be the concern of a health service? Many peoples' social lives centre around alcohol and its relaxing effect. Is this because the rest of their lives is so stressful, that they find it impossible to relax without alcohol? Should a health service try to change this? If so how? Are habits only of personal concern? Or are they moulded by our circumstances? Perhaps the smoker feels like the super-hero of the cigarette adverts every time he lights up? Would you try to stop this kind of advertising?

Should people have the right to opt out of the NHS and pay for treatment privately? We already pay for treatment in taxes, but are we getting our money's worth? Does the NHS provide equal treatment for everyone regardless of income?

Who decides where the money goes? The resources come from the patients, but they do not make the decisions, in fact they are not even consulted about them. Medical administrators have the major say in how the money is spent. So money may often go towards more equipment or buildings in the hospital sector which are used by few people, instead of improving health services at a community level. Far more sickness is treated by the community services than every reaches hospital. Who do you think should decide the priorities for health spending?

One thing leads to another

Your answers to all these questions will depend on several factors. How you define health and what you think causes illness (see Chapter 1) will affect what you decide the concerns of a Minister of Health should be. And of course Ministers of Health can't just wave magic wands. If you were Minister of Health you might find all sorts of difficulties in putting your plan into action. Other groups in society exercise power and influence too. Supposing you decided to introduce stricter factory legislation to control work conditions. What would you do if the factory owners turned round and said that complying with the new law would prove so expensive that they'd go out of business – and put people out of work? Supposing you decided to ban cigarette advertising which resulted in a drop in sales. This would result in less tax going to the government. How would you make up the lost revenue?

If you look back at all the things you've written down you'll probably find that some of them have an effect on each other. Can you say what other changes would have to happen so that the changes you'd like to carry out as Minister of Health would really occur?

Another factor is the issue of personal freedom versus the collective good. We have suggested there are some areas of health which an individual cannot easily change by himself because they depend on the way society is organised. But if changes were made would this mean too much restriction of personal liberty? How can we find the balance between freedom to 'do our own thing' and freedom to harm ourselves and perhaps others, thus costing society money? We have a law which says crash helmets must be worn but not one for seat belts. Their wearing is compulsory in many other countries. When sewage systems were first introduced to prevent diseases some people resented the loss of their freedom to throw slops out the window!

We think health *is* a political issue. Do you agree?

We hope you have enjoyed tackling this book and that it has opened your eyes to new ways of thinking about health. And we very much hope that it may have spurred you on to make some changes to your own lifestyle, where appropriate.

Maybe, by reading this book, an interest has been sparked off in some particular aspect of health. In that case, we trust you will find the *What next?* section useful. Or maybe you've acquired a taste for studying? If you are not already tackling this book as part of an Open University course, you might consider sending off an application to become a student of the 'Health choices' course. You can find out about this in the introductory pages of this book. There are also other courses in the Open University's Community Education programme you might enjoy.

Whatever you do,
Good luck.

What next?

This is a guide to sources of information and help that's available from people, places and books.

Finding people and places

1 In the community there are many places and people you can turn to. But you may have no idea whether or not an organisation exists that concerns itself with your particular health interest. In this case, your first line of investigation might be to contact one of these people or places locally:

Health Education Officer
Citizens Advice Bureau
Community Health Council
Social Services Department
Council of Social Service

More details of these are listed under the guide for Chapter 8, *A healthy community* page 251.

2 Alternatively, you could consult a reference book in your local library – or ask the librarian to do so for you. We list a few reference books on page 253. For example a book called *Voluntary social services: directory of organisations and handbook of information* covers all kinds of voluntary organisations. Your local library may well have a file of addresses of local groups or nationally run organisations.

3 Remember too, your doctor, health visitor and friends may know of a group of people sharing your health interest.

4 If you have the name and address of a voluntary organisation you wish to contact, write to them enclosing a large stamped addressed envelope. Otherwise it is an expensive business for people to post information back to you!

5 If you're unsure of an address, but know the full name of the organisation and the town it is in, or would prefer to make contact by phone, you could try ringing Directory Enquiries. This service can give you the address as well as the phone number. Or consult the appropriate telephone directory at your post office or library. Again a general agency like the Citizens Advice Bureau could probably provide you with an address and phone number.

Using a telephone directory

The telephone directory of one area may not follow the same pattern as that for another area, nor do names always come under the headings you would think of first. For example health centres may come under the general heading of your health authority (such as Bedfordshire Area Health Authority). As a start, look under the name of what you want first. If you can't find it then try headings such as your local health authority, local council or social services. If you have no success using the ordinary white pages directory, try the Yellow Pages entry 'Social service and welfare organisations' which usually yields a mine of information. Once again Directory Enquiries may be able to help if you have problems.

We often suggest contacting your local health education officer. You may find mention of a health education department number under the entry for your district or area health authority. If not ring the main number given for the health authority and ask to be put in touch with the health education department. Or write a letter care of the health authority at their main offices. The phone number of your health authority is often given in the 'useful numbers' section at the beginning of the white pages directory.

No organisation for your interest?

If there really is nothing which caters for your interest perhaps someone should start something new – *you* maybe. You can do this with the help of the Council of Social Services. You should first check whether an existing organisation could extend its scope to cover your needs. If it's a matter of setting up a new local branch of an existing national organisation, then their headquarters may be able to assist with publicity material that will help you draw together others who share your interest. Take another look at the topic on self-help in Chapter 8.

Finding books

We suggest some books you might find useful and interesting and have listed them according to the chapter they relate to most closely. You could try to borrow some of them from the library. If you want to read more about a particular subject:
○ see if other books are mentioned in a bibliography (book list) at the back of a book you have read on the subject. See if they are in the library, or if the library can get them for you.
○ ask what other books on that subject are in the library.

Using the library

If you are a new or infrequent library-user, go to the public library. (If you live in the country use the mobile library but try to find time to look in at the library in town when you go shopping.) Ask the staff to show you where books on the subjects you are most interested in are kept. They will also explain how to use the card index on subjects so that you can check if they have books that are not on the shelves at present but out on loan. You can ask to reserve a book that is out on loan so that it will be put aside for you when it is returned. The card index of authors will help you find the title of a book when you only know the author. Or it will tell you which other books written by an author whom you particularly like are stocked by the library. If the library does not have a book you want, staff may be able to obtain it from another library for you.
○ You may want to look at a reference book or directory to find the address of an organisation you are interested in, eg, British Association for Counselling. Look at the way entries are arranged. Some directories do not distinguish between 'for' and 'of' but pick up the first significant word afterwards, such as C for

Counselling. Others use all the letters, so that British Association *of* comes a long way after British Association *for*.
○ Your library may offer facilities for groups to meet. And may have a display board showing their activities.
○ If you haven't already joined the library, join now.

Buying books

You may wish to buy a book if you think you'll refer to it so often you want it at hand! You might be lucky and find it already in stock in a local bookshop. A local bookshop is probably better stocked and can be of more help than a chainstore. If you have to order the book have the full title, author, publisher and date or edition of the book ready for the bookseller. Before ordering:
○ ask how long the book will take to arrive
○ ask if it is the latest edition.
○ check what price the book will be.
○ try and see the book first before you order by looking at it in the library or seeing a friend's copy.

Guide to Chapter 1
A new look at your old life

Health Education Council
78 New Oxford Street
London WC1 1AH
The Council is concerned with health education in England, Wales and Northern Ireland. It produces posters and leaflets for the public on a wide variety of health subjects and interests. It organises campaigns to increase awareness of health. It also runs a library service and funds research.

Scottish Health Education Unit
21 Lansdowne Crescent
Edinburgh EH12 5EH
The Unit serves Scotland and has similar aims and functions to the Health Education Council.

Know Your Body
Michael Jeffries
(British Broadcasting Corporation, 1976)
Good if you're keen to know the exact whys and wherefores of what goes on in your body. Written to accompany a BBC series of the same name, this book has quite a detailed approach although it usually uses everyday terms – or at least defines the more complicated ones!

Living Well: The People Maintenance Manual
(Mitchell Beazley, 1977)
Well illustrated book aimed at alerting people to the dangers and stress of modern life. Emphasis on physical activity. Also particularly relevant to Chapters 3 and 6.

Our Bodies Ourselves
Jill Rakusen and Angela Phillips
(Penguin Books, 1978, First British Edition)
An unusual health book written for women by women. Concentrates on you finding out about yourself, your body and feelings.

The Sunday Times Book of Body Maintenance
Oliver Gillie and Derrik Mercer
(Michael Joseph, 1978)
Began life as a serial in the Sunday Times magazine and was developed and extended into a book. Takes mainly a physiological – how the body functions – approach.

Take Care of Yourself
D. M. Vickery and J. F. Fries
(George Allen and Unwin, 1979)
This book has been designed as a practical do-it-yourself guide to medical care. It will help you decide when you need to see a doctor. It succeeds at being both interesting to read and a useful reference book. It is also particularly relevant to Chapter 8.

Your Body
David Scott Daniel
(Ladybird Books Ltd, 1967)
A simple introduction to the structure and workings of our bodies. The information in Ladybird books is certainly not just for children!

Guide to Chapter 2
Person to person

Association for Humanistic Psychology
62 Southwark Bridge Road
London SE1 0AU
The Association aims to promote research and interest in developing people's individual potential. It will provide lists of individuals and organisations running groups or courses to help people improve their personal relationships.

British Association for Counselling
For details see *What next?* guide for Chapter 6, page 248.

Family Service Units
For details see *What next?* guide for Chapter 6, page 248.

Born to Win
Muriel James and Dorothy Jongeward
(Addison Wesley, 1971)
This book encourages awareness and understanding of one's own personality and behaviour.

A Complete Guide to Therapy
Joel Kovel
(Harvester Press, 1977)
A well informed guide to different kinds of therapy. Heavy going to read at times but worth the effort if you want to find out what's what in this confusing field.

Constructive Criticism
Gracie Lyons
(IRT Press)
This is a handbook on techniques for good communication. Although written for groups, it's also useful for individual relationships.

I'm OK – You're OK
Thomas A. Harris
(Pan Books, 1973)
An introduction to the theory of how you can gain control of yourself, your relationships and your future – no matter what has happened in the past. It emphasises our ability to change and to choose – not just adapt. Worth the effort of concentration to read this book which is at times complex in its ideas although written in non-technical language.

Ordinary Ecstasy
John Rowan
(Routledge Kegan Paul, 1976)
A partisan and sympathetic tour of the 'new therapies' as they're sometimes called. Everything you always wanted to know about encounter groups, gestalt therapy, bioenergetics, co-counselling and many others.

Person to Person – Ways of Communicating
Michael Argyle and Peter Trower
(Harper and Row, 1979)
This book is one of the 'Life Cycle' series, presenting psychology for the ordinary reader. *Person to person* discusses body language, expression, gesture, ritual, and social conduct and the roles they play in conversation, friendship and falling in love.

Health Choices
An Open University short course of which this book is a part. The TV and radio programmes that go with the course highlight various aspects of person-to-person communications. For details of the course see page 10.

Guide to Chapter 3
Looking after yourself

Amateur Swimming Association
Harold Fern House
Derby Square
Loughborough LE11 0A1
The Association provides information about swimming and also about the incentive award scheme which it runs.

British Cycling Federation
70 Brompton Road
London SW3 1EN
Information about clubs all over the country is available from this address. Membership of the Federation includes insurance cover for cyclists.

British Heart Foundation
57 Gloucester Place
London W1H 4DH
The Foundation aims to raise and provide money for research into heart conditions. It supplies leaflets giving advice to anyone who has suffered a heart attack or stroke.

British Nutrition Foundation
15 Belgrave Square
London SW1
Promotes education and research in the field of nutrition.

British Dietetic Association
305 Daimler House
Paradise Street
Birmingham B1 2BJ

British Paraplegic Sports Society
Stoke Mandeville Stadium
Harvey Road
Aylesbury

Bucks
The Society supports a regional network of clubs for the disabled.

British Sports Association for the Disabled
Stoke Mandeville Stadium
Harvey Road
Aylesbury
Bucks
The Association caters for a wide variety of sport for the disabled. Its work is organised in regions.

Central Council for the Disabled
34 Eccleston Square
London SW1V 1PE
Aims to develop services for the welfare of the disabled throughout the country. Runs an information service and encourages the formation of local associations. Publishes guides and leaflets and a monthly information bulletin, also a journal, *Contact*, which comes out every two months.

Chest and Heart Association
Tavistock House North
Tavistock Square
London WC1H 9JE
Concerned with the prevention of chest, heart and stroke illnesses, and to help people who suffer from them. Provides health education and counselling; promotes research; publishes books, booklets and leaflets.

Keep Fit Association
70 Brompton Road
London SW3
The Association has a central body which organises training courses for keep fit instructors, sends demonstration teams out to different parts of the country, and makes awards. It also co-ordinates the work of nine regions; the regions are autonomous and run their own classes and demonstrations. The organisation is for women only.

Ramblers Association
1–4 Crawford Mews
York Street
London W1H 1PT
If you want to go walking in the company of others or to attend organised events, the Ramblers Association is the place to contact. The Association has many town and district-based branches. It organises regular walks for members and also holds 'open events' from time to time.

Relaxation For Living
For details see *What next?* guide for Chapter 6, page 249.

Sports Council (England)
The Information Centre
70 Brompton Road
London SW3 1EX
The Council was established in 1972, and its aims are to:

○ make people more aware of the importance and social value of sport and physical recreation.

○ improve sports facilities and ensure that existing provision is used.

○ encourage more people to engage in sport.

○ raise standards of performance.

There are nine regional offices in England, and these are responsible for carrying out the Council's policies, taking into account local needs, interests and conditions. The Council should be able to give you the address of an organisation concerned with a specific sport. A considerable range of publications is available to people visiting the Information Centre. The Sports Council provides technical and advisory services to local authorities, voluntary sports bodies and other organisations. The separate Councils for Scotland, Wales and Northern Ireland share the same aims and perform the same functions.

Sports Council (Northern Ireland)
49 Malone Road
Belfast BT9 6RZ

Sports Council (Scotland)
1 St Colme Street
Edinburgh EH3 6AA

Sports Council (Wales)
The National Sports Centre for Wales
Sophia Gardens
Cardiff CF1 9SW

Wheel of Yoga
For details see *What next?* guide for Chapter 6, page 249.

Aerobics and **The New Aerobics**
Kenneth Cooper
(Bantam Books, 1972 and 1970)
Two books that investigate how much and how often you need to cycle, swim or jog if you want to get really fit.

Beat Heart Disease
Risteard Mulcahy
(Martin Dunitz, 1979)
An informative book in the 'Positive Health Guide Series' on how adopting a healthier lifestyle can beat heart disease. Includes practical advice on diet and exercise.

A Diet of Tripe
Terence McLaughlin
(David and Charles, 1978)
An historical look at the food man has eaten through the ages.

The Every Other Day Exercise Book
Fern Lebo
(Penguin Books, 1979)
A recommended book containing carefully arranged exercise programmes for everyone.

Deliberately avoids over-straining the body. Includes a 16 minute plan to get and keep in shape, pre and post natal exercises, and getting fit again after a heart attack.

The Famine Business
Colin Tudge
(Pelican, 1979)
Why do we eat what we eat? Is it good for us? Who benefits from the way agriculture is organised in this country? What's it got to do with poverty and famine and the third world? Colin Tudge argues that the Western diet is unsound nutritionally and that, by its demands on third world countries for particular kinds of imported foods, it creates poverty there. He analyses why this is so, proposes a more rational form of agriculture and indicates the economic and political problems that would make these changes difficult.

Fitness on Forty Minutes a Week
Michael Carruthers and Alistair Murray
(Futura, 1980)
An introduction to a graded exercise programme which aims to help you get fit and stay fit in only 40 minutes a week.

Food and Profit – It Makes You Sick
The Politics of Health Group
(British Society for Social Responsibility in Science)
A very forcefully stated pamphlet taking a strong line on the issue of what part the food industry plays in producing ill health in our society. More details of the British Society for Social Responsibility in Science and its publications are in the *What next?* guide for Chapter 8, page 251.

Keeping Up With Yoga
For details see *What next?* guide for Chapter 6, page 249.

Know the Game
(EP Publishing)
'Know the Game' is the title of a series of small books covering over 70 major sports and pastimes. Each book gives clear concise explanations of the rules and basic principles of the activity concerned.

Living Well
For details see *What next?* guide for Chapter 1, page 242.

Nutrition – Everything You Need to Know to Ensure Healthy Wholesome Eating
Paul Simons
(Thorsons Publishers, 1978)
A simple guide to nutrition.

Nutrition
John Yudkin
(Hodder and Stoughton, 1977)
This book in the 'Teach Yourself' series covers thoroughly the principles of nutrition and also includes chapters on issues like preservatives and additives, sugar and world food production.

Physical Fitness
Royal Canadian Air Force
(Penguin Books, 1970)
Graduated exercises for those who really want to build up their fitness to a high level.

The Sunday Times Book of Body Maintenance
For details see *What next?* guide for Chapter 1, page 242.

Health Choices
An Open University short course of which this book is a part. A cassette of a simple exercise routine set to music with accompanying illustrated notes and poster is included in the course. For details of the course see page 10.

Guide to Chapter 4
Breaking old patterns

Action on Smoking and Health (ASH)
27–35 Mortimer Street
London W1N 7RJ
ASH has three main functions: it is an information agency; it promotes research; and it is a pressure group campaigning for the interests of non-smokers and aiming to limit the influence of cigarette companies.

Alcoholics Anonymous
11 Redcliffe Gardens
London SW10 9BG
A nation-wide society made up of several hundred groups. The only qualification for membership is a sincere desire to stop drinking.

Al-Anon Family Groups UK and Eire
61 Great Dover Street
London SE1 4YF
An organisation which enables the relatives and friends of alcoholics to meet and learn from each other about ways of facing their common problem. Members have demonstrated that changed family attitudes can bring about recovery. A list of publications and details of group meetings are available from this address.

Al-Teen
61 Great Dover Street
London SE1 4YF
Al-Teen is an organisation under the wing of Al-Anon, but was formed especially for 12–20 year olds to enable them to discuss the problems and experiences of living in a family where a member has a drinking problem.

Anorexic Aid
Gravel House
Copthall Vorner
Chalfont St. Peter
Bucks
Offers support and information to anorexia nervosa sufferers and their families. Self-help groups are organised regionally and co-ordinated by a newsletter.

Gamblers' Anonymous
17–23 Blantyre Street
Cheyne Walk
London SW10
A fellowship of men and women who have joined together to try to overcome their own gambling problems and to help other gamblers to do the same. Compulsive gambling can be just as much of a problem as addiction to drugs.

National Council on Alcoholism
Hope House
45 Great Peter Street
Westminster
London SW1P 3LT
The Council has a network of regional centres which provide information and advice to alcoholics, their families or employers. Its main purpose is to create greater public awareness of the problems associated with alcoholism and its prevention.

Slimming Clubs
Many national organisations, clinics and local groups run slimming clubs, and the best way to find out about the ones in your area is to ask at the library.

Weight Watchers
1 Thames Street
Windsor
Berkshire SL4 1SW
A national organisation which runs classes all over the country to help people lose weight and maintain the loss. The association has a magazine that is an enjoyable, practical and reliable source of information.

Act Thin, Stay Thin
Richard B. Stuart
(Granada Publishing,
Hart Davis, McGibbon Ltd, 1978)

A very practical book that helps you look at why, when and how you eat and then helps you plan to lose weight. The author is a director of Weight Watchers International.

Fat is a Feminist Issue
Susie Orbach
(Paddington Press, 1978)
A practical book with the subtitle 'the anti-diet guide to permanent weight loss', it challenges accepted thinking about weight loss. The author discusses why women become compulsive eaters, why women often get fat, and why they regain weight after dieting. It includes interesting case histories.

Habits
John Nicholson
(Pan Books, 1978)
An interesting book dealing with things most of us do consciously, or unconsciously, everyday. Explains why we eat when we're not hungry, as well as why we smoke, tell lies and worry.

No Smoke
Robert East and Bridget Towers
(Kingston Polytechnic, 1979)
A manual based on research in the fields of behaviour modification and social psychology, offering guidance to the person who intends giving up smoking. It provides information which should clarify the aims of the reader and strengthen his or her resolve to stop smoking. It gives a series of activities which can be used to break the habit.
    Available from Botes Books, Brook Street, Kingston-upon-Thames or by ordering from a local bookshop.

Sleep
Ian Oswald
(Penguin, 1970)
A very interesting and readable book about all aspects of sleep and its mysteries.

Slimmers' Guides
(Tom Evton Ltd)
A series of slimmers' guides, for example, 'The Slimmers Guide to Carbohydrates' are published in association with

Slimming Magazine. They are very useful for reference in controlling your weight. They list food values of many items including brand name products.

Slimming Magazine
Burwood House
16 Caxton Street
London SW1H 6QH
The magazine is a popular and reliable source of information in the diet and weight control field. A network of clubs throughout the country are linked to the magazine.

What's Your Poison?
Paul Gwinner and Marcus Grant
(British Broadcasting Corporation, 1979)
This book was written to accompany a BBC Further Education TV series on drinking. It aims to enable readers to find out what sort of drinkers they are and encourages positive decisions to help the individual enjoy drinking but at the same time avoid difficulties with it. It is a practical book, though not so well presented and easy to follow as the TV series.

Which? Way to Slim
(Consumers Association, 1978)
An easy-to-read book full of information and advice on nutrition and slimming. Very practical.

Guide to Chapter 5
Work and health

British Safety Council
62–64 Chancellors Road
London W6 9RS
Provides training in industrial safety and
first aid. Publishes booklets, pamphlets
and guides to the latest safety regulations, also books, and the periodical,
Safety. Also concerned with all aspects of
public safety.

**Environmental Health Officers
Association**
19 Grosvenor Place
London SW1X 7HU
The Association is concerned with all
aspects of environmental health and its
resources and activities are aimed at
educating people in this field. The environmental health officer at your local
authority should be able to offer you help,
advice and information, particularly if
you have any complaints on the effect of a
workplace on the environment. He can
for example deal with problems of noise,
air pollution, food inspection and control,
and housing.

Friends of the Earth Ltd
9 Poland Street
London W1
Friends of the Earth is an organisation of
conservationists committed to preventing environmental abuse of all kinds. It
runs local groups and produces publications.

Health and Safety Executive
Regina House
Old Marylebone Road
London NW1

It is concerned with the health, safety and
welfare of nearly all persons at work. It is
involved with research, provides information and advice, helps develop policy regarding health and safety and
produces publications.

Pre-Retirement Association
69–73 Manor Road
Wallington
Surrey SM6 0DQ
Exists to encourage people to prepare for
retirement.

Trades Union Congress
23–28 Great Russell Street,
London WC1 3LS
The central co-ordinating body for trade
union activity in Britain. It is involved in
health and safety matters at work and
can give advice and information as well
as providing basic training courses for
safety representatives.

Changing Your Job
Godfrey Golzen and Philip Plumbley
(Kogan Page, 1978)
Practical advice on changing your job.

Democracy at Work
*(British Broadcasting Corporation, 1977/
Further Education Advisory Council)*
A book for active trade unionists orig-
inally written to accompany a series of
BBC Trade Union Studies programmes. It
looks at many basic questions on work
including some health related matters.

Hazards Bulletin
The Work Hazards Group
*(British Society for Social Responsibility
in Science)*
The Work Hazards Group produces a
regular Hazards Bulletin as well as various pamphlets. The aim of the bulletin is
to inform interested workers of recent
technical development and workplace
struggles over health and safety. The
group believes that proper working conditions can only be achieved by workers
becoming well informed and by their
participation in organising their places of
work. Further details of the British Society
for Social Responsibility in Science see
What next? Chapter 8, page 251.

**The Hazards of Work – How to
Fight Them**
Patrick Kinnersley
(Pluto Press, 1973)
Although some of the information needs
revising this remains a good guide to
health at work. Particularly good is the
section which discusses how health can
be affected by the way in which your
work is organised. A directory of toxic
substances provides a useful source of
reference.

Government Publications
HMSO bookshops stock many government publications concerned with work
and health, including copies of various
Acts of Parliament.

Health and Safety at Work Booklets
Department of the Environment
(HMSO)
A wide range of cheap booklets on many
aspects of health and safety. You may
well find a booklet describing your parti-
cular occupation as the booklets seem to
cover almost everything from 'Safety in
Laundries' to 'Safety in Use of Abrasive
Wheels' to 'Canteen, Messrooms and
Refreshment Services'.

**Health and Safety at Work – a TUC
Guide**
(Trades Union Council, 1976)
A useful small book looking at the basics
of the Health and Safety at Work Act, and
areas of concern in health and safety. It
includes checkpoints to help you assess
your workplace.

**Labour and Monopoly Capital – the
Degradation of Work in the
Twentieth Century**
Harry Braverman
(Monthly Review Press, 1974)
Despite its off-putting title, this is a highly
readable book. It explains how and why
automation has led to less interesting and
less skilled jobs for the majority of people
and suggests some solutions.

Living with Radiation
National Radiological Protection Board
(HMSO, 1973)
A small booklet providing information

and advice to people about radiation hazards.

Social Security Leaflets
You should be able to obtain DHSS leaflets on family benefits, low income benefits, benefits for the sick or unemployed, benefits for handicapped or disabled people, industrial injuries benefits, pensions and widows' benefits, national insurance and other miscellaneous leaflets from your local social security office. If you have difficulty obtaining any leaflets, write to: DHSS (Leaflets), P.O. Box 21, Stanmore, Middlesex HA7 1AY. The catalogue of social security leaflets is revised twice a year – usually in April and November – and can be obtained from the above address.

Work is Dangerous to your Health
Jeanne M. Stellman and Susan M. Daum
(Vintage Books, 1973)
A handbook of health hazards in the workplace and what you can do about them. Some of the references to legislation in the book only apply in the USA, but most of the book is relevant and very useful to people in every type of work in Britain. Includes a list of the chemical dangers found in different types of work.

Working
Studs Terkel
(Penguin, 1977)
The author interviewed American workers in a whole variety of occupations about how they felt about their jobs. This book contains their verbatim reports. They give a fascinating insight into the different ways people cope with the stresses of work.

Guide to Chapter 6
Stress and emotions

British Association for Counselling
1a Little Church Street
Rugby
Warwickshire
Gives up-to-date information on how to get help. Publishes a directory of psychosexual counselling agencies.

Cruse
The Charter House
6 Lion Gate Gardens
Richmond
Surrey TW9 2DF
A national organisation set up to help widows come to terms with their practical and emotional problems following bereavement.

Family Service Units
National Office
207 Old Marylebone Road
London NW1 5QP
FSU provides an intensive service for families in severe personal, social or financial difficulty. There are 22 units around the country.

Gingerbread
35 Wellington Street
London WC2
A nationally organised self-help association for one-parent families with a large number of local groups. Gingerbread offers practical help, information and advice on all kinds of problems faced by people bringing children up on their own.

MIND (National Association for Mental Health)

22 Harley Street
London W1N 2ED
Offers information, advice and counselling to people with all types of problems connected with mental disorder. It also runs several residential establishments for mentally ill or handicapped people.

National Federation of Womens' Institutes
39 Eccleston Street
London SW1W 9NT
This movement is organised at three levels: village, county and national with 9000 individual groups. It is an educational and social organisation for women. The fundamental aim is to improve the lot of women in society.

National Housewives Register
The National Organiser
South Hill
Cross Lanes
Chalfont St. Peter
Bucks SL9 0LU
Caters for housewives whose interests go beyond the concerns of home and family and has groups throughout the country. It publishes a National Newsletter twice a year and an introductory leaflet is available from the above address.

National Union of Townswomens' Guilds
2 Cromwell Place
London SW7 2JG
The Guilds cater for women in urban areas in a similar way to the Womens' Institutes in rural areas, and have similar aims. They enable women to meet and pursue various activities. There is a strong educational bias.

The Open Door
4 Manor Brook
Blackheath
London SE3
An information and contact service for those who suffer from agrophobia (fear of open spaces). A monthly newsletter is circulated among members through which they exchange experiences and symptoms and offer advice. Members can remain anonymous or can be put in touch with other members locally.

Relaxation for Living
Dunesk
29 Burwood Park Road
Walton-on-Thames
Surrey KT12 5LH
This association runs classes to help people learn to recognise the build-up of harmful tension in their bodies and to develop the skills of physical relaxation.

The Samaritans
17 Uxbridge Road
Slough SL 1SN
A national organisation with local branches all over the country. These advertise a telephone service which is manned 24 hours a day, seven days a week. Samaritans are ready to help people who are in despair over anything or who just need someone to talk to. The number of your local Samaritans is in the telephone directory, or ask the operator to put you through.

Society of Compassionate Friends
50 Woodwaye
Watford
Herts WD1 4NW
International organisation offering friendship and understanding to bereaved parents.

Westminster Pastoral Foundation
23 Kensington Square
London W8
Offers a counselling service to people in need of help with emotional problems of any sort.

Wheel of Yoga
Acacia House
Centre Avenue
Acton Vale
London W3 7JX
The organisation exists to co-ordinate the study and practice of yoga. It organises meetings, provides training for instructors and runs a library and information service.

Women's Therapy Centre
19a Hartman Road
London N7
Working from a feminist perspective, the Women's Therapy Centre offers individual and group psychotherapy to women only. There is a sliding scale of charges according to income.

Bereavement
Colin Murray Parkes
(Pelican Books, 1975)
A valuable book for people who've experienced some form of bereavement or for those who work with bereaved people. It describes what we know about the process of grieving, the ways in which people try to cope, and how they rebuild their world again.

Depression
Ross Mitchell
(Penguin, 1975)
A small book published in conjunction with MIND (it is in the MIND Specials series) that attempts to explain what is meant by the term 'depression'. It is interestingly illustrated by case histories.

How to Lift Your Depression
Dean Juniper
(Open Books, 1978)
A practical booklet giving day to day plans for coping with depression.

Keeping Up With Yoga
Lyn Marshall
(Ward Lock Ltd, 1976)
An introduction to yoga written to accompany a London Weekend TV series.

Kicking the Fear Habit
Manuel J. Smith
(Bantam Books, 1978)
A straightforward fun-to-read book on overcoming fears and phobias.

A Less Anxious You
Elizabeth Forsythe
(Mitchell Beazley, 1978)
A easy to read book looking at anxiety occurring in all sorts of situations.

Our Bodies Ourselves
For details see *What next?* guide for Chapter 1, page 242.

Richard Hittleman's 30 Day Yoga Meditation Plan
Richard Hittleman
(Corgi, 1978)
A clearly presented day by day meditation guide. During the daily 20 minute sessions you learn and apply many meditation techniques, such as breathing, mantra and visualisation. The value of each technique is discussed and photographs illustrate each daily routine.

Spare Rib
27 Clerkenwell Close
London EC1
A magazine that is a useful source of contacts for those wishing to join a local Women's group. Available at newsagents or on subscription.

Stress and Relaxation
Jane Madders
(Martin Dunitz, 1979)
A highly recommended book in the Positive Health Guide Series outlining self-help ways to cope with stress. The author has developed simple techniques of natural relaxation. The exercises can be done virtually anywhere – at home or at work.

Health Choices
An Open University short course of which this book is a part. A cassette on relaxation with accompanying text and pictures is also included. One of the television and one of the radio programmes associated with the course deal with stress at work. For details of the course see page 10.

Guide to Chapter 7
Your sex life

Albany Trust
16–18 Strutton Ground
London SW1P 2HP
Concerned to help people with psycho-sexual problems, especially those in sexual minority groups.

British Association for Counselling
For details see *What next?* guide for Chapter 6, page 248.

British Pregnancy Advisory Services
Head Office
Austy Manor
Wootton Wawen
Solihull
West Midlands B95 6DA
A non-profit making trust which offers information and help in matters relating to sex and birth control, specialising in the provision of an abortion counselling and referral service.

Brook Advisory Centres
233 Tottenham Court Road
London W1P 9AE
There are seven centres in different cities around the country. All run birth control clinics and offer psycho-sexual counselling.

Catholic Marriage Advisory Council
15 Lansdown Road
London W11 3AJ
Offers a counselling service similar to that of the National Marriage Guidance Council with, in addition, a legal and medical service. Like the NMGC, it also helps both married and single people.

Family Planning Association
Margaret Pyke House
27–35 Mortimer Street
London W1A 4QW
Offers a professional service of medical help and advice. It aims to educate people in methods of contraception and to promote sexual health.

The Forum Clinic
2 Bramber Road
London W14 9PB
A specialist agency for psycho-sexual counselling. It offers advice, information and therapy for any sex problem, as well as a referral service. The clinic specialises in helping single men but also runs a sex therapy course for couples.

Grapevine
296 Holloway Road
London N7
A sex education, information and counselling service for the under 30s.

Jewish Marriage Advisory Council
529b Finchley Road
London NW3
A counselling service for Jewish families.

Lifeline UK
53 Victoria Street
London SW1
Offers a professional counselling service for women with unwanted pregnancies. It works to avert the need for abortions, but also provides post-abortion counselling where necessary. Offices in major cities as well as in London.

Marie Stopes Memorial Centre
106 & 108 Whitfield Street
London W1P 6BE
Supplies information and advice on abortion, birth control and psycho-sexual problems.

National Marriage Guidance Council (NMGC)
Herbert Gray College
Little Church Street
Rugby
Warwickshire CU21 3AP
The Council co-ordinates the work of about 150 local marriage guidance councils, It offers a professional counselling service to people needing help in marriage and family relationships including, where necessary, counselling over separation and divorce. It has offices throughout the country, serving England and Wales.

Scottish Marriage Guidance Council
58 Palmerston Place
Edinburgh EH12 5AZ
The Council serves Scotland in the same way as the National Marriage Guidance Council serves England and Wales.

The Art of Sensual Massage
Gordon Inkeles and Murray Todris
(*Allen and Unwin, 1977*)
Profusely illustrated with photographs that you'll either love or dislike, this book shows good massaging techniques.

Human Sexuality
Leonore Tiefer,
(*Harper and Row, 1979*)
This book in the 'Life Cycle' series examines the interaction between the sexual customs of our society and the way in which individuals behave, and how feelings change with age.

The Joy of Sex
Alex Comfort
(*Quartet Books, 1975*)
A highly recommended book with a clear commonsense approach. Not just a book on techniques, but on happy relaxed lovemaking.

Living is Loving
Inge and Stan Heggler
(*Panther Books, 1974*)
A direct but casual book whose illustrations you'll either find amusing or off-putting.

The Massage Book
George Downing
(*Penguin Books, 1979*)
Excellent straightforward instructions on how to massage yourself and your partner.

Sex Therapy Today
Patricia and Richard Gillan

(Open Books, 1976)
An account of behaviour therapy for sexual problems that is clear to understand.

Toward Intimacy
Task Force on Concerns of Physically Disabled Women.
(Human Sciences Press, 1978)
A sensitive understanding book on sexuality and family planning for physically disabled people.

Treat Yourself to Sex
Paul Brown and Carolyn Faulder
(Penguin Books, 1980)
A self-help sex therapy guide by authors who believe firmly that good sex is based on the skills of relating together and that these skills can be learnt. It aims to help people with sex problems achieve good sex and those with a good sex life enjoy it even more. Highly recommended.

Guide to Chapter 8
A healthy community

The Acupuncture Association
2 Harrowby Court
Seymour Street
London W1
The association can supply lists of acupuncturists.

British Homoeopathic Association
27a Devonshire Street
London W1
Offers information on homoeopathy, an alternative to NHS therapy.

British Naturopathic and Osteopathy College and Clinic
6 Netherhall Gardens
London NW3
Can provide information on therapies and clinics.

The British Society for Social Responsibility in Science
9 Poland Street
London W1V 3DC
The BSSRS is a radical organisation providing information and advice on health matters, especially on hazards at work and in the community. Publications by some of their working groups are mentioned in the *What next?* guide for Chapters 3, 5 and 8.

Citizens Advice Bureau
Your local bureau: address in telephone directory.
Gives free confidential and impartial advice and information about services and rights. Staff will know what you are entitled to and who will be able to help among the official bodies or voluntary organisations. They will also help with filling in complicated forms, like applications for benefits. This is a good place to start if you don't know who to turn to. Just drop in or phone. They have trained staff, some paid but many volunteers, who keep themselves up-to-date with changes in the law and the kind of information people need.

Community Health Council
Headquarters
126 Albert Street
London NW1
Your local council: address in telephone directory.
There is a community health council in each district of the country. The council represents consumer interests in health. Contact them if you have problems or complaints about health facilities. They will also know about local organisations which may be of help. The council is staffed by representatives of the community, some elected by local organisations. In Scotland the equivalent are the local health councils.

Council of Social Service
Council for Voluntary Service
Community Council
Your local council: address in telephone directory.
These councils have different names in different areas of the country but work on the same principles. They find needs and opportunities for development within the community and initiate action to meet these needs.

Family Practitioner Committees
Your local FPC: address in the telephone directory or on your medical card.
Complaints can be made in writing to the administrator of the FPC within eight weeks of the occurrence of an incident involving your GP/opthalmic optician/ dentist or chemist. The kinds of complaints they deal with include:
○ difficulty in finding a new GP, dentist or optician.
○ difficulty in getting a home visit.
○ lack of room at a GP or dentist's surgery.

251

○ inadequate records of illness or treatment.
○ problems on issuing of medical certificate.
○ inadequate or lack of treatment.
○ problems in being referred to hospital.

The Community Health Council for your area may be able to help you with the wording of the letter. If your complaint seems reasonable it will then be investigated. At first it can be investigated quite informally and the problem may be solved just by correspondence between the administrator and the people involved. However, if this provides no solution, a formal procedure is then operated and a sub-committee of the FPC meets to investigate the complaint. The sub-committee consists of health professionals and members of the general public. Both the patient and the person who is the subject of complaint are asked to attend a meeting of the sub-committee and they can be represented by a friend or colleague, but not by a lawyer or official from a trades union or professional association.

In Scotland instead of complaining to FPCs, complaints should be made in writing to the Secretary of the Primary Care Division of the local area health board within six weeks of the event which is the reason for complaint. The Service Committee of the area board, on which both the general public and health professionals are represented, considers all complaints.

Healing Research Trust
5 Thorn Park
Plymouth
Promotes alternative medicine.

Health Education Departments
Your local health education service: address in telephone directory.
Most health authorities now have health education officers who promote information on health throughout an area or district. They will be able to provide you with names, organisations and usually pamphlets, posters and booklists.

Health Service Commissioner
There are offices in England, Scotland and Wales at:

Church House
Great Smith Street
London SW1P 38W
71 George Street
Edinburgh EH2 3EE

Queen Court
Plymouth Road
Cardiff CF1 4DA

The Health Service Commissioner is an ombudsman for the NHS and will deal with complaints about the health service.
○ The complaint should be made within one year of the incident.
○ Usually you should have first written to the area or regional health authority.
○ The Health Service Commissioner cannot investigate complaints on matters that the Family Practitioner Committee covers.

The Commissioner carries out his investigation. He sends a report to you and the health authority. He can make the report public. But it's up to the health authority to take any action on his report.

The National Institute of Medical Herbalists
68 London Road
Leicester
Can provide lists of herbalists.

The Patients Association
11 Dartmouth Street
London SW1H 9BN
The Association runs an information service and publishes *Self-help and the patient*: a directory of organisations concerned with particular diseases and handicaps (6th edn, 1978).

Professional Bodies
Listed below are the names and addresses of many of the main controlling bodies or councils and members' associations for health professionals. They often deal with general queries on professional training, health care provision and policies and health education. The councils for each profession can advise on the procedures for making complaints about practitioners' personal moral behaviour, although it is probably best to consult your local community health council or The Patients Association first.

British Dental Association
64 Wimpole Street
London W1M 8AL

British Dental Hygienists Association
Dental Department
Eastman Dental Hospital
Grays Inn Road
London WC1

British Medical Association
BMA House
Tavistock Square
London WC1H 9JP

Central Council for Education and Training in Social Work
Clifton House
Euston Road
London NW1

Chartered Society of Physiotherapy
14 Bedford Row
London WC1R 4ED

Council for the Education and Training of Health Visitors
Clifton House
Euston Road
London NW1

Environmental Health Officers Association
For details see *What next?* guide Chapter 5, page 247.

General Dental Council
37 Wimpole Street
London W1

General Medical Council
44 Hallam Street
London W1

General Nursing Council
23 Portland Place
London W1A 1BA

General Optical Council
41 Harley Street
London W1

Guild of Health Education Officers
7 Sandringham Road
Bromley
Kent BR1 5AR

Health Visitors' Association
36 Eccleston Square
London SW1V 1PF

Pharmaceutical Society of Great Britain
17 Bloomsbury Square
London WC1A 2NN

Royal College of General Practitioners
14 Princess Gate
Hyde Park
London SW7

Royal College of Midwives
15 Mansfield Street,
London W1M 0BE

Royal College of Nursing
1a Henrietta Place
Cavendish Square
London W1M 0AB

Royal College of Physicians
11 St Andrews Place
London NW1 4LE

Society of Chiropodists
8 Wimpole Street
London W1M 8BX

The General Council and Register of Osteopaths
16 Buckingham Gate
London SW1E 6LB
Can supply lists of trained and registered osteopaths.

Social Services Department
Your local authority: address in telephone directory.
They will advise on any benefits or allowances which can be claimed through the Department of Health and Social Security. They will know of any local organisations or groups that may provide support, information or facilities. Each social services department employs social workers, who look after individuals (this can include visiting them at home).

Women's Royal Voluntary Service
17 Old Park Lane
London W1Y 4AJ
Carries out a wide range of welfare and emergency work in the community.

Charities Digest
(*Butterworths, 1979*)
A list of charitable trusts and organisations, produced in conjunction with the Family Welfare Association.

Cuts and the NHS
Politics of Health Group
(*British Society for Social Responsibility in Science*)

This looks at the effect of financial cutbacks on the health service. The group will know of any organisations which already exist and which can be of use or help to you.

The Encyclopaedia of Alternative Medicine and Self Help
Malcolm Hulke
(*Rider, 1978*)
A comprehensive guide to alternative medicine in easy-to-consult reference book style. The first part of the book is a collection of articles describing various therapies. The second part is a directory of aids and services available to prospective patients.

Guide to the Social Services: a Book of Information Regarding the Statutory and Voluntary Services
(*Macdonald and Evans*)
Produced in conjunction with the Family Welfare Association, it covers official and voluntary services available to the community and contains a lot of legal information.

Health Rights Handbook
Gerry and Carol Stimson
(*Prism Press, 1978*)
A consumer's guide to medical facilities. Especially of interest for those who wish to have more control over the care they receive.

The Health Team in Action
(*British Broadcasting Corporation, 1974*)
Originally published in association with a BBC TV series in 1974, is now slightly out of date but remains a good explanatory book including a section on who's who in a health centre team.

Help I Need Somebody!
Sally Knight
Hertfordshire Library Service
County Hall
Hertford SG13 8EJ
This is a guide to national associations for people who need help. It is regularly updated and deals with all the main aspects of health problems and handicaps.

In Defence of the NHS
Radical Statistics Health Group
(*British Society for Social Responsibility in Science*)
An analysis of some of the proposals put to the Royal Commission on the National Health Service by medical organisations. It should be read in conjunction with the Government publication, *Prevention and health: everybody's business.*

Prevention and Health: Everybody's Business
(*HMSO, 1974*)
A Government publication which is a reassessment of public and personal health matters.

Take Care of Yourself
For details see *What next?* guide for Chapter 1, page 242.

Under the Axe
National Union of Public Employees
Civic House
Aberdeen Terrace
London SE3
Discusses the NHS very much from the union standpoint. Mainly on London but interesting for other areas too.

Voluntary Organisations: A National Council of Voluntary Organisations Directory
(*Bedford Square Press, 1980*)
This publication produced in conjunction with the National Council of Social Services covers all kinds of voluntary organisations.

Whose Priorities?
Radical Statistics Health Group
(*British Society for Social Responsibility in Science*)
This is a critique of a Government publication, *Priorities for health and personal social services in England.*

Health Choices
An Open University short course of which this book is part. One of the television programmes and one of the radio programmes in the course look at doctor–patient relationships. For details of the course see page 10.

Index

Illustrators

Philip Argent	pages 19, 67
Caroline Austin	pages 81 (top), 90–91, 92
Bob Cosford	pages 198, 199
Ken Cox	pages 54–55, 56–57, 86, 87, 88–89, 93, 102, 136–137, 148–149, 165, 178–179
Jerry Hoare	pages 26, 27, 28, 29, 38, 39, 48, 49, 52–53, 107, 113, 152–153, 160–161, 177, 188–189, 195, 220, 237
John Ireland	pages 36, 46, 47, 50–51, 114, 115, 128, 139, 141 (right), 181, 213, 231, 313
Tony McSweeney	pages 24, 42, 43, 60–61, 194
Nigel Osborn	pages 22–23
Ingram Pinn	pages 85, 112, 126–127, 143, 219, 221, 223, 229
Bill Prosser	pages 40, 117, 192, 193, 200–201, 202–203, 205, 207, 209
Juliet Stanwell-Smith	pages 121, 169, 189, 233
Dave Staples	pages 30–31, 68–69, 73, 135, 156–157, 190
Paul Stickland	pages 65, 98–99, 110, 111, 118, 119, 120, 141 (bottom), 147, 214, 215, 216–217, 238–239
Tristram Woolston	pages 18, 81 (bottom), 98–99 (diagram), 108, 129, 163, 171, 192–193
Kathy Wyatt	pages 14–15, 34–35, 62–63, 94–95, 122–123, 150–151, 182–183, 210–211

Photographs

Barnabys pages 18 and 70, BBC page 226 (© O.U.P.C.), Camera Press pages 17 (top right) and 160, Carl Purcell/Colorific page 83, Coloursport page 17 (top left), James Stevens Curl page 172, Daily Telegraph Colour Library/Ford Motor Company page 133, John Garrett 10, Tommy Hindley page 79, Kobal Collection pages 124, 130–1, John Melville pages 18, 32, 33, 36, 44, 45, 49, 58–59, 74–75, 76, 96, 100–101, 146, 158–159, 163, 186–187, 191, 225, 231, 235, Chris Schwarz page 166, The Morning Star page 143, Rex Features pages 174, 175, 194, Syndication International page 17 (bottom), Volvo U.K. page 132, Zefa page 145.

ONE FOR MY BABY (And One More For The Road)
from the film THE SKY'S THE LIMIT
Music by Harold Arlen
Words by Johnny Mercer
© 1943 Edwin H. Morris & Co. Inc.
Assigned to Harwin Music Corp.
British Publisher: Chappell Morris Ltd.
Reproduced by kind permission

The information on food and diet in Chapter 3 is based on *Happy Eating I, II, III*, material prepared by the Schools Council Project (Health Education 13–18, for trial use in schools 1979–80).